Inquiry in the Classroom

Realities and Opportunities

A volume in
Contemporary Research in Education

Series Editor:
Terry A. Osborn, *Fordham University*

Contemporary Research in Education

Terry A. Osborn, Series Editor

Celluloid Blackboard:
Teaching History With Film (2007)
edited by Alan S. Marcus

Inquiry in the Classroom

Realities and Opportunities

edited by

Eleanor Abrams
University of New Hampshire

Sherry A. Southerland
Florida State University

and

Peggy Silva
Souhegan High School

Information Age Publishing, Inc.
Charlotte, North Carolina • www.infoagepub.com

Library of Congress Cataloging-in-Publication Data

Inquiry in the classroom : realities and opportunities / edited by Eleanor Abrams, Sherry South-
erland, and Peggy Silva.
   p. cm.
 Includes bibliographical references.
 ISBN-13: 978-1-59311-834-1 (pbk.)
 ISBN-13: 978-1-59311-835-8 (hardcover)
 1. Inquiry-based learning. 2. Classroom management. I. Abrams, Eleanor. II. Southerland,
Sherry A., 1962- III. Silva, Peggy Clohessy.
 LB1027.23.I57 2007
 371.3--dc22

                                                              2007027617

ISBN 13: 978-1-59311-834-1 (pbk.)
         978-1-59311-835-8 (hardcover)

Printed in the United States of America

CONTENTS

ACKNOWLEDGMENTS

We want to thank the teachers who have opened the reality of their classrooms through the years. Our thanks to them for showing us what is possible as well as describing for us the day-to-day factors that make their work so challenging. Equally as important are our teachers and teacher candidates who have talked and argued and struggled with us to come to an understanding of inquiry. Anything we write is reflective of the time we've spent with them.

Thanks, too, the research group at Florida State University (Sherelle Lowe, Patrick Enderle, and particularly Cady Hall) for your technical help in preparing the manuscript as well as Erica Blatt at the University of New Hampshire.

INTRODUCTION

Inquiry in the Classroom: Identifying Necessary Components of a Useful Definition

Eleanor Abrams, Sherry A. Southerland, and Celia Evans

Even a casual glance at the literature focusing on science education allows one to see the prominent role *Inquiry* plays in discussions of science education reform—*Inquiry and the National Science Standards* (National Research Council [NRC], 2000), *Constructing Extended Inquiry Projects: Curriculum Materials for Science Education Reform* (Singer, Marx, Krajcik, & Chambers, 2000), *Designing Inquiry Pathways* (National Science Teachers Association [NSTA], 2004)—to name only a few. Indeed, current national reform movements (American Association for Advancement of Science [AAAS], 1989; NRC, 2000) and derivative state standards have embraced inquiry as the most authentic, relevant, and effective pathway for children to come to understand science. The prominence of inquiry seems to imply that the science education research and teaching communities wholeheartedly embrace it. Despite its prominence and acceptance by the science education research community, however, inquiry—at least in terms of its role in the science classrooms—continues to be the subject of much debate, both in how to define inquiry in the classroom and its merits (Barrow, 2006; Camins, 2001; DeBoer, 1991). Indeed, despite its prominence in current reform efforts, Settlage (2003) asserts that the term "inquiry" has been "one of the most confounding terms within science education" (p. 34).

Surprisingly, the lack of a clear and commonly held definition of inquiry in the classroom, the ambiguity in terms of kinds of knowledge it is to engender, and even nagging questions regarding its effectiveness as a pedagogical tool have not stopped the push by those involved in science education reform to integrate inquiry into K-12 classrooms. This widespread acceptance by the research and teacher education community in the face of such uncertainty leaves classroom teachers the burden of crafting their own definitions of inquiry in the classroom, selecting their own approach to this method and determining its strengths and weaknesses for their particular students, context and content. Placing such a nebulous construct at the center of science education reform effort with such scant support for teacher thinking about these constructs calls into question the eventual success of these reforms. Anderson (2007) explains that "if [inquiry] is to continue to be useful we will have to press for clarity when the word enters a conversation and not assume we know the intended meaning" (p. 808). Clearly, the educational research and teacher education communities must take on more of the "conceptual work" in defining and describing useful applications of inquiry in the classroom if teachers are to understand its appropriate role in their work. This text is an attempt to do some of this conceptual work, and in this introduction we will propose a frame to employ in discussions of inquiry in the classroom—a frame that makes more explicit the meanings of inquiry intended by the speaker.

A problem with trying to define inquiry in the classroom is the lack of consensus on what inquiry looks like. Inquiry in the classroom takes on several different forms and functions depending upon who is offering the definition. Inquiry can be conceived as a critical attribute in defining the nature of science, a content standard by which we can assess student understanding, and a teaching standard (Lederman, 2003). Anderson (2007) sees three different but related approaches to inquiry evidenced in the *National Science Education Standards* (NRC, 1996), scientific inquiry, inquiry learning, and inquiry teaching.

During the two symposia that led to the development of this text it became clear that even among a members of a relatively homogenous science education research community (*National Association for Research in Science Teaching*), we *each* held related but different definitions of inquiry. Although many of us saw inquiry as useful—we understood it useful for achieving *different* learning goals, and certainly the portrait of classroom inquiry that we held were remarkably variable. Every author operated from the belief that inquiry could be beneficial to the future lives of their science learners-but each of us understood inquiry in a slightly or very different manner. Our 3 years of discussion, writing, and ongoing research has not resulted in consensus about inquiry, instead we've each become much more aware of a continua of thought regarding inquiry, and the need to be explicit in situating our own discussions on inquiry if our work is to inform that of classroom teachers in an useful manner.

The goals of this text are to help you more successfully navigate the complex landscape that is inquiry in the classroom—and by and large our focus in on inquiry teaching, what its various forms are and what factors influence it. We hope that this text allows you to develop and refine your definitions about what is inquiry in the classroom; and explore how should it be used to support the success of students. This section will include the various definitions of inquiry offered in the research literature accompanied by what we see as a useful way to conceptualize the broad practices that can be included as inquiry in the classroom and the various factors that influence the use of inquiry. At the end of this section, we will describe the structure of the remainder of the text.

INQUIRY AND SCIENCE EDUCATION: AN INTIMATE AND LONG TERM RELATIONSHIP

As Rudolph (2005) so insightfully describes, "Few things in science education are as popular these days as inquiry" (p. 803). It is important to recognize that this popularity is not a "flash in the pan" but reflects science educations long engagement with inquiry. Early in the last century, philosopher John Dewey provided a critique of the dominant mode of teaching in an address to the AAAS. Echoing science educators of today, Dewey maintained that science teaching gave too much emphasis on the accumulation of information and not enough on science as a way of thinking and an attitude of mind (Dewey, 1910, as cited in NRC, 1996). The lead article in the first volume of *Science Education* (then called *General Science Quarterly*) was an article by Dewey (1916) in which he takes the position that "the method of science, problem solving through reflective thinking, should be both the method and valued outcome of science instruction in America's schools" (p. 18).

Although many in academia embraced Dewey's ideas, little changed in terms of science teaching and learning on a national level (DeBoer, 1991). This trend changed somewhat at the end of World War II when many in the United States recognized our military and economic success was due to our scientific expertise, the expertise that they felt was dwindling in the years after the war. During this period, two important figures held great influence in shaping ideas in science education, Jerome

Bruner (1962) and Joseph Schwab (1962). Bruner is significant for his role in organizing the Woods Hole conference of 1959, in which a group of scientists (largely physicists and biologists) and psychologists came together to discuss how science education might be made more interesting and engaging for students—with the ultimate aim of producing more scientists to add to the United States' scientific expertise. Bruner's efforts are important as he worked to make the structure of the discipline of science as viscerally important as the way it was taught, explaining:

> Mastery of the fundamental ideas of a field involves not only the grasping of general principles but also the development of an attitude toward learning and inquiry; toward guessing and hunches, toward the possibility of solving problems on one's own. Just as a physicist has certain attitudes about the ultimate orderliness of nature and a conviction that order can be discovered, so a young physics student needs some working version of these attitudes if he [sic] is to organize his learning in such a way as to make what he learns usable and meaningful in his thinking. (p. 20)

Bruner's argument is that science students should experience the doing of science in order to hone their disposition toward learning. In Bruner's work we hear the echoes of Dewey's conviction that the doing of science is essential for one to become a learner of science.

One of Bruner's contemporaries, the educational philosopher Joseph Schwab (1962), was also an early leader in the effort to weave the doing of science into the science classroom. Reaffirming Dewey's admonishment that science teaching placed too much emphasis on the accumulation of information and not enough on science as a way of thinking, Schwab protested the teaching of science as a presentation of final form facts. He worked to have science learning begin in the laboratory, with students asking questions, collecting data, and constructing explanations. His efforts, along with Bruner's and others, can be found in the National Science Foundation (NSF) sponsored curriculum of the 1970's, with their reliance on different forms of inquiry.

The mention of NSF's involvement in curriculum development is not off-handed. Indeed, Rudolph (2002) describes that scientists historically have played pivotal roles in the development of science education curricula, a role that continues with the efforts of both *American Association for the Advancement of* Science (AAAS) and the National Research Council (NRC) in the national reforms of science education. So the central role inquiry plays in these current reforms should come as no surprise, as for many scientists and others (Dewey, Schwab, Bruner), having students participate in science is a fundamentally important goal of science learning and a means to achieve that learning.

The Challenge of Defining Inquiry

It is one thing to suggest that inquiry should be central to a student's science learning, but quite another to actual define inquiry. Discussions about "inquiry" in classroom are reminiscent of discussions we have had with other ecologists about the terms "sustainability" or "forest health" or "ecosystem integrity." To those in the field, these terms represent concepts whose meanings are easy to understand in a very general way. However, they are so multifaceted that they are nearly impossible to define, let alone apply. Comparing the outcomes of ecological studies that seek to determine the impact of some event or activity on "sustainability" or "ecosystems integrity" is difficult because different researchers often use different criteria to answer their questions. We argue that classroom inquiry is equally multifaceted, equally difficult to define, and the outcomes are equally difficult to compare among all the different versions that are being practiced. In this section of the text, we explore how can we take the necessarily broad concept of inquiry in the classroom and structure it so that it is not vague and nebulous yet still maintains the flexibility it must have to be accessible to all potential practitioners.

Inquiry in the classroom can be conceived as a complex set of ideas, beliefs, skills, and/or pedagogies. It is evident that attempting to select a singular definition of inquiry may be an insurmountable and fruitless task. Any single definition of inquiry in the classroom would necessarily reflect the thinking of a particular school of thought, at a particular moment in time, or a particular goal, and such a singular definition may serve to limit legitimate and necessary components of science learning. However, operating without a firm understanding of the various forms of inquiry leaves science educators often "talking past" one another, and often results in very muddled attempts in the classroom. We argue that agreeing on the necessary components of a useful description of inquiry for us to proceed with this book. We suggest that one important aspect of such description is the goal a teacher has for inquiry in the classroom.

Three Instructional Goals of Inquiry in the Classroom

The two *National Science Education Standards* were created by two national science organizations in the 1990s. They both describe inquiry in the classroom similarly. The first national science education standard was *Project 2061: Science for all Americans* (AAAS, 1989). In the publication, inquiry is defined largely as a process.

Over the course of human history, people have developed many interconnected and validated ideas about the physical, biological, psychological, and social worlds. Those ideas have enabled successive generations to achieve an increasingly comprehensive and reliable understanding of the human species and its environment. The means used to develop these ideas are particular ways of observing, thinking, experimenting, and validating. These ways represent a fundamental aspect of the nature of science and reflect how science tends to differ from other modes of knowing. (p. 1)

The second reform document, constructed by the National Research Council (NRC, 1996), defines inquiry somewhat differently but again captures the essence of inquiry as a process.

Scientific inquiry refers to the diverse ways in which scientists study the natural world and propose explanations based on the evidence derived from their work. Inquiry also refers to the activities of students in which they develop knowledge and understanding of scientific ideas, as well as an understanding of how scientists study the natural world. (p. 23)

Both standards euphemistically define inquiry in the classroom around the idea of students "doing" science to learn about the world. As one looks at such descriptions with an eye for more detail, it is clear that inquiry enjoys three goals in science education discussions; (a) understanding how scientific inquiry proceeds, (b) being able to successfully perform some semblance scientific inquiry, and (c) understanding how inquiry results in scientific knowledge (NRC, 2000).

Learning About Inquiry

Perhaps the most traditionally familiar goal of inquiry is for students to learn about inquiry as an investigative process. In this usage, "inquiry refers to the diverse ways in which scientists study the natural world and propose explanations based on the evidence derived from their work" (NRC, 1996, p. 23). It is this use that harkens back to the "scientific method" that many people experienced as learners. However, it is important to recognize that the portrait of inquiry as conveyed in the reforms is fundamentally different than this lock-step method. Instead, when students come to learn about science as a process of inquiry they are to learn how scientists go about constructing explanations of natural phenomena and come to recognize that these methods are appropriate for questions posed in their own lives (Flick, 2003).

Learning to Inquire

It is around this goal that both sets of reform are most explicit—that is the argument that students must become capable of participating in inquiry that bares some semblance to the activities that are on going in science. The *National Science Education Standards* (NSES) (NRC, 1996) state:

> Inquiry is a multifaceted activity that involves making observations; posing questions; examining books and other sources of information to see what is already known; planning investigations; reviewing what is already known in light of experimental evidence; using tools to gather, analyze, and interpret data; proposing answers, explanations, and predictions; and communicating the results. Inquiry requires identification of assumptions, use of critical and logical thinking, and consideration of alternative explanations. (p. 23)

Each of the reform efforts are quite clear, one must participate in inquiry if one is to become familiar and adept at performing such activities to make sense of the world. Thus, although the first aspect of inquiry in the reforms requires that inquiry be the focus of study and discussion, this second aspect of inquiry requires that students participate in such activities—and not solely read or talk about them. It is important to note that this development of inquiry skills is fundamentally linked with Bruner's (1962) goal of developing the disposition to use such skills.

Inquiry and Constructing Learner's Scientific Knowledge

It is important to note that learning *about* inquiry and learning to do inquiry is distinct from using inquiry to learn science content—although some authors and some teachers seem to conflate the three. The last goal of the use of inquiry—that of allowing for the construction of more robust content knowledge—is tied to understandings of how individuals learn (Bransford, Brown, & Cocking, 2000). This research suggests instruction that is more inductive, where students are actively involved in the construction of explanations, will result in more meaningful, retrievable, and applicable knowledge. In this vein, inquiry has been used to describe a wide variety of curriculum projects and programs (Moss, Abrams, & Robb-Kull, 1998; Rivet & Krajcik, 2004), teaching techniques (McCarthy, 2005), and overall approaches to teaching science (Druva & Anderson, 1983).

It seems prudent to note that this point, however, that the effectiveness of inquiry in engendering student learning has been inconclusive, with some studies suggesting marked improvement in students' test scores while others report no significant improvement (Chang & Mao, 1999; Edmondson & Novak, 1993; Gibson, 1998; Hall & McCurdy, 1990; Leonard, 1983; Marx et al., 2004; Russel & French, 2001). Settlage and Blanchard, in their essay in Section V of this book "Requisite Teacher Knowledge About Inquiry: Resources for Thinking About Inquiry," appropriately describe this the lack of strong empirical evidence for inquiry supporting student science learning. Much more research is needed that empirical explores the effectiveness of inquiry as a pedagogical approach—however, such research can only be as useful if the framework for inquiry that is used to support it is clearly explicit.

Describing how Inquiry is Enacted in the Classroom

In our discussions with our cocontributors for the preparation of this text, and in our work with preservice and inservice teachers, it has become clear that even if one shares the same goal for the use of inquiry (i.e., learning about inquiry, learning to inquire, or learning scientific knowledge), there still can be a bevy of approaches to achieving this goal. Thus, identification of a goal for the use of inquiry in the classroom is only part of a full descriptions—goals must be accompanied by a description of how the inquiry is to be structured. There are a number of categorization schemes for the way inquiry is structured, and we will provide the most prominent in this section.

Essential Characteristics of Inquiry

The NRC recognized the difficulty in integrating inquiry in the classroom and published a companion book, *Inquiry and the National Science Education Standards* (NRC, 2000). Interesting, much of this companion focuses on using inquiry as a teaching approach. In this text, they outline inquiry in the classroom along five essential characteristics, each of which varies according to the degree of teacher to student centeredness (see Table 1).

Five characteristics about the learner are placed on a continuum from teacher directed on one end, guided inquiry in the middle, to student generated on the other end. Using this chart, teachers can score their curriculum, their teaching approach, or their assessment in terms of how inquiry-oriented it is. Although this approach reflects the complexity of trying to integrate inquiry into the classroom, we have found it too inclusive in practice. This approach does not complete the defini-

Table 1. The National Science Education Standards' "Essential Features of Classroom Inquiry" (NRC, 2000, p. 29).

Essential Feature	Variations			
1. Learner engages is scientifically oriented questions	Leaner poses a question	Learner selects among questions, poses new questions	Learner sharpens or clarifies question provided by teacher, materials, or other source	Learner engages in question provided by teacher, materials, or other source
2. Learner gives priority to **evidence** in responding to questions	Learner determines what constitutes evidence and collects it	Learner directed to collect certain data	Learner given data and asked to analyze	Learner gives data and told how to analyze
3. Learner formulates **explanations** from evidence	Learner formulated explanation after summarizing evidence	Learner guided in process of formulating explanations from evidence	Learner gives possible ways to use evidence to formulate explanation	Learner provided with evidence
4. Learner connects explanations to scientific knowledge	Learner independently examines other resources and forms the links to explanations	Learner directed toward areas and sources of scientific knowledge	Learner given possible connections	
5. Learner communicates and justifies explanations	Learner forms reasonable and logical argument to communicate explanations	Learner coached in development of communication	Learner provided broad guidelines to sharpen communication	Learner give steps and procedures for communication
	More ——— Amount of Learner Self-Direction ——— Less			
	Less ——— Amount of Direction from Teacher or Material ——— More			

tion of inquiry because it seems that every piece of curriculum, every instructional methodology, and every assessment can be fit into this understanding inquiry in the classroom. If inquiry is everything, how can the notion of inquiry guide science teachers' practice? Instead, we argue that other approaches to describing the specific inquiry approach are required.

Schwab's/Colburn's Levels of Inquiry

Schwab's (1962) and Colburn's (2000) description of inquiry in the classroom are similar. We will describe Schwab's approach and show how Colburn's definitions map on Schwab's structure. Schwab offers a way to understand the various ways in which inquiry can be enacted in a classroom (Table 2). His analysis focuses on three activities: asking questions, collecting data, and interpreting those data. He understands these three activities as being fundamental and suggests that a useful way of understanding differences of classroom enactment of inquiry hinges on who is responsible for these activities. Once again, the three activities fall along a continuum between the student and the teacher. In Level 0 inquiry, the teacher provides the students with the question to be investigated and the methods of gathering data. The conclusions are not immediately obvious to the students during the activities, but the teacher is there to guide them toward an expected conclusion. Despite any variety in the students' data, the teacher will help them to interpret those so everyone understands the importance of the results. This aligns with Colburn's structured inquiry.

In Schwab's (1962) Level 1 and Level 2 more and more responsibility for the central activities of inquiry are given to the students. Activities might move toward Level 1 or 2 as students' inquiry skills and dispositions develop. Schwab's Level 1 and 2 correspond to Colburn's (2000) guided activity.

Finally, there is Schwab's (1962) Level 3 inquiry, in which the responsibility for all the major facets of a lesson is left to the responsibility of the students. This would correspond to Colburn's (2000) *open inquiry*. A somewhat familiar example of a Level 3 inquiry would be a

Table 2. Schwab's Levels of Inquiry

	Source of the question	*Data collection methods*	*Interpretation of results*
Level 0	Given by teacher	Given by teacher	Given by teacher
Level 1	Given by teacher	Given by teacher	**Open to student**
Level 2	Given by teacher	Open to student	**Open to student**
Level 3	**Open to student**	**Open to student**	**Open to student**

students' science fair, in which the student decides the procedures necessary to collect data, and the student is responsible for interpreting the
findings.

OTHER PROMISING "TAKES" ON INQUIRY

What we have described to this point represents the most common understandings of inquiry currently represented in the research and science
teacher education literatures—and we argue that much of the confusion
surrounding inquiry and its applications to actual classrooms resides in
contrasting goals or means of reaching those goals—contrasts that go
unrecognized or addressed. Although the portrait we're creating is
already sufficiently complex, we would be remiss in not describing some
of newly emerging "takes" on inquiry—-approaches that may hold some
promise for science teachers and learners.

Reasoning in Inquiry: Simple Versus Authentic Tasks

Many researchers focus on inquiry as a means to hone scientific reasoning abilities of students. In this framework, classroom inquiry activities
are to serve as vehicles through which students hone their reasoning abilities—and activities that echo those performed by scientists would be
ideal for such purposes. However, as Chinn and Malhotra (2002) suggest,
what scientists do (authentic inquiry) and what happens in the classroom
(simple inquiry) are fundamentally different in quality and epistemology,
going so far to suggest that the epistemology of common classroom
inquiry activities is antithetical to that of authentic science.

In the framework presented by Chinn and Malhotra (2002), authentic
scientific inquiry include tasks in which questions are not necessarily
determined, there is often more than one variable, procedures must be
designed, and there is usually a need for multiple studies. School inquiry
tasks involve investigating the effect of a single independent variable on a
single dependent variable accompanied by careful observations and
descriptions guided by a specified procedure. These differences in the
cognitive thought involved in authentic inquiry and typical school inquiry
"imply a different epistemology"—that is, the set of beliefs about what
knowledge is and how it can be changed (Chinn & Malhotra, 2002,
p. 186). The nature of simply school inquiries may lead students to belief
that knowledge can and should only be changed as a result of a simply,
definite experiment—something in stark contrast to a more robust epistemology of authentic science. Their findings suggest that common

approaches to classroom inquiry actually draw students further from a sophisticated understanding of science and its culture.

Chin and Malhotra (2002) reported that inquiry activities developed by scientists rather than teachers contained a higher percentage of tasks that were included in authentic. It is interesting that few of scientist-designed tasks allowed students the flexibility to generate their own questions. Scientist designed tasks allowed students to choose variables within a data set to study (also known as guided inquiry). Scientists developed tasks also scored higher on having students control variables, making multiple observations, summarizing or graphing data, and conducting multiple studies on the same question (Chinn & Malhotra, 2002). Their findings suggest three implications for classroom inquiries: (1) the need for the inclusion of more tasks that allow for authentic reasoning, (2) the need for a better understanding of scientists' strategies when reasoning when engaged in inquiry, and (3), the inclusion of instructional strategies that will ensure that students learn to reason scientifically when they are engaged in school inquiry tasks.

Although these are provocative findings and the framework is insightful, we need to ask ourselves how cognitively complicated can/should inquiry conducted by first, second, third, or fourth graders be? Certainly when students have built up the cognitive skills, it makes sense to incorporate research challenges based on more complex models (multiple hypotheses, several steps in a process that help to clarify what the next step in the experiment should be etc.). Although there is the potential danger of expecting K-12 students to work at these higher cognitive levels when they lack the more foundational skills and conceptions, we must recognize the need for a carefully scaffolded approach to such authentic tasks if student are to be able to reason scientifically.

Inquiry as Argumentation

Another perspective on inquiry in the classroom focuses on inquiry as a means of interacting with competing knowledge claims. This perspective on inquiry suggests that teachers should shift their focus from "doing" more traditional hands-on science activities to developing classroom activities that focus the students on constructing evidence-based rationales that will be tested and critiqued by their peers and others—certainly activities that are central in formal science. Gallagher and Tobin (1987) stated inquiry in the classroom tends to be a largely procedural set of activities, lacking opportunities for students to understand how scientific knowledge is constructed through reflection, debate, and argument. The limited opportunity to develop scientific argumentation skills prevents students from practicing the scientific thinking skills needed to understand how scientific knowledge is created and the role of inquiry in that creation (Park & Kim, 2006).

Larry Yore and his coauthors in Section II of this volume, "Selecting and Using Inquiry Approaches to Teach Science: The Influence of Context in Elementary, Middle, and Secondary Schools," articulate that inquiry should be presented as an interactive process where people attempt to search out, describe, and explain patterns of events occurring in the natural universe (cf. Good, Shymansky, & Yore, 1999). These authors suggest that the prevailing discursive pattern in scientific communities is rhetorical persuasion (i.e., the construction of explanations, the production of compelling arguments with coordinated evidentiary claims). These rhetorical activities extend to the common practice of the rebuttal of counterclaims through the use of evidence. It is through such rhetoric that the scientific community seeks to establish physical causality and make generalized claims. Newton, Driver, and Osborne (1999) state that argumentation—focusing on developing those rhetorical practices in students—is important within the social practice of inquiry in the classroom because students need to both develop knowledge and understand the evaluative criteria used to establish scientific theories. If students are to become capable of judging the utility of scientific explanations in their own lives, they must gain skill in participating in such practices. Therefore, Kuhn (1993) and others (Driver, Newton, & Osborne, 2000; Duschl Schweingruber, & Shouse, 2007) advocate that students need to experience inquiry as argumentation as well as inquiry as exploration if they are to fully understand how science is done.

What does this approach to inquiry mean for classroom practice? Teachers could use argumentation as a way to help students to develop the ability to differentiate evidence from data during their inquiry-based lessons. Students' scientific conceptions can be developed when they practice describing and justifying their evidence-based conclusions, presenting alternative theories, presenting counter-arguments, and providing rebuttals through argumentation with peers and teachers.

Inquiry as a Means of Drawing Students Into the Culture of Science

Some educators see science as a culture with particular habits of mind, value systems, and ways of knowing (Lee, 2003; Settlage & Southerland, 2007). Using this notion, participation in inquiry-based activities is understood to be a way to enculturate students into science—to bring them into the ways of thinking, doing and knowing that are endemic to science. In this approach, it is thought that by participating in inquiry, students will gain first hand knowledge of how scientific knowledge is created and will learn how to create that knowledge themselves (AAAS, 1989, 1993; National Research Council, 1996, 2000). It is thought that by immersion in inquiry (a central action of the culture of science), students will be better able to navigate the complex societal problems that involve science. This advantage will enhance their ability to participate in the democratic process as well as break down the barriers for students to pursue certain careers.

Although a host of researchers and policy groups emphasize the need to bring students into the culture of science, others see the prominent role of inquiry as a cornerstone of the culture of science in a much more negative manner. They argue that the reliance on inquiry as a means of defining science can serve to limit entry for nontraditional, nonmainstream students (Snively & Corsiglia, 2001). Liza Finkel in her essay in Section III of this volume, "Accommodating Student Diversity Within Inquiry," expresses her concern that using inquiry in the classroom may be problematic because it is derived from a traditional model of science a way of thinking that emerges from Western European male traditions. Lee (2003), a researcher that focuses on the intersections of underserved students' cultures and ways of knowing and those of science, explains that teachers' mono-cultural view of science must be reformed, allowing for a balance between the best of what science has to offer with other ways of knowing. Although she recognized that inquiry may be more difficult for nontraditional students due to its limited instructional congruence with their home lives, Lee advocates that diverse students need to become fluent in the culture of science as well as in their own cultures, and much of her work is an attempt to describe how that trans-cultural fluency can be supported by teachers (Lee, Hart, Cuevas, & Enders, 2004; Lee, Maerten-Rivera, Penfield, LeRoy, & Secada, in press).

Bridging cultures is difficult and selecting inquiry-based experiences that are open to all students can be a challenging task for teacher. A dangerous path to tread is to think you know what is relevant to another person without asking—as typically that judgment is based on the cultural norms of the teacher, thus providing for instruction that is much more congruent for students with a background similar to the teacher and much more foreign (and thus difficult) for students different from the teacher (Settlage & Southerland, 2007).

Too, making curricular decisions based on implicit assumptions can also lead to stereotyping of gender and race. For example, would an inquiry-based project based upon the topic of makeup interest girls any more than one focused on cars be of interest to boys? Should we expect our Latina/o students to participate more enthusiastically if cooperative groups were employed? Inquiry-based science can be an opportunity for students to explore the questions that are relevant to the complex persons they are. A wonderful example of this is described in Jose Rios essay on "Inquiry for Diverse Student Populations: Promises and Pitfalls." The question selected by one group of students was connected to the boy's lives and culture. Their project on racial profiling bridged the everyday with the scientific world so the students could see the power of science to make sense of their world. The students were allowed to select the specific question they were to pursue—a teaching act that may allow for a smoother transition between cultures for some of our traditionally underserved students.

This model of science as a culture forces science teachers to go beyond inquiry as a set of process skills or as a scripted approach to the presentation of science lessons and points to the need to ask and answer some harder questions about science. Whose knowledge is this? Who does it benefit and who does it exclude? What information is missing if we use this one way of knowing? As one employs the lens of the culture of science and inquiry as a means of enculturating students into this culture, it becomes necessary to create spaces for student discourse about the creation of scientific knowledge—not simply creating that knowledge. So again, this approach of science as culture overlaps with and draws much from the other approaches that emphasize the role of argumentation in inquiry and the role of inquiry as the process for one type of knowledge creation, science. Thus, when one steps away from the focus on levels of classroom inquiry or the essential features of such inquiries, certainly there is an emphasis on students participating in the wide variety of scientific activities, with particular emphases on argument and the manner in which inquiry serves to generate one kind of understanding of the physical world—both of which become essential if students are to be drawn into the culture of science.

INQUIRY IN THE CLASSROOM: A *WIDE* VARIETY OF INSTRUCTIONAL APPROACHES

Emphasizing the wide variety of definitions of inquiry as well as the various goals different groups have for these definitions is important as we deal with teachers' conceptions about inquiry. Often in our methods classes and graduate courses, discussions of inquiry in the classroom have fallen on deaf ears, as teachers reject the possibility of using inquiry in their classroom. As we have investigated this reluctance, we found many teachers conceive classroom inquiry as only open inquiry/Schwab's Level 3/ or that situated only on the student centered continua for each of the five essential characteristics, perhaps a residual belief left over from the largely open inquiry of the post-Sputnik era curriculum (Barrow, 2006) or the early influence of scholars such as Bruner (1962) who emphasized the need for students to engage with phenomena under their own direction. Regardless of its source, many teachers conceive of inquiry as a "free-for-all" in which they supposed to allow students to interact with materials with little, if any, guidance. And much like Lee Meadow's description in his essay, "Teacher Knowledge About Inquiry: Incorporating Conceptual Change Theory," they reject such an approach, recognizing the need for students to have adequate process skills and dispositions for inquiry as well as rejecting the possibility that such open-ended exploration could result in any substantial meaning-making.

It is important for teachers to recognize that inquiry in the classroom represents a much broader array of approaches than solely that of Level 3/open-inquiry. Instead, the NRC (2000) is clear in suggesting that dependent on the ability of the students in the class and the nature of the material to be taught; often one must begin at a much more teacher-centered fashion. A teacher may approach a Level 3 inquiries in her classroom perhaps only 2 or 3 times in a year. Before this, students must have a wealth of opportunities to hone their skills if they are to be successful in completing such inquiries and learning from their activities.

As a research community we moved past the notion that inquiry is equivalent solely to Schwab's Level 3/open inquiry—and we must successfully make that shift as science teacher educators. Instead, as will be described throughout the student knowledge, student diversity, and teacher knowledge sections of this text, we as science educator must have a much more sophisticated understanding of range of approaches to inquiry—and we must help teachers learn to use these understandings to decide which approach is appropriate given the ability of their students and the nature of the content to be taught.

The Need for a Flexible Structure of Classroom Inquiry

Rop (2003) presents a startling juxtaposition between the ideal classroom atmosphere and the reality that most teachers face. The contrast reinforces how important it is to identify aspects of science inquiry that result in enhanced: content, process skills and cognitive skills. At the same time, it needs to be flexible enough to accommodate the needs and constraints of all educators:

> In the ideal [high] school classroom, students and teachers who learn with them would follow intellectually intriguing byways, model scientific thinking

for each other, celebrate the art of questioning and challenge each other by articulating different points of view. Thought patterns would include mustering evidence, using argumentation effectively and testing one another's ideas. Both teachers and students would be given the freedom and time to learn, and the knowledge and confidence that real intellectual engagement is compatible with both immediate and future goals. Participants would learn and understand deeply a wide range of ideas and concepts. (p. 30)

In most real-world science classrooms, however, participants are caught between demands for breadth of content coverage and desires for depth of content understandings. Time constraints, pressures to teach to high-stakes proficiency tests, concern for national and state curricular standards, limited resources, tradition and the resulting resistance to change are real and powerful. (p. 30)

The first quote paints a picture of a learner-centered classroom in which the teacher is the facilitator of student-directed learning and where high level cognitive skills are developed through questioning, evidence gathering, testing/challenging ideas, and collegial interaction. There are no time or curriculum constraints. This classroom would be a model of open-ended, Level 3 inquiry. Although scientists are not without constraints in their practice, many of the attributes represented in this classroom would be in-line with components of authentic science practice.

In the "reality-check" quote, we are reminded that the typical classroom is far from the idealized one. In addition to the challenges articulated in the quote, the organizational structure of a school day, a teacher's learning objectives, and comfort level with content vary between classrooms. Different combinations of these aspects make for innumerable versions of inquiry in the classroom. Overlaying the sociocultural axes (gender, ethnicity, etc.) make the variety almost unfathomable. What can and should the real-world teacher take into the classroom from the ideal scenario?

What do Classroom Inquiries Look Like?

In a college setting, the time frame in which inquiry can be conducted can range from one-time, 3-hour laboratory experiences within an otherwise lecture dominated course, to semester-long research immersion programs where independent research projects developed by students are the focus. Public school classroom time lines may be more constrained than college inquiry, but the models are still exceedingly variable and depend on the class time available during the day/week for particular content.

Examples of inquiry include those tasks that cause students to observe and record natural and experimental phenomena, formulate questions, design experiments, analyze and evaluate data, draw conclusions and present scientific results (AAAS, 1993). They also include activities that generate student discussion, argumentation, and the linking of related ideas and concepts (Biological Science Curriculum Studies [BSCS], 1993).

Chinn and Malhotra (2002) differentiate what scientists do as "authentic inquiry" from what happens in classrooms ("simple inquiry"). Traditionally the "scientific method" is taught as approximately 5 steps: Observe, question, experiment, interpret results, and accept or reject a hypothesis. In reality, this definition is extremely oversimplified to describe the work of scientists (McComas, 1998). For example, some research does not present hypotheses for testing; instead, some scientists state research objectives. Many studies are designed to test a single hypothesis and others pose multiple working hypotheses and develop experiments or collect data that can bring information to bear on all of them. Large parts of the process involve reading and interpreting the literature, redesigning experiments, writing about related theories, providing explanations, linking information to models, and so forth (Grandy & Duschl, 2005).

When students have an opportunity to practice some of these skills and use various sources of information (data, discussion, lecture, observation, literature) to generate meaning, they engage in activities that echo the authentic science process. Overall, these processes are either deductive (creating specific predictions/hypotheses from a broad body of knowledge, as in the "if"…. "then"… phrasing of hypotheses) or inductive (combining individual occurrences or ideas into a broader conceptual framework).

Models of inquiry in the classroom, like the practice of science by scientists in different contexts, have multidimensional complexity. As suggested by both the NRC (2000), Schwab (1962) and Colburn (2000), the practice of inquiry in the classroom includes components of the scientific process that are very teacher guided as well as open-ended inquiry projects that are completely student-owned. The complexity of the inquiry approach should be determined by the scientific literacy of the students. Some activities can be completed in very short time frames (a lab experience or classroom activity), others might take up the better part of a semester or school year (observing changes in leaf pigments from September through October).

How is Inquiry Linked to Science Literacy?

As mentioned previously, the approach to inquiry might differ given a teacher's immediate goals, however, the ultimate goal of public education is for students to become scientifically literate by graduation. Although there is no single agreed upon published definition of science literacy (Hodson, 1999), the components of science literacy most often described in the education literature include: the nature of science, conceptual knowledge, ethics of science, interrelation between science and society, and science and technology, and science in the humanities (DeBoer, 1991). A scientifically literate individual has an understanding of science that allows her to apply it to novel situations, societal problems and issues (Hurd, 1958 as cited in DeBoer, 1991), or is one who can use knowledge and skills in science, technology and mathematics to think about and make sense of the ideas and claims that that she is faced with each day (AAAS, 1993). The BSCS (1993) identifies the following four levels of scientific literacy:

Nominal Literacy – Students know when a term is scientific and can provide simple explanations of concepts and misconceptions are common (literate in name only)

Functional Literacy – Students have a scientific vocabulary and can define terms, but primarily memorize these. There is a lack of personal experience with scientific concepts

Structural Literacy – Students understand terms in context, are developing procedural knowledge and skills of the field and can explain scientific concepts in their own words. Students construct meaning from their experiences. Students begin to link concepts

Multidimensional Literacy – Students can work independently, link ideas across scientific disciplines, understand the history and nature of science as a process, and understand links between science and society

It is easy to see that developing inquiry skills in students throughout their education (or enculturating students into inquiry) and developing science literacy are parallel, and both are "building" processes. Science literacy and inquiry activities progress along a continuum of increasingly more complex thinking/reasoning skills. For example, observing and recording those observations in a notebook is a critical, yet relatively simple task in the process of science and this activity would help develop a nominal level of science literacy. Reading an article and discussing the important information with classmates (or colleagues) is also critical to conducting inquiry on a subject and develops/requires a functional level of literacy. Synthesizing the literature on a topic and discussing the interpretation of data in the context of the other information in the field is also a critical component of inquiry and requires a more complex level of thinking (structural literacy). Certainly taking this information, designing and interpreting a scientific study and communicating it in the context of the discipline demonstrates a multidimensional level of science literacy. In this conceptual framework, learners are thought to construct content knowledge as they construct explanations to account for their findings. The appropriate assessment for such inquiries would vary according to the goal for the inquiry and would vary according to the expected level of literacy of the students.

Affective Requirements for Successful Classroom Inquiry

Although there is a range of issues to consider as one considers whether a classroom inquiry is appropriate (many of which—student ability, student prior knowledge, time, materials, and the nature of the content to be learned—are discussed throughout this text), one also must focus on how best to integrate inquiry-based activities given the "atmosphere" of the classroom. There are the subtle ways in which teachers develop the "climate of inquiry" in the classroom, among their students. On a coarse-scale this topic may seem to be analogous to classroom management; however we are referring to the more personal side of managing, and nurturing students' engagement in inquiry. Teacher behaviors that engender a "climate of inquiry" may include a respect for student ideas (giving students ownership), the ability to listen and ask reflective questions, genuine interest in student thoughts, flexibility, giving thoughtful and regular constructive feedback, confidence in students' abilities, and the ability to be fallible as the expert. With young students these characteristics lead to a feeling of caring in the classroom (Agne, 1992; Mills, 1997). Barbara Crawford's (2000) work in describing a teacher's role in establishing a community of learners for inquiry is particularly insightful here. Although traditional understandings of inquiry may describe that teachers are less involved in inquiry than they would be for a traditional lesson, Crawford's work suggests otherwise. She explains that given the different nature of student roles in inquiry that teachers are actually MORE involved in inquiry lessons than they are otherwise—the antithesis of their role in more discovery approaches to material. Much of teachers involvement has an affective dimension: their role as a motivator, a guide, a modeler of scientific attitudes and attributes, a supportive mentor requires teachers in inquiry classroom to be highly engaged, and to be very sensitive, and responsive to the affective dimensions of learning. Given the significance of these affective concerns in learning in general (Alsop, 2005), and inquiry specifically, we argue that this is an area in need of much more empirical and pedagogical attention.

The Optimal Form of Inquiry as a Niche

Rather than abandon the concept of 'inquiry' because complexity, we have looked to the natural world for an analogue, as a way to construce an analogy. We have found that in the work of Hutchinson (1957) with his construct of a niche. Let us start with a brief overview of niche theory and then discuss how niche theory may be a helpful lens by which to view inquiry in the classroom.

Niche is a biological population's "profession," the way in which a population makes use of a habitat. For example, in the Northeastern woods, there are two similar species of woodpeckers, the Downy and the Hairy. These woodpeckers look similar in size and appearance, inhabit the same forests and coexist. However, the Downy and the Hairy Woodpeckers have different niches. The Downy Woodpecker uses smaller branches of trees while the Hairy Woodpecker tends to spend more time on the trunk. Indeed, their target food species vary enough so they can overlap and individuals of both species can exist even on the same tree. To a novice birder, these birds seem identical but it is not until you start analyzing the complex and competing factors that influence the Downy and Hairy Woodpeckers selection of its "optimal" niche do you see the differences.

Hutchinson (1957) realized this complexity when he was trying to describe the factors that bounded the niches of various animals. He realized they needed to be conceptualized beyond the 3 factors or dimensions (something he referred to as "n-dimensional"). He explained that the location of a niche is at the junction of some number (n) of resource axes. He also realized the size and location of a niche may vary somewhat given a particular location and time. For example, niches of certain populations might expand if there is a lack of competition from another species or if there is more food types. "Optimal" is not a fix quality but is contextually dependent when describing the niche of a population.

If we use this analogy to conceptualize inquiry, then we could say that the way inquiry is enacted in any single classroom occurs at a point at the intersection of numerous resources axes. Just as the optimal niche for a population varies according to a number of variables, the nature of the classroom inquiry to be enacted will vary according to a number of variables.

In a more robust description of the factors influencing the optimal form of classroom inquiry, we understand that the actual classroom inquiry will "fall" somewhere in multidimensional space. (To conceptualize this hyperspace, think about a cube). The position of the inquiry is determined by the intersection of a number of axes in that classroom hyperspace can be placed within 5 broad, composite categories (1) logistical, (2) sociocultural, (3) cognitive ability/literacy, (4) nature of the content and (5) goals. Just as in any multivariate research environment, there are surely correlations between some of the 5 composite axes described and also significant interactions between these axes and the way in which learning is supported in a classroom climate (both explicitly and subtly) that affect learning outcomes. These labels are not effective ways to describe particular contexts. In this book's examples of inquiry in the classroom, teachers had particular reasons for their curricular choices. The niches for inquiry in the examples were often "optimal" given the resources (internally and externally) available. Rather we use these broad categories here as a way to think through all the variables that might influence the kind of inquiry that is enacted in a classroom.

Niche theory can help us think through why inquiry in the classroom does not always reach its full potential as espoused by reform efforts, science educators, and curriculum developers. Niche theory distinguishes between fundamental and realized niches. Fundamental includes all the possible conditions under which a population thrives and reproduces. A realized niche is the actual niche exhibited in a particular time and place. Realized niches will always be a subset or smaller than the fundamental niche for a variety of reasons. It is easy to envision a classroom where the resources will define the limits to how inquiry can be implemented in the classroom.

What Determines the Optimal Form of Inquiry?

We understand that the optimal form of enactment of classroom inquiry (i.e., Level 1, 2, 3, open versus structured, simple versus authentic task) must be determined by considering a large number of interacting factors, many of which will be discussed in this text: student ability and knowledge, contextual constraints, nature of the content to be learned, goals for the inquiry, to name a few. The way in which we understand this interaction is shown in Figures 1a and 1b. Imagine a teacher approaching a common activity/content—a pendulum laboratory in which students investigate the factors that influence the rate of swing of a pendulum. Teacher A's goal in this inquiry-based activity is to have her students learn specific content knowledge. She has limited time to prepare and teach this material, limited classroom space and limited materials—she will have to raid her desk and garage at home to locate the paperclips, washers and string. Her students enter the classroom with limited inquiry skills. Her content knowledge is adequate in both physical science and experimental design and our teacher recognizes that this activity could allow for a very high level inquiry. However, the other limiting factors (time, space and materials) shape the manner in which she approaches instruction.

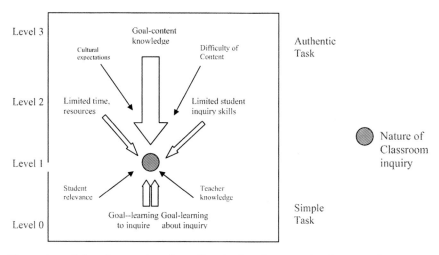

Figure 1a.   Select factors that shape Level 1 inquiry as optimal approach.

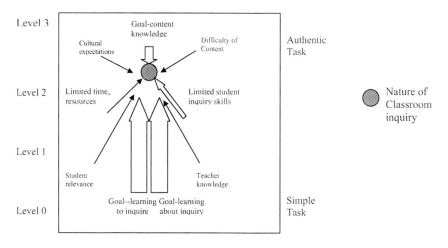

Figure 1b.   Select factors that shape Level 3 as optimal approach.

In such a situation, Teacher A chooses a straightforward approach in which the students are given the question to be answered, predetermined directions for collecting their data, and the teacher guides their sense making—that is a Level 1 inquiry. It is our argument, given her many constraints and content goals for the lesson, Level 1 is the optimal form of inquiry to enact in this context.

Figure 1b describes another set of factors for this same activity. The activity is the same but Teacher B has the overarching goals of learning to inquire and learning about inquiry. Time and materials are adequate in this classroom and she recognizes that her students bring with them developing inquiry skills. Under these conditions, a much more open, Level 2 or 3 inquiry could be accomplished with the same basic activity. For instance after the appropriate engagement activity, the teacher may allow her students to pose a number of questions about pendula, they could go on to design and conduct a variety of investigations, and they could determine answers to their questions based on these investigations. This is clearly a very different lesson than the Level 1 inquiry, with very different learning outcomes.

We use this example to show how the interaction of factors shape what form of inquiry is optimal, or if inquiry is optimal. By this example, we are not suggesting that the nature of the content to be learned does NOT play an important role, but in this example we held it constant to allow for our comparison. We see that the optimal form of inquiry is determined by a number of factors, and a specific context may call for a different form of inquiry to be enacted. We would expect that the nature of support that is needed in inquiry activities will vary as the level of the inquiry is shifted (Crawford, 2000), but we must be clear in our explanation that open ended, Level 3 inquiry is **NOT ALWAYS** the optimal approach to teaching science in all cases. The level of inquiry should vary as the different contextual and content factors vary.

To truly understand the relationships between these many dimensional variables and how they come together to determine the optimal for of inquiry may require large-scale multivariate analyses, such as those commonly used when scientists are trying to understand food webs, or ecosystem processes. But such empirical investigations into classroom inquiry can only be accomplished if we become much more systematic, rigorous and detailed in the ways we describe the inquiry events. Our broad definition of classroom inquiry is:

> Any cognitively appropriate activity that echoes some subset of the practices of authentic science in which students are expected to engage with resources (literature, people, environment) around the generation or answering of questions or the solving of problems.

Note here what is not included in this definition. We have deliberately left the goal of inquiry open. Likewise, the way in which inquiry is to be enacted remains unclear. That is because the nature of the inquiry will and should vary dependent on factors in our n-dimensional hyperspace of the classroom. To operationally define and to understand the influence of the hyperspace of the classroom, we need to revisit the principles that guide authentic practice and think about which parts of those principles and practices are appropriate in different inquiry models. The real matrix should be multidimensional, including the five composite axes discussed earlier—(1) logistical, (2) sociocultural, (3) cognitive ability/literacy, (4) nature of the content and (5) goals.

WHAT TO DO WITH ALL THIS?

Those of us who practice some version of classroom inquiry ALL have some intuitive sense of what it is when we are doing it and the degree to which it engages our students—whether they are third graders involved in a unit on decomposition, high schoolers engrossed in a forensics unit, science methods student struggling to understand the phases of the moon, or budding scientists involved in their own research projects. Many approaches to inquiry allow students to construct understandings of science content and the nature of the scientific enterprise as well and hone inquiries skills better than, or as well as, other pedagogies. We hope that by formally recognizing about how variable inquiry in the classroom can and should be, we can free ourselves from expectation that our students should be able to design and conduct, unique and novel, independent research projects and present us with their flawless reasoning and perfect interpretations when they have completed a few (or many) of our wonderful classroom "inquiry" activities.

Even if we agree that inquiry in the classroom is qualitatively or quantitatively different from what scientists experience in their practice (Chinn & Malhotra, 2002), and that real classroom environment is far from ideal for promoting the practices of authentic science, it is important to recognize that inquiry can be effective in achieving each of its formal goals (learning about inquiry, learning to inquire, and learning scientific knowledge).

As this introduction demonstrates, inquiry in the classroom is a very complex proposal. And like most complex proposals, it is difficult to describe and disseminate in a systematic manner. We argue that science educators must be willing to acknowledge this complexity and find tangible, systematic ways in which to discuss inquiry if we are to support teachers in appropriating this practice into their classroom repertoire. We have identified what we understand to be the central components of useful description of inquiry, and we argue there is a very real need for any discussion of inquiry to be prefaced with where that discussion resides on our n-dimensional hyperspace. Thus, throughout this book, we will situate each of the sections along what we understand to be the most immediately salient resource axes of this hyperspace. Where other aspects become salient (i.e., role of argument, inquiry as a way of knowing, authenticity of the task), those too should be identified. It is our hope that the recognition of the wide variation in inquiries will spark educational researchers and curriculum designers to compose useful exemplars of this variation (Songer, Lee, & McDonald, 2003) to further inform teachers' practice. Recognizing inquiry does exists as an n-dimensional hyperspace, each exemplar and discussion of inquiry should be accompanied at a minimum by the identification of its instructional goal and means of enactment so that the reader can recognize where this exemplar resides along the broad description of inquiry.

FURTHER FLESHING OUT THE COMPLEXITIES: THE REST OF THE BOOK

The purpose of this text is to further flesh out some of the factors—specific dimensions of our n-dimensional hyperspace—important to inquiry in the classroom. As such, some of the of the factors have already been introduced, others will be new to the conversation. In our discussions that lead to the preparation of this manuscript, it became clear that each of us was interested in classroom inquiry, and so we each wanted to situate our analysis in these classrooms. For that purpose, our discussions are organized into sections. Each section begins with one (or more) vignette—snippets of science classrooms—that the authors then discuss how this vignette demonstrates some aspect of the specific dimension that they are charged with discussing. Because inquiry is so multifaceted and its portrayals are often complex and nuanced, the discussion of the dimension is broken into separate essays—each of which addresses the focal dimension in different ways. Following the essay, a broader discussion across the essays is offered to support your sense making.

As we began this effort, we selected what we understood to be the most influential dimensions of inquiry in the classroom. But certainly there are others that can and should have been included, (i.e., the role of curriculum in supporting (or confining) the enactment of inquiry, the manner in which inquiry can shape students' knowledge, the role systemic efforts can have in enabling inquiry). But given the confines of one text, we have chosen what we understood to be the central components, and these have been arranged into 6 sections. Our vision is that each of these sections can be self-supporting, so their appearance in the text does not represent the order in which they must be read. Ideally, the reader would engage in the introduction, then select the section that addresses the dimension influencing classroom inquiry that is of greatest importance. The only exception to this is Section VI, which is a specific form of enactment of classroom inquiry; engagement with this section may be best augmented after reading the sections that interest you.

Section I. Students' Knowledge About and Skill With Inquiry

Norman G. Lederman, Sandra K. Abell, and Valarie Akerson

The authors of Section I focus on the dimension of student knowledge and its influence on what students learn from inquiry experiences, as well as how recognition of this knowledge should influence the manner in which inquiry in the classroom is enacted. They work to describe the "challenges and obstacles" students face during classroom inquiry.

Section II. Selecting and using Inquiry Approaches to Teach Science: The Influence of Context in Elementary, Middle, and Secondary Schools

Larry D. Yore, Laura Henriques, Barbara Crawford, Leigh Smith, Susan Gomez-Zwiep, and John Tillotson

The authors of Section II describe that the context in which teachers make decisions about the use of inquiry. Beyond the obvious physical structure of the school, school culture, grade-level norms, politics, and beliefs about science, science teaching, and science literacy have significant influences on teachers' abilities to implement inquiry teaching. Three sources of structure that that influence the success of inquiry teaching includes: students' cognitive influences (discussed in Section I), content influences (content structure), and contextual influences (i.e., teacher structure, institutional structure, curricular priorities, schedules). The authors work helps us understand that the sole focus on the inclination of teachers to enact inquiry (discussed in Section V) or students' abilities to learn through inquiry (discussed in Section I) is incomplete without recognizing the powerful influences institutional influences play on classroom inquiry. We must recognize how these factors change across grade levels.

Section III. Accommodating Student Diversity Within Inquiry

Liza Finkel, Kathleen Greene, and Jose Rios

Section III points to the need to bridge the culture between the students' worlds (particularly underserved students) and that of science (which has traditionally excluded those very persons underserved by schooling). The authors of this section explain how inquiry in the classroom is insufficient in and of itself to engage underserved students in science. If we are to allow all students the opportunity to participate in school-based science, we must go beyond simplistic models of inquiry in the classroom. They argue that we must also find ways in which students not only learn science concepts, but also begin to explore the sociocultural aspects of that knowledge and its production—exploring the social implications, ethical complications, and personal meanings of the science they learn.

Section IV. Standardized Test and Inquiry: The Accountability Movement and science education reforms

Sherry Southerland, Eleanor Abrams, and Todd Hutner

The authors of Section IV describe how standardized assessments currently employed in the push toward accountability in schooling and inquiry based science teaching are often seen as having contradictory and mutually exclusive goals. Following this description, they ask two important questions: How we do find ourselves in this position? How can we resolve this dilemma in ways that will allow for better student understanding of science? For this discussion, the authors recognize that any reform of teaching, and particularly science teaching, is a very difficult, long-term process that requires both structural changes in the system and personal changes in the knowledge and beliefs of teachers, administrators, and policy makers that work within and influence that system The first essay will focus primarily on some of the structural changes required, and the second essay will focus primarily on the personal changes required.

Section V. Teacher's Knowledge and Enacting Inquiry

John Settlage, Lee Meadows, Mark Olson, and Margaret Blanchard

Researchers' understandings about student inquiry are useful inasmuch as these are translated into classroom practice. In Section V, the authors examine the knowledge teachers require in order to be effective when implementing inquiry within science classrooms from very different perspectives with very different outcomes. The first essay in the section focuses on the pedagogical knowledge a teacher needs to effectively enact inquiry for student learning. The second centers on aspects of the content knowledge a teacher may need for successful enactment of inquiry. The third contribution within this section considers a particular approach to pedagogical knowledge is needed, namely that inquiry be removed from the realm of pedagogy and be conceived as a skill set that students should acquire.

Section VI. Student-Scientists Partnerships: Exploring One Example of Inquiry in the Classroom

David M. Moss, Catherine Koehler, and Barrett N. Rock

Section VI represents a departure from the other parts in the book in that it focuses on exploring a specific, and not atypical, form of inquiry in the classroom. Moss and his colleagues discuss student-scientists partnerships (SSPs) using the GLOBE program as the prototypical example of such partnerships. Their exploration allows for a close examination of how inquiry is often vague construct that is enacted in many classrooms which yields a fruitful analytical frame for identifying the benefits and limitations of inquiry in the classroom.

SUMMARY

Following our own proposal, at the outset of each section, we will situate the section's discussion of inquiry, highlighting the goals of inquiry employed by the authors, and the means through which they proposed inquiry is to be enacted in the classroom. We will indicate where each of these dimensions of inquiry overlap and interact with one another in significant ways. At the outset of this section, we have suggested that the educational research and teacher education communities take on more of the "conceptual work" in defining and describing useful applications of classroom based inquiry. It is our hope situating each section's discussion of inquiry via the lens of n-dimensional hyperspace, we will serve to make discussions of inquiry more rigorous, more systematic, and more useful for science teachers.

REFERENCES

Agne, K. (1992). Caring: The expert teacher's edge. *Educational Horizons, 70*(3), 120-24.

Alsop, S. (2005). *The affective dimensions of cognition: Studies from education in the sciences.* Dordrecht, The Netherlands: Kluwer.

American Association for Advancement of Science. (1989). *Science for all Americans.* Washington, DC: Author.

American Association for the Advancement of Science. (1993). *Benchmarks for science literacy.* New York: Oxford University Press.

Anderson, R.D. (2007). Inquiry as an organizing theme for science education. In S. K. Abell & N. G. Lederman (Eds.), *Handbook of research on science education* (pp. 807-830). Mahwah, NJ: Erlbaum.

Barrow, L. (2006). A brief history of inquiry: From Dewey to Standards. *Journal of Science Teacher Education, 17,* 265-278.

Biological Science Curriculum Studies (BSCS). (1993). *Developing biological literacy.* Dubuque, IA: Kendal/Hunt.

Bransford, J., Brown, A., & Cocking, R. (2000). *How People Learn: Brain, Mind, and Experience & School.* Washington, DC: National Academy Press.

Bruner, J. (1962). *The process of education.* Cambridge, MA: Harvard University Press.

Camins, A. H. (2001). Dimensions of inquiry. *FOSS Newsletter, 18.* Retrieved July 10, 2006, from http://lhsfoss.org/newsletters/archive/FOSS18 .InquiryDimensions.html

Chang, C., & Mao, S. (1999). Comparison of Taiwan science students' outcomes with inquiry-group versus traditional instruction. *The Journal of Educational Research, 92*(6), 340-346.

Chinn, C., & Malhotra, B. (2002). Epistemologically authentic inquiry in schools: A theoretical framework for evaluating inquiry tasks. *Science Education, 86,* 175–218

Colburn, A. (2000). An inquiry primer. *Science Scope, 23*(6), 42-44.

Crawford, B. A. (2000). Embracing the essence of inquiry: New roles for science teachers. *Journal of Research in Science Teaching, 37*(9), 916-937.

DeBoer, G. (1991). *History of idea in science education: Implications for practice.* New York: Teachers College Press.

Dewey, J. (1916). Method in science teaching. *The Science Quarterly, 1,* 3–9.

Driver, R. A., Newton, P., & Osborne, J. (2000). Establishing the norms of scientific argumentation in classrooms. *Science Education, 84*(3), 287-312.

Druva, C. A. & Anderson, R. D. (1983). Science teacher characteristics by teacher behavior and by student outcome: A meta-analysis of research. *Journal of Research in Science Teaching, 20*(5), 467-479.

Duschl, R. A., Schweingruber, H., & Shouse, A. W. (2007). *Taking science to school: Learning and teaching science in grades K-8.* Washington, DC: National Academy Press.

Edmondson, K. M. & Novak, J. D. (1993). The interplay of scientific epistemological views, learning strategies, and attitudes of college students. *Journal of Research in Science Teaching, 30,* 547-559.

Flick, F. B. (2003, March). *Inquiry as cognitive process.* Paper presented at the annual meeting of the National Association for Research in Science Teaching, Philadelphia.

Gallagher, J. J., & Tobin, K. (1987). Teacher management and student engagement in high school science. *Science Education, 71,* 535-555.

Gibson, H. L. (1998). *A study of the long term impact of an inquiry-based science program on students' attitudes towards science and interest in science careers.* Unpublished doctoral dissertation, University of Massachusetts, Boston.

Good, R. G., Shymansky, J. A., & Yore, L. D. (1999). Censorship in science and science education. In E. H. Brinkley (Ed.), *Caught off guard: Teachers rethinking censorship and controversy* (pp. 101-121). New York: Allyn & Bacon.

Grandy, R., & Duschl, R. (2005). *Reconsidering the character and role of inquiry in school science: Analysis of a conference.* Paper presented at the annual meeting of the International History, Philosophy, Sociology and Science Teaching Conference, Leeds, England.

Hall, D. A., & McCurdy, D. W. (1990). A comparison of a biological science curriculum study (BSCS) laboratory and a traditional laboratory on student achievement at two private liberal arts college. *Journal of Research in Science Teaching, 27*(7), 625-636.

Hodson, D. (1999). Building a case for a sociocultural and inquiry-oriented view of science education. *Journal of Science Education and Technology, 8*(3), 241-249.

Hutchinson, G. E. (1957). Concluding remarks. *Cold Spring Harbor Symposium on Quantitative Biology, 22,* 415-427.

Kuhn, D. (1993) Science as Argument: Implications for Teaching and Learning Scientific Thinking. *Science Education, 77*(3), 319-337.

Lee, O. (2003). Equity for linguistically and culturally diverse students in science education: A research agenda. *Teachers College Record, 105*(3), 465-489.

Lee, O., Hart, J. E., Cuevas, P., & Enders, C. (2004). Professional development in inquiry-based science for elementary teachers of diverse student groups. *Journal of Research in Science Teaching, 41*(10), 1021-1043.

Lee, O., Maerten-Rivera, J., Penfield, R., LeRoy, K, & Secada, W. (in press). Science Achievement of English Language Learners in Urban Elementary Schools: Results of a First-Year Professional Development Intervention. *Journal of Research in Science Teaching.*

Lederman, N. G. (2003). Never cry wolf. *School Science and Mathematics Journal, 103*(2), 61-65

Leonard, W. H. (1983). An experimental study of a BSCS-style laboratory approach for university general biology. *Journal of Research in Science Teaching, 20(9),* 807-813.

Marx, R. W., Blumenfeld, P. C., Krajcik, J. S., Fishman, B., Soloway, E., Geier, R., et al. (2004). Inquiry-based science in the middle grades: Assessment of learning in urban systemic reform. *Journal of Research in Science Education, 41*(10), 1063-1080.

McCarthy, C. B. (2005). Effects of thematic-based, hands-on science teaching versus a textbook approach for students with disabilities. *Journal of Research in Science Teaching, 42*(3), 245-263.

McComas, W. (Ed.). (1998). *The nature of science in science education.* Dordrecht, The Netherlands: Kluwer.

Mills, R. A. (1997). Expert teaching and successful learning at the middle level: One teacher's story. *Middle School Journal, 29,* 30-39.

Moss, D. M., Abrams, E. D., & Robb-Kull, J. (1998). Can we be scientists too? Secondary students' perceptions of scientific research from a project-based classroom. *Journal of Science Education and Technology, 7*(2) 149-161.

National Research Council. (1996). *National Science Education Standards.* Washington, DC: National Academy Press.

National Research Council. (2000). *Inquiry and the National Science Education Standards*. Washington, DC: National Academy Press.

National Science Teachers Association. (2004). *Designing inquiry pathways*. Last downloaded Feb. 12, 2007, http://science.nsta.org/enewsletter/2004-01/member_high.htm

Newton, P., Driver, R., & Osborne, J. (1999). The place of argumentation in the pedagogy of school science. *International Journal of Science Education, 21*(5), 553-576.

Park, Y. S., & Kim, C. J. (2006). *The opportunity of scientific argumentation in the classroom: Claim evidence approach*. A paper presented at the annual conference of Public Communication of Science and Technology, Seoul Korea.

Rivet, A. E., & Krajcik, J. S. (2004). Achieving standards in urban systemic reform: An example of a sixth grade project-based science curriculum. *Journal of Research in Science Teaching, 41*(7), 669-692.

Rop, C. J. (2003). Spontaneous inquiry questions in high school chemistry classrooms: perceptions of a group of motivated learners. *International Journal of Science Education, 25*(1), 13-33.

Rudolph, J. L. (2005). Inquiry, instrumentalism, and the public understanding of science. *Science Education, 89*(5), 803-821.

Rudolph, J. (2002). *Scientists in the classroom: The cold war reconstruction of American science education*. New York: Palgrave Macmillian.

Russell, C. P., & French, D. P. (2001). Factors affecting participation in traditional and inquiry-based laboratories. *Journal of College Science Teaching, 31*(4), 225-229.

Schwab, J. (1962). The teaching of science as enquiry. In *The teaching of science* (pp. 1-103). Cambridge, MA: Harvard University Press.

Settlage, J. (2003, January). *Inquiry's allure and illusion: Why it remains just beyond our reach*. Paper presented at the annual meeting of the National Association for Research in Science Teaching, Philadelphia.

Settlage, J., & Southerland, S.A. (2007). *Teaching science to all children: Using culture as a starting point*. New York: Routledge.

Singer, J., Marx, R. W., Krajcik, J., Chambers, J. C. (2000). Constructing extended inquiry projects: Curriculum materials for science education reform. *Educational Psychologist, 35*(3), 165-178.

Snively, G., & Corsiglia, J. (2001). Discovering indigeneous science: Implications for science education. *Science Education, 85*, 6-34.

Songer, N. B., Lee, H. S., & McDonald, S., & McDonald. (2003). Research towards an expanded understanding of inquiry science beyond one idealized standard. *Journal of Researchg in Science Teaching, 87*(4), 490-516.

SECTION I

STUDENT'S KNOWLEDGE AND SKILL WITH INQUIRY

Norman G. Lederman, Sandra K. Abell, and Valarie Akerson

EDITORS' NOTE

Describing Section I's Use of
Inquiry in the Classroom

Section I focuses on a particularly influential dimension of the classroom hyperspace for inquiry—that of student knowledge and skills. It is important to recognize that although many of us conceive of essential student knowledge and skills to be essential to he development of the relevant content and science process skills, the authors of Section I insightfully highlight the need for other little-mentioned aspects of this dimension, procedural and social skills. As we work to determine the optimal form of inquiry to be enacted in the classroom we must be mindful of this much more robust (and affectively informed) understanding of student knowledge and skills. These issues are again tackled in Section III ("Accommodating Student Diversity Within Inquiry") and Section V ("Teachers' Knowledge and Enacting Inquiry") and the lack of such understanding and its detrimental results in Section VI ("Student-Scientists Partnerships").

Some of the goals of the vignette presented at the outset of Section I are **learning to inquire** and **learning about inquiry.** Inquiry in the pursuit of science content knowledge is also touched upon, it is but only briefly. Thus, this vignette closely reflects the open inquiry dimensions of the classroom hyperspace as discussed in Figure 1b in the Introduction. The vignette that

Inquiry in the Classroom: Realities and Opportunities, pp. 3–35
Copyright © 2008 by Information Age Publishing
All rights of reproduction in any form reserved.

is the focus of Section I and its discussion do beg the question of the relationship between the various goals of inquiry—often it seems that the goal of the construction of scientific knowledge and the other two (learning to inquiry and learning about inquiry) are antithetical. As suggested in Norm Lederman's essay in Section I, one must wonder, must it be that way? Can one teach for all three goals in the same lesson?"

We have mentioned that the dimensions of the classroom hyperspace in the opening vignette do largely parallel that described in Figure 1B (see Introduction). The optimal form of inquiry mindful of the interaction of these various dimensions is a Level 3 inquiry. This is a relationship that we will see reflected throughout the text: an emphasis on learning to inquiry, learning about inquiry, along with adequate classroom resources, time and student abilities allow for a Level 3/open inquiry. What is novel about Section I, however, is that it does thoughtfully call into light the one aspect of the classroom hyperspace that is particularly temporal in nature, student skill level. Section I helps us understand that student skill levels need to be seen through a developmental lens. And the level of inquiry that is optimal at the beginning of a school year will transform as students' knowledge and skills transform and teacher planning needs to account and allow for this.

VIGNETTE

Ms. Pinto's seventh grade students enter the science classroom and notice that there is a 10-gallon fish tank on the front desk that is 3/4 filled with water. There is also an orange and a banana on the desk next to the fish tank. Once the students are settled, Ms. Pinto asks the students to raise their hands if they think the orange will float or sink in the fish tank. Most students think the orange will sink and a few are undecided. Ms. Pinto places the orange in the fish tank and it floats. The students, regardless of their predictions, react with glee. They seem to have enjoyed making the prediction and then seeing the result. Now Ms. Pinto peels the orange and asks the students to again predict whether it will float or sink. This time, most students think the orange will float and there are no students who are undecided. The students predicting it will float explain their prediction on the grounds that the orange now weighs less than when the skin was on and that it floated with the skin. Those thinking it will sink have made their prediction based on the assumption that Ms. Pinto would not be showing them the demonstration unless the results were different than what they would think.

Ms. Pinto places the peeled orange in the fish tank and it quickly sinks to the bottom. Surprised by the result, the students react with laughter and excitement. The students are now asked to predict what will happen to a banana when it is placed in the fish tank. The banana appears to be perfectly ripe, yellow with no black spots. Vir-

tually all of the students predict that the banana will float. Ms. Pinto asks the students for a reason and the most popular answer is that since the orange floated with its skin on, so will the banana. The banana is placed in the fish tank and, as predicted by most students, it floats. Noticing the pattern of events in this lesson, the students begin asking Ms. Pinto to peel the banana. After students have made predictions, Ms. Pinto obliges by placing the peeled banana in the fish tank. The peeled banana floats. There is a short discussion of how the banana behaved differently than the orange and then Ms. Pinto takes a cardboard box full of bananas from underneath her desk. The bananas are of different sizes; some are still green, some are perfectly yellow, and some are clearly beginning to spoil. Ms. Pinto peels several bananas and illustrates to the students that some peeled bananas float, some sink, and some remain suspended below the surface of the water. In addition, when Ms. Pinto slices some peeled bananas in half, the two parts may behave differently; that is, one part floats and one part sinks.

The students are very excited at this point. Ms. Pinto tells the class that they are going to have a chance to try to explain what they have just seen. The students will work in groups of four. Each group will have its own fish tank, a variety of bananas, and a butter knife. Ms. Pinto has the student groups develop a question they want to ask and then develop a design to answer their question. As the students work, Ms. Pinto walks around the room so she can get some idea of what the different groups have in mind. Before students can begin their investigation, Ms. Pinto must approve what the students have planned, but wants students to feel that they have maximum flexibility in terms of the question to be answered and the research design. This means that Ms. Pinto will approve just about any approach as long as it is not dangerous to students.

After about 15 minutes of planning, all groups are getting their materials and beginning the investigation. Ms. Pinto circulates as the students work and periodically asks students questions as they proceed with their investigations. Each group is also expected to write a laboratory report that includes the question(s) to be answered, procedures, results, and discussion. With about 10 minutes left in the class period, the students are asked to begin cleaning up. Because of the length of this laboratory, the students are told to be prepared to discuss their group's investigation the next day.

At the beginning of the class period the next day, the students are given 15 minutes to organize their presentation in groups. This is followed by a brief presentation by each group that summarizes the investigation performed. Although all groups did not investigate the same question, the investigations fell into three categories: comparisons of level of ripeness to floating and sinking, comparisons between full banana sizes, and comparisons between pieces of bananas. There is clearly variation in research designs as well as differences in groups' conclusions within the same category of research investigation. Ms. Pinto summarizes the lesson by engaging the students in a discussion of the importance of having a clear connection between evidence and conclusions. Ms. Pinto does not provide the stu-

dents with the "correct" answer because she does not have a definitive answer to explain the behavior of the bananas.

INTRODUCTION

Scientific inquiry has become a revitalized concern for science teaching and learning since the unveiling of Benchmarks for Science Literacy (1993) and the *National Science Education Standards* (National Research Council, 1996). Nevertheless, there remains much confusion among teachers about what scientific inquiry looks like in the classroom and what skills and knowledge students need to successfully participate in scientific inquiry. Consequently, it is not surprising that little has changed relative to the inclusion of scientific inquiry in actual classroom practice. In the following chapters of Section I three university science educators and former teachers consider the challenges and obstacles students face when asked to participate in scientific inquiry in response to the provided classroom vignette. Although the focus is on what students need to know and be able to do, we also comment on what teachers need to consider and do when designing and implementing inquiry experiences for their students.

In addition to focusing on the "doing" of inquiry (e.g., generating questions, designing investigations, collection, and analysis of data), each author will also focus on the often ignored knowledge "about" inquiry. This knowledge includes, but is not limited to such understandings as:

- All scientific investigations begin with a question, but do not necessarily test a hypothesis.
- There is no single set and sequence of steps followed by all scientific investigations (i.e., there is no single scientific method).
- Inquiry procedures are guided by the question asked.
- All scientists performing the same procedures may not get the same results.
- The "best" explanation is built by the community on the basis of the evidence collected, the beliefs of the community, the parsimony of the explanation, and so forth (as opposed to a vote or by consensus).

The authors take diverse perspectives on the key issues involved in the classroom vignette, sometimes overlapping on certain aspects. In the end, we hope the reader will be left with a richer appreciation for the considerations and tensions inherent in the implementation of inquiry into the science curriculum. We begin with a discussion of essential skills students must have in order to navigate an inquiry-based lesson, followed by a discussion of skills students need prior to participation in inquiry; the chapters end with a discussion of what students actually end up learning as a result of the inquiry vignette provided.

WHAT STUDENTS NEED TO KNOW AND DO IN INQUIRY-BASED INSTRUCTION

Sandra K. Abell

Although never directly stated, Ms. Pinto's goals for the activity described in the vignette in chapter 1 seems to have included improving students' inquiry abilities and understandings. Ms. Pinto seems to believe that this will happen merely by engaging students in the activity. Like many teachers, she sees the value in the doing, and assumes if students do inquiry, they learn inquiry. This view fails to take into account that inquiry abilities and understandings need to be nurtured explicitly if students are to improve (Abd-El-Khalick, Bell, & Lederman, 1998; Abell, 1999; Abell, Martini, & George, 2001). Furthermore, this view does not take into account students' incoming knowledge and skills (Bransford, Brown, & Cocking, 1999) that could influence what they learn in the lesson. That is, if students do not have the prerequisite inquiry knowledge and abilities assumed by their teacher, they will not be successful in this lesson.

What Ms. Pinto reasonably can expect of her seventh grade students will depend in part on their previous school science experiences. Ms. Pinto could look to the *National Science Education Standards* (NSES) (National Research Council, 1996) for guidance. The NSES could help her realize what students might already know and be able to do when they enter her class, as well as what inquiry abilities and understandings she might need to help them develop. The purpose of this essay is to examine the inquiry abilities and understandings with which students could be expected to enter seventh grade, and compare them with reasonable inquiry learning goals for Ms Pinto's lesson.

Inquiry Abilities

Inquiry abilities are those performances that we expect of students, either as a prerequisite for or as an outcome of inquiry-based instruction. They encompass the essential features of inquiry (National Research

Council, 2000) and include such abilities as asking questions, designing investigations, collecting and analyzing data, using evidence to construct explanations, and communicating explanations. Table 1 displays the NSES for Grades K-4, 5-8, and 9-12 related to these inquiry abilities. It would be reasonable for Ms. Pinto to expect that her seventh graders have achieved the inquiry abilities in the first column, but she will need to find explicit strategies to help them acquire the abilities in the second column. She could also use this table to help her think about the best ways to prepare her students for Grades 9-12.

Developing Questions

Involving students in scientific questions is an essential feature of inquiry. By grade four students should be able to ask scientific questions and answer them through a variety of methods. However, they might not be able to refine ill-defined problems or to figure out which questions require scientific investigations to address. Research with university level students demonstrates that collaborative group work can contribute to the formulation of questions guide investigations (de Jesus, de Souza, Teixeira-Dias, & Watts, 2005). Ms. Pinto expects her students to take a rather fuzzy problem about sinking and floating fruit and construct a researchable question. Unless students have had previous instruction and practice in constructing and refining researchable questions, they will have problems with this lesson, although working in groups might help students refine their questions. Ms. Pinto might provide explicit instruction about what makes a good research question. As preparation for later grades, Ms. Pinto will want to help students begin to connect their research questions to specific science concepts under study (see also Lederman's essay in Section I).

DESIGNING INVESTIGATIONS

Ms. Pinto expects students to design investigations in response to their questions. Experimental design is a challenging task that requires students to understand fair testing, to be able to sort dependent and independent variables, and to decide appropriate ways to observe and measure variables. To be successful, students need to be able to think through a series of steps ahead of time, and make logical connections between their question and the data they will collect. Young children need guidance in understanding the meaning and value of repeated trials in designing experiments (Varelas, 1997). According to the NSES

Ask a Question About Objects, Organisms, and Events in the Environment	Identify Questions That can be Answered Through Scientific Investigations	Identify Questions and Concepts That Guide Scientific Investigations
This aspect of the standard emphasizes students asking questions that they can answer with scientific knowledge, combined with their own observations. Students should answer their questions by seeking information from reliable sources of scientific information and from their own observations and investigations.	Students should develop the ability to refine and refocus broad and ill-defined questions. An important aspect of this ability consists of students' ability to clarify questions and inquiries and direct them toward objects and phenomena that can be described, explained, or predicted by scientific investigations. Students should develop the ability to identify their questions with scientific ideas, concepts, and quantitative relationships that guide investigation.	Students should formulate a testable hypothesis and demonstrate the logical connections between the scientific concepts guiding a hypothesis and the design of an experiment. They should demonstrate appropriate procedures, a knowledge base, and conceptual understanding of scientific investigations.
Plan and Conduct a Simple Investigation.	*Design and Conduct a Scientific Investigation*	*Design and Conduct Scientific Investigations*
In the earliest years, investigations are largely based on systematic observations. As students develop, they may design and conduct simple experiments to answer questions. The idea of a fair test is possible for many students to consider by fourth grade.	Students should develop general abilities, such as systematic observation, making accurate measurements, and identifying and controlling variables. They should also develop the ability to clarify their ideas that are influencing and guiding the inquiry, and to understand how those ideas compare with current scientific knowledge. Students can learn to formulate questions, design investigations, execute investigations, interpret data, use evidence to generate explanations, propose alternative explanations, and critique explanations and procedures.	Designing and conducting a scientific investigation requires introduction to the major concepts in the area being investigated, proper equipment, safety precautions, assistance with methodological problems, recommendations for use of technologies, clarification of ideas that guide the inquiry, and scientific knowledge obtained from sources other than the actual investigation. The investigation may also require student clarification of the question, method, controls, and variables; student organization and display of data; student revision of methods and explanations; and a public presentation of the results with a critical response from peers. Regardless of the scientific investigation performed, students must use evidence, apply logic, and construct an argument for their proposed explanations.

Table continues on next page.

Table 1. Standards for Inquiry Abilities, K-4, 5-8, and 9-12 Continued

K-4	5-8	9-12
Employ Simple Equipment and Tools to Gather Data and Extend the Senses	*Use Appropriate Tools and Techniques to Gather, Analyze, and Interpret Data*	*Use Technology and Mathematics to Improve Investigations and Communications*
In early years, students develop simple skills, such as how to observe, measure, cut, connect, switch, turn on and off, pour, hold, tie, and hook. Beginning with simple instruments, students can use rulers to measure the length, height, and depth of objects and materials; thermometers to measure temperature; watches to measure time; beam balances and spring scales to measure weight and force; magnifiers to observe objects and organisms; and microscopes to observe the finer details of plants, animals, rocks, and other materials. Children also develop skills in the use of computers and calculators for conducting investigations.	The use of tools and techniques, including mathematics, will be guided by the question asked and the investigations students design. The use of computers for the collection, summary, and display of evidence is part of this standard. Students should be able to access, gather, store, retrieve, and organize data, using hardware and software designed for these purposes.	A variety of technologies, such as hand tools, measuring instruments, and calculators, should be an integral component of scientific investigations. The use of computers for the collection, analysis, and display of data is also a part of this standard. Mathematics plays an essential role in all aspects of an inquiry. For example, measurement is used for posing questions, formulas are used for developing explanations, and charts and graphs are used for communicating results.
Use Data To Construct a Reasonable Explanation	*Develop Descriptions, Explanations, Predictions, and Models Using Evidence*	*Formulate and Revise Scientific Explanations and Models Using Logic and Evidence*
This aspect of the standard emphasizes the students' thinking as they use data to formulate explanations. Even at the earliest grade levels, students should learn what constitutes evidence and judge the merits or strength of the data and information that will be used to make explanations. After students propose an explanation, they will appeal to the knowledge and evidence they obtained to support their explanations. Students should check their explanations against scientific knowledge, experiences, and observations of others.	Students should base their explanation on what they observed, and as they develop cognitive skills, they should be able to differentiate explanation from description–providing causes for effects and establishing relationships based on evidence and logical argument. This standard requires a subject matter knowledge base so the students can effectively conduct investigations, because developing explanations establishes connections between the content of science and the contexts within which students develop new knowledge.	Student inquiries should culminate in formulating an explanation or model. Models should be physical, conceptual, and mathematical. In the process of answering the questions, the students should engage in discussions and arguments that result in the revision of their explanations. These discussions should be based on scientific knowledge, the use of logic, and evidence from their investigation.

Think Critically and Logically to Make the
Relationships Between Evidence and Explanations

Thinking critically about evidence includes deciding what evidence should be used and accounting for anomalous data. Specifically, students should be able to review data from a simple experiment, summarize the data, and form a logical argument about the cause-and-effect relationships in the experiment. Students should begin to state some explanations in terms of the relationship between two or more variables.

Recognize and Analyze Alternative
Explanations and Predictions

Students should develop the ability to listen to and respect the explanations proposed by other students. They should remain open to and acknowledge different ideas and explanations, be able to accept the skepticism of others, and consider alternative explanations.

Recognize and Analyze Alternative
Explanations and Models

This aspect of the standard emphasizes the critical abilities of analyzing an argument by reviewing current scientific understanding, weighing the evidence, and examining the logic so as to decide which explanations and models are best. In other words, although there may be several plausible explanations, they do not all have equal weight. Students should be able to use scientific criteria to find the preferred explanations.

Table continues on next page.

Table 1. Standards for Inquiry Abilities, K-4, 5-8, and 9-12 Continued

K-4	5-8	9-12
Communicate Investigations and Explanations	*Communicate Scientific Procedures and Explanations*	*Communicate and Defend a Scientific Argument*
Students should begin developing the abilities to communicate, critique, and analyze their work and the work of other students. This communication might be spoken or drawn as well as written	With practice, students should become competent at communicating experimental methods, following instructions, describing observations, summarizing the results of other groups, and telling other students about investigations and explanations.	Students in school science programs should develop the abilities associated with accurate and effective communication. These include writing and following procedures, expressing concepts, reviewing information, summarizing data, using language appropriately, developing diagrams and charts, explaining statistical analysis, speaking clearly and logically, constructing a reasoned argument, and responding appropriately to critical comments.
	Use Mathematics in all Aspects of Scientific Inquiry	
	Mathematics is essential to asking and answering questions about the natural world. Mathematics can be used to ask questions; to gather, organize, and present data; and to structure convincing explanations	

Source: From National Research Council, 1996

(National Research Council [NRC], 1996), entering seventh graders should be able to consider fair testing, but they may have "trouble identifying variables and controlling more than one variable in an experiment" (p. 143). Ms. Pinto should engage her students in a range of experiences with planning investigations; she will need to find ways to teach the planning process while students do the planning. For example, using an investigation design worksheet (Abell, 1999; Harlen, 2001) will help prepare students for more sophisticated planning required in later grades (see Table 1).

Data Collection, Analysis, and Explanations

In the early grades, students typically have the opportunity to use various tools to observe and measure, so that by seventh grade, Ms. Pinto should expect her students to know which tools will be best for collecting the kinds of data they need. Students will have had some experiences using technology tools to organize information. By seventh grade, Ms. Pinto will need to teach students more sophisticated data organization tools (e.g., spreadsheets, databases) and analysis techniques (e.g., descriptive statistics). In later grades, students will use mathematics more frequently throughout an investigation.

Another essential feature of inquiry (NRC, 2000) is that students use evidence to build explanations. According to the NSES (NRC, 1996), it is reasonable to expect that students in grades K-4 can use data as evidence to support and compare explanations. At these grades, student explanations are often descriptive. Elementary students understand various types of uncertainty in their data and can posit strategies for modifying experiments to remove uncertainty (Metz, 2004). By seventh grade, we want students to move beyond description to demonstrate a logical flow between cause and effect. Teachers may need to be mediators between scientific ideas and experimental data during inquiry (Varelas, 1996). In her lesson, Ms. Pinto will need to help students state their explanations in terms of the relationship between variables. Ms. Pinto should expect her students to have had some experiences with comparing different explanations for a phenomenon by the time they get to seventh grade. She may need to help them remain open to ideas that are different from their own, and be able to analyze and evaluate the explanations in terms of the quality of the evidence. Explanations may take the form of models of how the phenomenon works, paving the way for students to use a variety of types of models (physical, conceptual, and mathematical) in later grades.

Communicating

In Grades K-4, we hope that students have had a variety of experiences in communicating their scientific ideas through writing, drawing, and speaking (Varelas, Becker, Luster, & Wenzel, 2002). They may have begun to critique their work and that of others. By seventh grade, Ms. Pinto should expect more details in these communications related to experimental questions, methods, and findings. For example, she might have students practice writing conclusions based on a variety of data sets, and then apply this skill in the sinking/floating lesson. In addition, seventh graders should add mathematics to their communication tool box. Ms. Pinto might eventually present students with the formula for density and expect students to incorporate it into their explanations of floating and sinking fruit. All of these communication skills will be built on in subsequent grades (see Table 1).

Summary

Students come to science classes at every grade with a range of experiences with inquiry—either within the formal school science setting or beyond. They have developed abilities to do inquiry related to asking questions, designing investigations, collecting and analyzing data, and developing and communicating explanations. Teachers must take these incoming abilities (or lack thereof) into account when planning inquiry-based lessons. They must find ways to support students to enhance their abilities in these areas through explicit instruction that occurs within the context of inquiry. Researchers have found that practicing inquiry skills does help to improve those skills (Hofstein, Shore, & Kipnis, 2004).

Ms. Pinto should not assume that all students can generate testable questions and design fair tests without support from the teacher. Instead, she should provide scaffolding for investigations. For example, introducing an investigation-planning sheet (Abell, 1999; Harlen, 2001) can help students identify the important variables in their study and focus on how their proposed procedures will provide evidence related to their questions. Teacher checkpoints during the process can help ensure that students develop specific abilities. Ms. Pinto should provide explicit instruction around specific inquiry abilities as partial inquiry activities throughout the school year. For example, students can practice writing and refining researchable questions, even if they never pursue them. Students can practice writing conclusions based on data provided by the teacher. Then when they undertake a full inquiry, such as in this vignette, they will be able to apply these skills confidently and successfully.

Inquiry Understandings

At the same time that students are developing abilities for doing inquiry, they are building understandings about scientific inquiry (see Table 2). The understandings are often the result of metacognition in relation to inquiry-based activities (Bransford, Brown, & Cocking, 1999; Zion, Michalsky, & Mevarech, 2005). That is, good teachers help students think about the thinking processes that they have used and focus students on knowing how to improve.

In the case of Ms. Pinto's class, it is clear that she expects students to come to her class with a set of understandings about inquiry that parallel the NSES for Grades K-4. She expects them to know that scientific investigations involve asking questions, collecting information, developing explanations, and sharing their work. These are relatively easy ideas to develop because they are the foundation for every science investigation. By the seventh grade, she might try to develop more advanced understandings of scientific inquiry, and to help students understand how scientific inquiry differs from inquiry in other fields. For example, in the sinking and floating lesson, she might emphasize the role of skepticism in science by asking students to examine the evidence collected by different groups and comment on the quality of the evidence. She might demonstrate the importance of the scientific community by helping students respectfully challenge each others' explanations and reasoning.

These types of teacher guidance can help students move from the K-4 understandings about inquiry to the more in-depth understandings expected in Grades 5-8, and ready them for Grades 9-12 expectations. Explicit instruction about inquiry can help students recognize that the enterprise of science involves both doing and thinking. Newly developed understandings about inquiry will help students recognize both the potential and limitations of scientific ways of knowing.

CONCLUSION

The vignette about Ms. Pinto illustrates some common ways that teachers engage students in inquiry. Embedded in these methods are common assumptions about students. For example, teachers assume that students possess a repertoire of inquiry abilities and understandings, and predict that they will be able to carry out investigations without difficulty. Oftentimes, teachers are disappointed when students do not meet their expectations in inquiry-oriented settings. However, rather than blame the students, teachers might reconsider their assumptions about students,

Table 2. Standards for Inquiry Understandings, K-4, 5-8, and 9-12

K-4	5-8	9-12
• Scientific investigations involve asking and answering a question and comparing the answer with what scientists already know about the world	• Different kinds of questions suggest different kinds of scientific investigations. Some investigations involve observing and describing objects, organisms, or events; some involve collecting specimens; some involve experiments; some involve seeking more information; some involve discovery of new objects and phenomena; and some involve making models.	• Scientists usually inquire about how physical, living, or designed systems function. Conceptual principles and knowledge guide scientific inquiries. Historical and current scientific knowledge influence the design and interpretation of investigations and the evaluation of proposed explanations made by other scientists.
• Scientists use different kinds of investigations depending on the questions they are trying to answer. Types of investigations include describing objects, events, and organisms; classifying them; and doing a fair test (experimenting).	• Current scientific knowledge and understanding guide scientific investigations. Different scientific domains employ different methods, core theories, and standards to advance scientific knowledge and understanding.	• Scientists conduct investigations for a wide variety of reasons. For example, they may wish to discover new aspects of the natural world, explain recently observed phenomena, or test the conclusions of prior investigations or the predictions of current theories.
• Simple instruments, such as magnifiers, thermometers, and rulers, provide more information than scientists obtain using only their senses.	• Mathematics is important in all aspects of scientific inquiry.	• Scientists rely on technology to enhance the gathering and manipulation of data. New techniques and tools provide new evidence to guide inquiry and new methods to gather data, thereby contributing to the advance of science.
• Scientists develop explanations using observations (evidence) and what they already know about the world (scientific knowledge). Good explanations are based on evidence from investigations.	• Technology used to gather data enhances accuracy and allows scientists to analyze and quantify results of investigations.	• The accuracy and precision of the data, and therefore the quality of the exploration, depends on the technology used
• Scientists make the results of their investigations public; they describe the investigations in ways that enable others to repeat the investigations.	• Scientific explanations emphasize evidence, have logically consistent arguments, and use scientific principles, models, and theories. The scientific community accepts and uses such explanations until displaced by better scientific ones. When such displacement occurs, science advances.	
• Scientists review and ask questions about the results of other scientists' work.		

- Science advances through legitimate skepticism. Asking questions and querying other scientists' explanations is part of scientific inquiry. Scientists evaluate the explanations proposed by other scientists by examining evidence, comparing evidence, identifying faulty reasoning, pointing out statements that go beyond the evidence, and suggesting alternative explanations for the same observations.
- Scientific investigations sometimes result in new ideas and phenomena for study, generate new methods or procedures for an investigation, or develop new technologies to improve the collection of data. All of these results can lead to new investigations.
- Mathematics is essential in scientific inquiry. Mathematical tools and models guide and improve the posing of questions, gathering data, constructing explanations and communicating results.
- Scientific explanations must adhere to criteria such as: a proposed explanation must be logically consistent; it must abide by the rules of evidence; it must be open to questions and possible modification; and it must be based on historical and current scientific knowledge.
- Results of scientific inquiry—new knowledge and methods—emerge from different types of investigations and public communication among scientists. In communicating and defending the results of scientific inquiry, arguments must be logical and demonstrate connections between natural phenomena, investigations, and the historical body of scientific knowledge. In addition, the methods and procedures that scientists used to obtain evidence must be clearly reported to enhance opportunities for further investigation.

Source: From National Research Council, 1996.

determine the abilities and understandings that are necessary for student success in inquiry, and provide supports that will lead to student success.

We know that not all students are equally prepared for classroom inquiry (see chapter on diversity, this volume). For some reason, they have not developed the prerequisite inquiry knowledge and skills. Perhaps their elementary schools did not emphasize science as inquiry. Perhaps their teachers did not understand the interplay of student background and success in inquiry (Lee & Luykx, 2005). Perhaps the students did not receive implicit instruction about inquiry abilities and understandings.

The *National Science Education Standards* (NRC, 1996) provide guidance for the kinds of inquiry abilities and understandings that teachers of various grades levels should aim to build. These abilities and understandings do not arise naturally from the doing of inquiry. Instead, they must be encouraged, supported, and coached by teachers. Inquiry requires a lot from students; finding ways to build students' inquiry abilities and understandings through explicit attention to them throughout science lessons is key to student success.

HOW DO I DO THIS? SKILLS STUDENTS NEED FOR INQUIRY

Valarie Akerson

To be able to design and carry out a classroom inquiry, students require many different skills beyond the cognitive abilities required to engage in inquiry. Sunal and Sunal (2003) state that middle school students need to be involved in making observations, gathering and communicating evidence, and hands on science experiences to participate in inquiry. Being able to conduct a scientific investigation, therefore, requires much in the way of abilities beyond thinking about the problem at hand. Classroom inquiry also requires facility with many other skills. Students need to have the skills that allow them to attend to detail and not get off task or distracted and be able to work in a lab. They also need to have an understanding of the kinds of equipment and technology that is available and will help them to answer their questions within their investigation. They need to be aware of what is available in their classrooms to use, and know how to use that material, as well as have an understanding of which equipment is most reasonable to provide them the support they need in their investigations. They need to have the social and communications skills that allow them to work collaboratively and cooperatively, and to possess the time management skills that enable them to design an investigation that fits within the given time frame.

Learner characteristics influence the content that students are able to glean from instruction (Akerson & Buzzelli, in press), and thus it is important that students possess the characteristic skills necessary to engage in inquiry. Teaching and assessing, both formally and informally, these myriad skills is the work of school. The complex layers of skills involved in completing inquiry tasks are the focus of this essay.

Attention Skills

As we know from middle school classrooms, middle school students often have trouble attending to coursework in favor of just about any other kind of distraction. Thus, staying focused on the classroom task is an important skill that middle school students need to develop. The demonstration that Ms. Pinto used (see chapter 1) at the beginning of the class period seems to draw all the students' attention, and to kindle their interest in the investigation. A tangible excitement permeates the classroom and the students appear to be interested in continuing the investigations with the fruit independently. At this point in the class the students need to change their attention from the demonstration to a focus on the investigation and the variables they could explore, such as the levels of ripeness in the bananas, pieces of bananas, and banana sizes, versus simply being swept away by the "coolness" of the activity. Rather than attending to the idea that the fruit in the tank is "cool," they need to be able to shift their attention to what the teacher wants them to investigate in terms of density and buoyancy. While they are planning, carrying out, and writing up their investigation, they need to be able to be able to attend to one another's ideas regarding deciding the research focus, the plan for the investigation, and interpreting the results, with a minimum of distractions and off-task behavior. Ms. Pinto must have clear classroom expectations that she communicates to the students, as well as a classroom management plan that is understood and followed by the students (Marzano, Marzano, & Pickering, 2003).

If we think about what students in Ms. Pinto's class are concerned about in terms of Maslow's hierarchy of needs (Huitt, 2004), it makes sense that they are more focused on interacting with one another rather than initially attending to the classroom task. Students' "belongingness" and "self-esteem" needs are lower on the hierarchy than their "need to know and understand" needs, meaning these concerns about belonging to their group are stronger, and need to be met through their interactions before they are ready for the cognitive challenge set forth as a problem for their investigation. Additionally, they must sense that engaging in the classroom investigation makes them part of the group, and will not alienate them from their belonging to the group.

The students' attention to this problem needs to carry over to the day after the investigation. They need to be able to recall the previous day's investigation so they can share their designs and results on the second day. Attention needs to be made of the kinds of details that should be shared with others to allow them to understand the group's design and interpretations.

The middle school students in Ms. Pinto's class also need to be able to attend to the details of their peers' research designs and interpretations during the second day's presentations. They must be able to focus on these presentations and be able to draw out common themes, or differences among research designs and interpretations. Thus, they will be able to have the concluding discussion that Ms. Pinto wishes them to have regarding how inquiry is done by scientists, and how their work was like what scientists do.

Lab Skills

As an experienced teacher Ms. Pinto has probably set up some kind of classroom procedure for retrieving and storage of classroom materials. Students need to be aware of these procedures to use in labs. They need to know where to find materials, which materials they can readily use, and which require the permission of the teacher. There are certainly safely procedures and rules set up in the class. They should understand the procedure for cleaning up their lab areas, lab materials, and storing the materials. Again, Ms. Pinto should have a classroom management plan set up to enable smooth organization, retrieval, and clean up of materials (Marzano, Marzano, & Pickering, 2003).

Technology and Materials Selection Skills

The middle school students in Ms. Pinto's class need to be able to think about the kinds of materials and technology that they have available to them that would help them with their investigations. Krajcik, Czerniak, and Berger (2003) indicate that middle school students need to be taught how to use technology to develop meaningful understandings, and to explore scientific ideas, as well as have the skills to simply navigate the technology, such as using the Internet as a search tool. Students need to think about the kinds of tools they might need to help them in this investigation, such as knives to cut the bananas, or perhaps discussing and deciding whether mass scales could help them determine any differences in the bananas. They need to have the skills not only to select the kinds of tools that can help them with their investigations, but the understandings of and abilities to properly use them. Ms. Pinto needs to provide direct instruction for how and when to use the different instruments so students will be able to self select the instruments during investigations, and then know how to use them appropriately.

For their work in recording data and also for writing their lab report the students may require the use of technology, specifically a computer. Perhaps they could use a graphing program to enable them to record the density of different bits of banana and whether it sinks or floats to help them interpret the differences in bananas. To word-process their lab reports the students would need keyboarding skills. They would need to know how to format their reports. Some of these computer skills may be taught by Ms. Pinto in the context of her science course, while other skills may be taught in other classes.

Social Skills

As we know, middle school students are very social beings who enjoy talking and interacting with one another. Some would state that it is within social interactions that science learning takes place (Cazden, 2001; Edwards & Mercer, 1987; Lemke, 1990). During an inquiry investigation, however, their social skills need to extend to work groups. Students need to be able to follow any cooperative learning procedures and assigned roles set up by Ms. Pinto for group work (Slavin, 1994). Particularly effective groups for inquiry would be small groups of two to four students within an environment of collaboration. In cooperative learning groups students are often assigned tasks such as "recorder," "equipment gatherer," "experimenter," and so forth. Students in cooperative groups must understand teamwork, how to support one another and accept differences, be active and reflective listeners, provide positive feedback, reach consensus, and how to coach and tutor others. If the teacher chooses cooperative groups, the students need to understand those roles, and be able to undertake the tasks associated with the roles, such as recording ideas, or ensuring that all group members are involved and get to share ideas. Ms. Pinto needs to provide explicit instruction as to the duties required of each role. If Ms. Pinto has not assigned specific tasks to individual group members there are still numerous social skills that these seventh grade students need to have to be able to undertake the inquiry task given them. Possibly a first task would be to decide who will do which tasks—who will record ideas, who will retrieve materials, who will be their spokesperson, and who will take the lead in clean up.

All of the students need to be able to share and take turns with materials and conducting the tests that they have planned. They need to be able to negotiate ideas when planning and conducting the investigation, and while interpreting the results. The students need to be able to interact well with each other whether or not Ms. Pinto is standing near and listening to their group.

In addition to their small group social skills, these middle school students need to have the social skills required of large group discussion. They need to be able to listen to peer groups' discussions of their research designs and results on the second day of this lesson. They need to be able to draw common themes and distinctions between ideas that are presented by their peers.

Communication Skills

Closely related to social skills are communication skills that contribute to sharing ideas in both written and oral forms (Saul, 2004). Gee (2004) describes the use of language in the science classroom as an academic language, that needs to be learned by students. The social language that students generally use is a different style than the academic language that they are learning for communicating their scientific ideas. Lemke (2004) indicates that scientific literacy is related to the use of language and print and spoken language. While middle school students enjoy communicating with one another, there are multiple communications skills necessary for them to engage in a classroom inquiry. Students in Ms. Pinto's class need to be able to communicate their ideas with one another. For instance, when deciding the focus of their investigations, students need to be able to describe their idea for the topic, and justify why their idea would be a good one for investigation. One hopes that the students in the class would be able to select the most appropriate idea for investigation based on sound ideas rather than whether or not the proposer of the idea held some kind of social status in the classroom. Students' communications with one another can provide insight into what they are learning, so their discussions must be on task (Edwards, 1993). Monitoring the interactions between the students will help the teacher to discern their understandings, as well as to keep students on task.

Once the focus of the investigation is selected, students must communicate feasible ideas for procedures of the investigation. These ideas need to be communicated to the group members; as well as to Ms. Pinto as she listens to them share their designs for approval. The students need to communicate their ideas for making observations and recording data, and then they need to communicate their ideas for what they believe is happening in their investigations as they are making inferences. These ideas need to be shared with each other in their group to help each other draw reasonable conclusions and see many sides of a conclusion.

The communication skills mentioned already are verbal, yet written communication skills are required of these students as well. Students must make written records of their observations. These observations need to be recorded in an organized way that enables the students to draw reasonable inferences and conclusions.

In addition to recording the observations in writing, the students need to be able to communicate their entire investigation in a written form through the lab report that is part of the lesson. They need to write clearly in their questions, procedures for answering the questions, results of the investigation, and then a discussion section regarding the interpretation of those results. This written communication needs to follow writing conventions and the format given them by Ms. Pinto. The students need to be able to decide what details are necessary to include in the report so the reader can understand their investigation and their conclusions. They need to include enough detail, and need to leave out any extraneous information that does not help them describe their investigation. Akins and Akerson (2002) and Nixon and Akerson (2004) have both found that writing can support student learning in connection with inquiry focused curricula. In each case teachers found that writing helped students conceptualize and communicate content in both physical and life science lessons.

A final formal verbal communication is required in this lesson. The students in this class are required to formally present their investigations verbally to their peers. They are given only 5 minutes to do this brief presentation. Similar to writing their lab report, to make this presentation they need to decide which details are necessary to share with their peers so they understand the full investigation and conclusions. They need to be able to briefly describe their investigation in a comprehensible fashion to others who were not part of the investigation.

Time Management Skills

One skill that eludes even experienced teachers is time management (Harlen, 2000). It is always difficult to negotiate different tasks in classroom in a way that fills the time appropriately. It is likely more difficult for middle school students to estimate the amount of time required for different tasks as part of their inquiry. Ms. Pinto led the first part of the lesson with a demonstration. She then gave the students 15 minutes to decide on a question and devise a plan for investigation. These students need to have skill in managing the 15 minutes given them to do two tasks: (a) identify the questions they want to answer and (b) plan a procedure for how they want to answer those questions.

These middle school students also need to use time management skills while they carry out their investigation. The investigation needs to fit within the remaining amount of the class period, leaving 10 minutes for clean up at the end. This limited time may eliminate any tangential investigations that they would like to do in conjunction with their planned investigations; however if they do not have good time management skills they may undertake related investigations and not have enough time to complete their planned investigation. They students must also plan to use their time during their investigation to write their lab report as they go during the same class period—recording their procedures, results, and a discussion of ideas that convey an organized report of their work and communicates their ideas in a written form.

On the following day the students must use the 15 minutes allotted at the beginning of the class period to organize their oral presentation of their results. This planning for the presentation also uses time management skills. In 15 minutes they must decide what details are necessary to share with their peers so they understand the investigation and conclusions, and they must also decide how they are going to present the information in a manner that is interesting to their peers and best conveys their message. During the presentation itself they need to use time management skills so they are best filling the time with the appropriate information without going over the allotted time. These skills are difficult for expert presenters, and are certainly equally difficult for middle school students.

Conclusion

The acquisition of the varied skill sets that students need to engage in learning within an academic community is not solely Ms. Pinto's responsibility; hopefully, these students have been practicing these skills in each of their classrooms. However, Ms. Pinto needs to prepare this investigation with an understanding of which skills require introduction, reinforcement, and mastery. She needs to establish clear parameters of expectations so that a culture of inquiry can prevail in her science classroom. Her students will need to rely on her instruction to guide them in their fledgling explorations of scientific inquiry.

WHAT DID YOU DO IN SCIENCE TODAY?

Norman G. Lederman

Ms. Pinto's lesson in chapter 1 certainly appears to contain many of the positive attributes often associated with inquiry-oriented instruction. The students are clearly engaged and motivated. They are working with familiar materials and they are given relative freedom to develop research questions, although the teacher has provided a general question concerning the different floating behavior of different bananas. On the other hand, students are given almost complete freedom to design the investigations to answer their questions. The teacher is the proverbial "guide on the side" instead of assuming the role of dispenser of information. However, there is always a tension between student engagement and student learning when it comes to such lessons. That is, one might wonder what the students have really learned. Was any science content learned? Was anything about inquiry learned? Can students learn about inquiry independent of learning some science subject matter? When they meet their friends in the hallway or at lunch, how will these students answer the question, What did you do in science today? Will they just say they had a lot of fun or will they talk about what they learned?

Initial Stages of the Lesson

The lesson begins with a demonstration by the teacher. Of critical importance is that the demonstration has students make predictions. These predictions are sometimes based on prior knowledge and at other times are based on intuition. However, students' predictions, in general, are eventually incorrect. This discrepancy piques students' interest in the lesson (Joyce, Weil, & Showers, 1992). In this case, the predictions are made publicly, but if the predictions were made "secretly" on paper the effect would have been similar. The predictions give the students some vested interest in the subsequent behavior of the orange and banana. Most would agree that the beginning of the lesson is a good exemplar of inquiry in the science classroom. The students have become engaged in a problem, the proverbial "hook." On the other hand, it can be argued that the problem created is unrelated to any science content that students are studying. Or, perhaps, the teacher has not made the connection for the students and has not asked the students to make any connections. For example, if the students had been studying floating and sinking or density, students could have been asked to make connections to these topics in their comments about the behavior of the banana and orange. So, the first issue that immediately surfaces is the relative balance given to student engagement and a focus on subject matter. Can the lesson be successful without any connection to subject matter included in the curriculum? Is giving students the opportunity to further develop their observation and inferential skills enough? Some may argue that of more importance is whether the inquiry is related to a social issue of interest, so that relevancy is established. It is clear in this vignette, and in everyday classroom life, that student engagement is not contingent upon relevancy. It is also clear that valid inquiry is not contingent upon whether the investigation is related to a social issue (although many good investigations can focus around a social issue); it can be related to a scientific phenomenon in and of itself.

Debrief of the Demonstration

Following the demonstration, the students, in groups, are asked to develop a question of interest that is derived from the demonstration. From an inquiry perspective, this next phase directly fits espoused theory. In inquiry-oriented instruction, we want students to work with a question provided by the teacher, or better yet, a question of particular interest to the students. At this point, what Ms. Pinto has done builds quite nicely on the interest generated by the demonstration. She has allowed the students to pursue a question of their own interest, instead of having to answer a question provided by the teacher. If the question is provided by the teacher, there is the possibility that the question will lose the interest of at least some of the students. On the other hand, without any guidance there is a concern that the students will not learn any science or the specific science that the teacher intends. For example, what if some students decide to investigate the effects of the color of the fruit skin or flesh on floating and sinking. The students will eventually learn that the color is not important, but will they learn anything about what makes an object float or sink? The tension that teachers often deal with in an inquiry lesson is whether to sacrifice high student interest in favor of a stronger focus on subject matter. All too often, teachers (especially those at the elementary level) will opt in favor of student engagement and enjoyment as opposed to the teaching of science subject matter. Of course, if the students are bored and inattentive, will they be learning the desired subject matter? As mentioned before, many educators believe that inquiry lessons should be connected to a relevant social issue. This is one way to engage students, but it is not a necessary component of what constitutes authentic scientific inquiry.

Launching Into Open Inquiry

Ms. Pinto has decided to let the students have maximum freedom in designing their investigations. The only exception would be an investigation that entails safety issues. From an inquiry perspective, the lesson is following the ideal. Students are now getting an opportunity to develop their investigation skills, not just manipulative skills but also the abilities needed to develop a research design to answer a specific question. However, is it not important to consider students' thinking as they develop their research questions and associated research designs? At the root of this situation is whether scientific inquiry is considered a set of generic problem solving skills, applicable to all contexts, or whether inquiry is context, subject matter specific. In Ms. Pinto's lesson, it appears that the relevance of subject matter is not considered important. She has made no attempt to have students relate their questions or research designs directly to any science subject matter. All that appears important is the logic and safety of students' investigations. Alternatively, is not one of the weaknesses of the "students as scientists" approach to curriculum and instruction the lack of attention to subject matter? Do not scientists bring in-depth knowledge of subject matter to their investigations that students can not? Is this not why students looking at the same data set will not come to the same conclusions as a scientist? At best, K-12 students can only simulate what scientists do. In particular, we can provide students opportunities to do the types of thinking and skills exhibited by scientists. But, wouldn't Ms. Pinto's lesson be a more accurate portrayal of scientific inquiry if she had students make explicit reference to relevant subject matter in the development of their research questions and related research designs? Some emerging research supports the notion that attention to subject matter provides a valuable context for the learning of inquiry and nature of science (Khishfe & Lederman, 2006).

Following the performance of their investigations, students are told to analyze their data and prepare for a public presentation of their results. Ms. Pinto is still following an instructional approach that most would consider as consistent with inquiry teaching. The students are given maximum flexibility to interpret their data relative to the questions they have asked. The only restriction is that each group will need to defend their conclusions to the rest of the class. Again, this portion of the lesson is meant to simulate the communication/dissemination phase of scientific inquiry. The teacher remains in the role as facilitator, seemingly helping to maintain student engagement in the activity. After all, the students have been allowed to pursue an answer to a question of their own development. They have been allowed to develop ownership of the activity and the results. At this point, others would be concerned that the students will not have had a focused opportunity to learn any science. That is, the groups will arrive at answers to their questions, but the foci of their investigations were necessarily concerned with readily observable characteristics of the fruit (e.g., color, ripeness, size). In short, it appears that this scientific inquiry will only give students an opportunity to learn about the relationship between empirical data and conclusions. It will not, as designed, give them any opportunity to learn about density or buoyancy.

Debriefing the Investigation: Opportunities and Missed Opportunities

The next day the student groups are given the opportunity to present their research questions, investigation, and their conclusions. This experience has clearly provided students with an opportunity to develop their inquiry skills. The students are motivated and the teacher is pleased with their engagement in the lesson. To many, this lesson/experience might represent the essence of inquiry in the science classroom. To others, there may be some concern about what was learned by the students. Students are given almost total freedom to pursue their interests regarding the behavior of the fruit. They developed questions of interest and research designs to answer their questions. In the end, each group came up with answers to their questions about which variables (e.g., fruit size, ripeness) were related to whether the banana floated or sunk in water. The post-lab discussion gave students an opportunity to defend their conclusions with data that they collected and to critically analyze the results of other groups' investigations. But what else did the students learn? What science did they learn? What did they learn about scientific inquiry?

Herein lies the tension with Ms. Pinto's inquiry lesson. Technically, the students did actively participate in the development of a scientific investigation. The students did experience scientific inquiry. From the teacher's perspective, the students were highly engaged and eagerly completed their assigned task. But, what did they learn? What could they have learned? The overall format and appearance of scientific inquiry in the classroom can often hide critical problems. In many ways, the problem is the same as the distinction between "hands-on" and "minds-on" science.

At the beginning of the lesson, the students could have been asked to relate the behavior of the orange to other objects that they have seen floating and sinking. This would have helped focus student attention on the science behind the demonstration and could have hopefully been used to focus student attention on the same science concepts when it comes to asking questions about the behavior of the banana. Students have vast knowledge about their environment and surroundings, but they do not automatically bring these to bear when asked to explain a demonstration that a teacher presents. Consequently, one of the obstacles students face when asked to engage in inquiry is knowing what knowledge is relevant to the problem at hand and how to apply this relevant knowledge to solve the problem. Ms. Pinto could have provided some structure to assist students in this regard, but she was also fighting against providing so much structure that it would stifle students' enthusiasm and engagement.

The discussion following the students' presentations of their investigations is a critical point of the lesson. As presented in the vignette, little science was learned other than a single understanding about scientific inquiry—there needs to be consistency between evidence and conclusions. Without structuring by the teacher, students will not naturally reflect on their investigations and thought processes (Abd-El-Khalick & Lederman, 2000). The students will not naturally compare what they have done in the present investigation to what scientists do in their investigations. The students could have been lead into a discussion about why different groups chose different questions to investigate. They could have also discussed how groups investigating the same question approached their research design differently. This could have lead to a discussion of how research design can impact results and this might explain why scientists often disagree about solutions and explanations for the same problem. Given that different groups arrived at different explanations, students could have also been engaged in a discussion about how two scientists looking at the same data may arrive at different conclusions because of differences in data interpretation. At a more simplistic level, the students could have been engaged in a discussion of how all scientific inquiry begins with a question and that there is no single set or sequence of steps that was followed in all investigations. Similar discussions could have focused on how variables were operationalized and how data were analyzed. The purpose of all these discussions could have been to provide students with a concrete understanding of why scientific claims are subject to revision and why replication is valued within the scientific community. Again, however, addressing these issues instructionally structures the two days much differently than Ms. Pinto structured her lesson. What students could have learned about inquiry would have been increased significantly, but what would have been sacrificed is the freedom students are supposed to have when participating in scientific inquiry.

It is also important to note that having students learn about inquiry requires the metacognitive activity of stepping back and analyzing one's thoughts and actions (Lederman, 1998). Do students know how to do this? If not, the reflection being asked will present a large obstacle to the success of the lesson. It is one thing to have students perform an investigation to answer a question. It is a different matter having students analyze their own thinking and behavior to arrive at a generalization of how science is done.

There still remains the issue of inquiry devoid of subject matter. Ms. Pinto's lesson appears to be an attempt to teach students inquiry skills and knowledge without any regard to subject matter. Naturally, the purpose of scientific inquiry is to answer questions of scientific concern. So, at one level it makes little sense to teach about inquiry and ignore subject matter. On the other hand, there is some logic to the notion of cognitive overload. Can students learn about a scientific phenomenon and simultaneously pay attention to how they are learning about that phenomenon? There is a tendency for students and teachers to separate the two and this can become an obstacle to learning within a context of scientific inquiry. Learning science in a context of scientific inquiry is purported to have the advantage of helping students understand subject matter as well as learn about scientific inquiry. The students in Ms. Pinto's class could have learned about density and/or buoyancy as they were observing the orange with and without its skin. They could have done the same with the extension involving the banana. However, there was no attempt to have students discuss why objects float and sink and how the scientific principles involved might be related to the structure of the fruit's skin, and what the skin adds to the fruit as a "system." The point is that the students could have learned some science subject matter while they were learning about scientific inquiry. And, the linking of subject matter with inquiry would have been a more accurate portrayal of the scientific enterprise. But, there is always the tension between letting students' creative juices flow and putting a wet blanket on an otherwise enjoyable experience. Put another way, there is always the tension between doing science and learning about science.

In summary, there are many obstacles for student success in science, let alone doing and understanding scientific inquiry. Inquiry instruction is designed to free students to pursue questions of interest and allow students to express their creativity, not to mention giving them an understanding of how science is done. However, in our attempts to engage students in inquiry, we often sacrifice the true purpose of scientific inquiry for fear of placing too many restrictions on students' behaviors. Ms. Pinto's lesson appears to be a clear example of this tension. She has provided a very engaging and enjoyable lesson for her students. The lesson generally follows anyone's conception of scientific inquiry, but it ends with the students probably learning very little science. Requiring students to structure their design of research questions and requiring them to reflect on their thoughts and actions may remove the freedom and enthusiasm students feel when allowed to proceed in a self-directed manner. The tension in Ms. Pinto's classroom is probably unavoidable. But, the need to provide equal and appropriate attention to both the doing of science and knowledge of science is also unavoidable.

Quo Vadis?

If there is one thing highlighted by the diverse perspectives of Ms. Pinto's inquiry lesson it is the complexity of integrating scientific inquiry into classroom instruction. However, this conclusion is not particularly illuminating or helpful. A common theme that runs through the comments of all three of our science educators is the importance of students' prior knowledge, dispositions, and skills relative to successfully navigating an inquiry activity. Sandra Abell in her essay, "What Students Need to Know and do in Inquiry-Based Instruction," focuses on a variety of issues regarding students' readiness to think and perform the tasks as needed to complete the inquiry activity. Valerie Akerson in her essay, "How do I do this? Skills Students Need for Inquiry," concentrates more on motivation, affective issues, and students' social skills, among others. I speculate in this essay about what students may or may not have learned as a result of the described lesson and spoke of the importance of bringing students' prior knowledge of subject matter and inquiry to the forefront.

Overall, it is clear that students are not capable of succeeding in inquiry if they are left on their own with no guidance. It is also clear that there is much knowledge and skills that students need to learn and develop that enable them to successfully complete a scientific inquiry experience (American Association for the Advancement of Science, 1993; National Research Council, 1996). In their chapter on science teaching and learning in the *Second Handbook of Research on Teaching*, Shulman and Tamir (1972) present a framework for evaluating the level of inquiry in a science curriculum. The framework is adapted from the work of Schwab (1962) and Herron (1971) and is primarily used to evaluate the level of inquiry in the 1960s "alphabet" science curriculum approaches (e.g., BSCS, ESSP, ISCS). However, the same framework is useful to summarize the messages of our science educators, and to offer advice to teachers attempting to integrate more inquiry into their science programs. The inquiry scale is based on the recognition that all science activities/tasks consist of a minimum of three parts: the question/problem, procedures, and solutions. One can discriminate the level of inquiry involved in any science activity by considering how many of these three the students know in advance. A brief "visual" of the scale was presented in the introduction to this text in Table 2 (see pp. xx).

Using the scale, a Level "0" involves the least amount of inquiry because students are given the question and procedures in advance. They also know the answer, or what they are supposed to find, because it was studied previously in their class or was part of a homework assignment previously completed. The Level "0" is a verification activity or the proverbial "cookbook" laboratory. It is still inquiry because it is similar to what scientists spend a lot of time doing. Research results must be replicated. But, the level of inquiry is very low. In a Level "1" is a bit more open-ended in that the students do not know in any formal way the solution to the question/problem. Levels "2" and "3" systematically remove more information in advance with students eventually being asked to develop their own questions, design, and solutions.

In addition to being used as an analysis, the framework also communicates the ideas expressed by the authors of this section. The process is developmental in that students need to learn how to develop solutions from data. They need to learn how to develop a research design to answer a given question. And they need to learn how to ask scientific questions. So, within a course, or across students' science programs, teachers need to consider how students will develop the knowledge and skills needed to succeed in inquiry. Instruction should gradually and systematically move from Level "0" activities with the ultimate goal being some Level "3" activities. It is not appropriate to expect students to immediately succeed in a Level "3" activity. Teaching and learning needs to build toward Level "3" not begin with Level "3."

Ms. Pinto's lesson would be rated as a Level 2 on the inquiry scale. Some might argue that the lesson was a Level 3, but there really was a general question provided by the teacher—why did certain bananas and banana parts sink while other floated? In terms of students' backgrounds and knowledge, this lesson is probably at the most realistic level as possible. Giving the students some parameters with a general question focused their attention appropriately. However, Ms. Pinto may want to consider integrating some reference to density, nature of science, and knowledge about inquiry into her lesson.

The message that students need certain skills and knowledge to succeed in inquiry and that these skills and knowledge need to be taught, was common to the discussions of our science educators. That is, students' incoming knowledge and skills can be significant barriers to success in an inquiry lesson. The teacher needs to consider students' background knowledge and skills and plan for when the necessary knowledge and skills will be developed so inquiry can proceed.

REFERENCES

Abd-El-Khalick, F., Bell, R. L., & Lederman, N. G. (1998). The nature of science and instructional practice: Making the unnatural natural. *Science Education, 82*, 417-436.

Abd-El-Khalick, F., & Lederman, N. G. (2000). Improving science teachers' conceptions of the nature of science: A critical review of the literature. *International Journal of Science Education, 22*(7), 665-701.

Abell, S. K. (1999). What's inquiry? Stories from the field. *Australian Science Teachers Journal, 45*(1), 33-40.

Abell, S. K., Martini, M., & George, M. D. (2001). That's what scientists have to do: Preservice elementary teachers' conceptions of the nature of science during a moon investigation. *International Journal of Science Education, 23*, 1095-1109.

Akerson, V. L., & Buzzelli, C. A. (in press). Relationships of preservice early childhood teachers' cultural values, ethical and cognitive developmental levels, and views of nature of science. *Journal of Elementary Science Education*.

Akins, A., & Akerson, V. L. (2002). Connecting science, social studies, and language arts: An interdisciplinary approach. *Educational Action Research, 10*, 479-497.

American Association for the Advancement of Science. (1993). *Benchmarks for science literacy: A Project 2061 report.* New York: Oxford University Press.

Bransford, J. D., Brown, A. L., & Cocking, R. R. (Eds.). (1999). *How people learn: Brain, mind, experience, and school.* Washington, DC: National Academy Press.

Cazden, C. B. (2001). *Classroom discourse: The language of teaching and learning* (2nd ed). Portsmouth, NH: Heinemann.

de Jesus, H. P., de Souza, F. N., Teixeira-Dias, J. J. C., & Watts, M. (2005). Organising the chemistry of question-based learning: A case study. *Research in Science & Technological Education, 23*, 179-193.

Edwards, D. (1993). But what do children really think?: Discourse analysis and conceptual content in children's talk. *Cognition and Instruction, 11*, 207-225.

Edwards, D., & Mercer, N. (1987). *Common knowledge: The development of understanding in the classroom.* London: Meuthen.

Gee, J. P. (2004). Language in the science classroom: Academic social languages as the heart of school-based literacy. In E. W. Saul (Ed.), *Crossing borders in literacy and science instruction: Perspectives on theory and practice* (pp. 13-32) Newark, DE: International Reading Association.

Harlen, W. (2000). *The teaching of science in primary schools* (3rd ed.). London: David Fulton.Harlen, W. (2001). Helping children plan investigations. In W. Harlen (Ed.), *Primary science: Taking the plunge* (2nd ed., pp. 58-74). Portsmouth, NH: Heinemann.

Hofstein, A., Shore, R., & Kipnis, M. (2004). Providing high school chemistry students with opportunities to develop learning skills in an inquiry-type laboratory: A case study. *International Journal of Science Education, 26*, 47-62.

Herron. M. D. (1971). The nature of scientific inquiry. *School Review, 79*, 171-212.

Huitt, W. (2004). Maslow's hierarchy of needs. *Educational Psychology Interactive.* Retrieved April 13, 2006 from, http://chiron.valdosta.edu/whuitt/col/regsys/maslow.html

Joyce, B., Weil, M., & Showers, B. (1992). *Models of teaching.* Boston: Allyn & Bacon.

Khishfe, R., & Lederman, N. G. (2006). Teaching nature of science within a controversial topic: Integrated versus non-integrated. *Journal of Research in Science Teaching, 43*(4), 395-418.

Krajcik, J. S., Czerniak, C. M., & Berger, C. F. (2003). *Teaching science in elementary and middle school classrooms: A project-based approach.* New York: McGraw-Hill.

Lederman, N. G. (1998). The state of science education: Subject matter without context. *Electronic Journal of Science Education, 3*(2). Retrieved from http://ejse.southwestern.edu/original%20site/manuscripts/v3n2/articles/guest%20editorial/lederman.html

Lee, O., & Luykx, A. (2005). Science education and student diversity: Synthesis and research agenda. Mahwah, NJ: Erlbaum.

Lemke, J. L. (1990). *Talking science: Language, learning, and values.* Norwood, NJ: Ablex.

Lemke, J. L. (2004). The literacies of science. In E. W. Saul (Ed.), *Crossing borders in literacy and science instruction: Perspectives on theory and practice* (pp. 33-47) Newark, DE: International Reading Association.

Marzano, R. J., Marzano, J. S., & Pickering, D. J. (2003). *Classroom management that works: Research-based strategies for every teacher.* New York: Association for Supervision & Curriculum Development.

Metz, K. (2004). Children's understanding of scientific inquiry: Their conceptualization of uncertainty in investigations of their own design. *Cognition and Instruction, 22,* 219-290.

National Research Council. (1996). *National Science Education Standards.* Washington, DC: National Academy Press.

National Research Council. (2000). *Inquiry and the National Science Education Standards.* Washington, DC: National Academy Press.

Nixon, D. T., & Akerson, V. L. (2004). Building bridges: Using science as a tool to teach reading and writing. *Educational Action Research, 12,* 197-217.

Saul, E. W. (2004). *Crossing borders in literacy and science instruction: Perspectives on theory and practice.* Newark, DE: International Reading Association.

Schwab, J. J. (1962). The teaching of science as enquiry. In J. J. Schwab & P. F. Brandwein (Ed.), *The teaching of science* (pp. 1-103). Cambridge, MA: Harvard University Press.

Shulman, L. S., & Tamir, P. (1972). Research on teaching in the natural sciences. In R. M. W. Travers (Ed.), *Second handbook of research on teaching* (pp. 1098-1148). Chicago: Rand McNally.

Slavin, R. (1994). *Cooperative learning: Theory, research and practice.* Boston: Allyn & Bacon.

Sunal, D. W., & Sunal, C. S. (2003). *Science in the elementary and middle school.* New Jersey: Merrill Prentice Hall.

Varelas, M. (1996). Between theory and data in a seventh-grade science class. *Journal of Research in Science Teaching, 33,* 229-263.

Varelas, M. (1997). Third and fourth graders' conceptions of repeated trials and best representatives in science experiments. *Journal of Research in Science Teaching, 34,* 853-872.

Varelas, M., Becker, J., Luster, B., & Wenzel, S. (2002). When genres meet: Inquiry into a sixth-grade urban science class. *Journal of Research in Science Teaching, 39,* 579-605.

Zion, M., Michalsky, T., & Mevarech, Z. R. (2005). The effects of metacognitive instruction embedded within an asynchronous learning network on scientific inquiry skills. *International Journal of Science Education, 27,* 957-983.

SECTION II

SELECTING AND USING INQUIRY APPROACHES TO TEACH SCIENCE: THE INFLUENCE OF CONTEXT IN ELEMENTARY, MIDDLE, AND SECONDARY SCHOOLS

Larry D. Yore, Laura Henriques, Barbara Crawford,
Leigh Smith, Susan Gomez-Zwiep, and John Tillotson

EDITORS' NOTE

Describing Section II's Use of
Inquiry in the Classroom

Section II is a useful survey of a wide variety of dimensions in the classroom hyperspace for inquiry. Using a broad definition of context, Section II focuses on a myriad of contextual factors (both internal and external to the teacher) that influence a teacher's decision making in terms of how inquiry is used in a classroom: teacher knowledge, curriculum, learning theory, time, materials, nature of the content to be taught, community expectations, accountability concerns to name only a few. But perhaps most pointedly, Section II articulates how the culture of the school and requirements of a particular grade level serve to influence the nature of inquiry that would be optimal in that hyperspace. Thus Section II is divided into three sections each reflecting a different level of schooling (elementary, middle, high)—and the authors offer useful insight into how the interactions of the grade level and the expectations it carries with it shape the kind of classroom inquiry that is possible.

As importantly, Section II introduces to our discussion a useful pair of constructs for science education: fundamental and derived senses of scientific literacy. Echoing the discussion of enculturation into the practices of a community touched upon in the introduction and the emphasis on

Inquiry in the Classroom: Realities and Opportunities, pp. 39–87
Copyright © 2008 by Information Age Publishing
All rights of reproduction in any form reserved.

communication mentioned in Section I ("Student Knowledge and Skills With Inquiry"), the fundamental sense of scientific literacy refers to a learner's ability to read, write and communicate within the culture of science. The derived sense of literacy refers to knowledge of the content of science, scientific inquiry and the nature of science. It is the argument of the authors of Secton II and others (Norris & Phillips, 2003) that both fundamental and a derived sense of literacy are required for one to be considered as fully scientifically literate.

The authors of Section II point out that one aspect of our necessary description of inquiry, that of the goals of inquiry, is insufficient at least in terms of serving as the goals for science education. The question becomes, what is the intersection of the fundamental sense of scientific literacy and classroom inquiry. The emphasis on communication in Section I and the discussion of science learning as enculturation into a community would suggest that science learning must be more broadly conceived than a sole emphasis on classroom inquiry as it is traditional conceived.

GOALS FOR INQUIRY

Both the elementary and middle school essays focus on the goal of **inquiry as a means of constructing scientific knowledge**. It is unclear what learning goal many of the secondary teachers had for inquiry-instead they seemed compelled to employ inquiry simply because it was a new, frequently discussed teaching approach. The lack of goals certainly helps us understand the lack of clarity in much the ensuing conversation. It is important to note that the one teacher that did have clear goals (that of **learning to inquire** and the **construction of scientific knowledge**) seemed to enjoy a more coherent and successful use of inquiry.

Means of Enactment of Inquiry

Both the elementary and middle schools, with their emphasis on content knowledge construction, employed a Level 1 or 2 version of inquiry (via some version of a learning cycle), in which students are provided some guidance both in terms of the questions to be asked and the methods to be employed in constructing the answers. This optimal enactment of inquiry does correspond to our evolving pattern, that lessons with more traditional content goals are often better suited to lower level levels of inquiry. Mindful of this goal combined with this means of enactment of inquiry, it is not surprising that the effectiveness of the lesson is often jeopardized by one dimension of the classroom hyperspace, the limitation of time. The lack of time often "cut short" the debriefing, the necessary sense making about the inquiry experience. Too, the lack of time and the emphasis on activities that many teachers feel compelled to adopt does serve to limit the development of students' development of scientific literacy in the fundamental sense of scientific literacy.

What is important to note about the high school setting (and what may hold true for many settings) is the common misconception of the privileged position of open, Level 3 inquiry. The high school vignette allows us to understand how that pedagogical misconception often serves to prevent teachers' full exploration of inquiry—as they reject open inquiry as implausible and inappropriate—thus this misconception is a significant barrier to teachers' adoption of classroom inquiry. This idea will be further discussed in Section V ("Teachers' Knowledge and Enacting Inquiry").

INTRODUCTION

chools are likely one of the most widely established, distributed, and familiar learning organizations in the world—but they are often misunderstood in terms of their internal culture and systemic operations. Frequently, people talk about K-12 schools as being a universal system and somewhat of a monoculture embodied in bricks and mortar; but, in fact, schools are composed of several worlds or subsystems, with each having unique institutional characteristics flowing from their structures, priorities, peoples, environments, and climates. These characteristics are more than numbers on a budget, enrollment lists and other statistics, vision statements, or strategic plans. Their influence resides in both the internal and external stakeholders—students, parents, teachers, administrators, and politicians—who are products of their experiences in and with schools and their preparations to fulfill their stakeholder responsibilitie—teacher education, sociopolitical agenda, and other cultural features. Local institutional decisions about school organization, buildings, programs, approaches, funding, and vision are open to the influence of these related, second-order factors and community traditions, customs, expectations, and priorities. This section will clarify some of the institutional and related factors discussed elsewhere in this book that influence decisions about science inquiry teaching in elementary, middle, and secondary schools.

BACKGROUND

Teachers' selection of an approach to teaching science is influenced by pragmatic factors, while science educators and reformers are frequently driven by idealistic views of science, inquiry, teaching, and classrooms. The internal and external institutional factors that influence teachers' interpretation and selection of inquiry include their views of the nature of science; models of learning and teaching; local policy, priority, and parents; student population; instructional resources; and physical factors of the classroom. In the United States—and increasingly in other countries —the interpretations of the No Child Left Behind Act of 2002 (NCLB) that stress accountability and testing over teaching and learning have effects that counter much of the message included in science education reforms (e.g., Science Literacy for All Students). Many large-scale tests continue to reflect a 1950s interpretation of science literacy (low-level content knowledge) rather than a contemporary interpretation involving a symbiotic relationship between a fundamental sense and derived sense (Yore & Treagust, 2006). The fundamental sense, *the classic sense of be a literate person able to read and write the discourse of science*, includes abilities, thinking, habits-of-mind, language, and information communication strategies to construct understanding of the big ideas in science and the communications to inform and persuade other people to take actions based on these big ideas. The derived sense, *the traditional sense of being an informed person knowing the content of science*, includes understanding of the nature of science, scientific inquiry, the relationship among science, mathematics and technology, and the major unifying concepts in science such as outlined in the national science standards (American Association for the Advancement of Science [AAAS], 1989; Hand, Prain, & Yore, 2001; National Research Council [NRC], 1992; Norris & Phillips, 2003; Yore, Bisanz, & Hand, 2003;). Furthermore, the phased enactment of policy has changed the priorities of schools. Because the early implementation of NCLB emphasized language arts and mathematics to the exclusion of science, social studies, and other disciplines, in some schools only discipline areas that are tested are actually taught! This may change when science becomes a required testing area (2007-2008 school year) in grades 3-5, 6-9, and 10-12. The influence may not be as strong as for language arts and mathematics, however, because the science test results will likely not be factored into the school's adequate yearly progress (AYP) or performance report; if it is factored, it is likely that it will be done so at significantly lower levels.

In spite of science not receiving the same status in the accountability movement, science is still being taught in school; and inquiry is seen as one of the main ways to teach science content and skills to children. However, the images of *science as inquiry* and inquiry teaching and learning described elsewhere in this book and other reform documents outline experiences that are similar to authentic scientific explorations (Minstrell

& van Zee, 2000; NRC, 1996, 2000). Unfortunately, *science as argument*—a critical epistemic and discourse feature of science—does not receive parallel consideration in these documents. We hold that science should be presented as an interactive-constructivist process where people attempt to search out, describe, and explain patterns of events occurring in the natural universe (Good, Shymansky, & Yore, 1999). The search is driven by inquiry, limited by human abilities and technology, and guided by hypotheses, observations, measurements, plausible reasoning and creativity, and accepted procedures that try to limit the potential influence of nontarget variables by utilizing controls. However, the prevailing discourse pattern in scientific communities is rhetorical persuasion, that is, explanations attempt to produce compelling arguments with coordinated claims, evidence, backings, counterclaims, and rebuttals and seek to establish physical causality and make generalized claims. Science as people's attempt to search and describe evolving toward general claims and exploration around physical causality provides a developmental framework for elementary, middle, and secondary school science teaching, while lower levels focus on searching and describing and the higher levels focus on searching, describing, and explaining causality (Yore, Hand, & Florence, 2004).

The images of science inquiry in the reform documents describe a range of learning experiences (NRC, 2000). A difficulty for teachers is that science inquiry takes on several connotations (focus and form)—inquiry as a critical attribute in the nature of science, science inquiry as a content standard, and science inquiry as a teaching standard (Henriques, 1997; NRC, 1996). Henriques' categories parallel the full, partial, or inquiry-like forms (NRC, 2000); but she considers nature of science, ontological, epistemological, cognitive, pedagogical, and discourse influences and the realities of classrooms composed of a single teacher and 20–30+ students. An analysis of the images of inquiry and the related pedagogical, cognitive, and functional demands indicates that the ability to meet these demands varies across the perspectives of generalist and specialist teachers, students, and elementary, middle, and secondary schools and that idealized images may have been too optimistic for most teachers of science and classrooms where science is taught (Anderson, 2002; Colburn, 1998; Rudolph, 2005). Furthermore, the intellectual, technological, and physical resources in their classrooms are drastically different than in world-class research laboratories.

Contextual elements that influence implementation of inquiry teaching are either internally constructed or externally imposed (Jones, 1997). Internal forces, which include teachers' preparation, goals, beliefs, knowledge, and perspectives, are discussed elsewhere in this book. External forces, the major focus of this section, are described as the institutional structures, environmental circumstances, and social and cultural exchanges that occur within and through the physical setting of the school (Bullough & Baughman, 1997; Firestone & Louis, 1999; Fullan & Stiegelbauer, 1991; Gregoire, 2003; Hargreaves, 1994; Sarason, 1996). Three sources of structure appear to be influencing the success of inquiry teaching/learning: *students' cognitive influences* (learner structure), *content influences* (content structure), and *contextual influences* (teacher structure, institutional structure, curricular priorities, timetable, school environment and classroom climate, instructional resources). Cognitive and content influences, addressed elsewhere in this book, vary across students, grade levels, content areas and target science topics of elementary, middle, and secondary schools. Contextual influences and external forces are not well documented in today's schools and classrooms.

Anderson (2002, p. 5) used attractive descriptors and metaphors for the teacher's role in inquiry teaching, for example, "helps," "communicates," "coaches," "facilitates," and "models," that may mask the complexity of implementing inquiry instruction into real classrooms and schools. It is easy to overestimate the simplicity of these comfortable sounding descriptors when, in fact, the demands of these ideas are significant. The crux of the current concerns about inquiry science teaching in schools focuses on whether it is reasonable to expect teachers to implement complex inquiry teaching strategies in underserviced schools and poorly equipped classrooms with ill-prepared learners. The systemic demands on schools, classrooms, families, and communities required to implement inquiry science programs are significant. School budgets, policies, and staffing practices do not appear to cover the initial investment in materials, the procedures and structures to maintain supplies, nor the professional support for teacher development (Johnson, 2007; Sandall, 2003; NRC, 2006). Many of the concerns in elementary, middle, and secondary schools are based on whether all types of inquiry teaching can be internalized and utilized by teachers with minimum science and teaching experience in multicultural classrooms and also whether these inquiry modes enhance science literacy and improve science achievement on state and national tests (Lee, 2005; Yerrick, Parke, & Nugent, 1997). A variety of institutional influences that promote the promises and delineate the barriers to inquiry science teaching in elementary, middle, and secondary schools are described in the vignettes and unpacked in the discussions of the following essays. Some factors vary across school level and others do both—encourage and discourage the use of inquiry teaching.

The organizational structure of this section varies from the other sections of the book. This section is divided into three essays on how institutional factors affect the integration of inquiry into the classroom at the elementary, middle, and secondary school level. The institutional structure varies so greatly between the three types of schools, there was a need to address the unique characteristics of each. There is also a vignette at the beginning of each essay describing a typical scene at each school. At the end of the three essays, there is a summary designed to look at the commonalities among elementary, middle, and secondary schools.

INQUIRY IN ELEMENTARY CLASSROOMS

Vignette

Catherine is a member of a team of third grade teachers at a large elementary school situated in the outskirts of a midsize city. Now in her fourth year of teaching, Catherine assumes the role of science advocate, with the responsibility for representing her grade-level team at school and district-wide curriculum and resources selection meetings. This assignment came to her by default upon her arrival at Eastside Elementary School. The more experienced members of her team had previously decided that they would become the social studies, health/physical education, and art/music advocates. (Language arts and mathematics were too "important" to have a single teacher representative.)

Catherine teaches science to 26 students in 30-minute blocks 3 times a week, in addition to teaching literacy, mathematics, and all other subjects. This particular morning, with 45 minutes remaining until the school day begins, Catherine moves about her classroom making final preparations for the day's science lesson. She locates and places into small plastic bags differently shaped magnets, nails, coins, brass fasteners, a crayon, a plastic straw, a Popsicle® stick, a piece of copper wire, a paper clip, a square of aluminum foil, and a chunk of steel wool. After making a final check that all bags contain the prescribed items, she carries a handful of half-sheets of paper—to be used as data sheets—to the front of the room and places them on her desk.

Catherine's portable classroom, without running water and bathrooms, is small and gives the impression of interrupted activity. Twenty-six student desks of varying heights are arranged in six groups and take up most of the space in the room. Catherine's desk, a personal computer, and a filing cabinet are situated at the front of the room, toward the corner furthest from the door. The perimeter of the room is lined with mismatched classroom furniture, including a large wooden playground equipment box (filled with basketballs, footballs, soccer balls, jump ropes, etc.); a row of hooks for students' backpacks and coats; bookcases of varying sizes; two large, locked wooden cabinets; two large classroom tables; a wall unit of student cubby holes or mailboxes; two banana chairs in a reading corner; a lighted grow table with a partially used bag of potting soil sitting in one of the trays; a television and VCR; and an overhead projector. Stacked below the tables and on top of the wooden cabinets are a number of large, rectangular clear plastic boxes covered with lids filled with science supplies—paper plates, boxes of foil, plastic cups, pipettes, plastic jugs, and miscellaneous other materials. Large plastic buckets filled with smaller supplies (straws, toothpicks, plastic spoons, wooden sticks, etc.), some spilling their contents, are also stacked on cabinets and bookcases.

Large whiteboards cover most of two walls, although one is used as a bulletin board to display student language arts projects and the other is partially covered by a map of the world. Two smaller bulletin boards cover much of the back wall and emphasize the importance of science in Catherine's curriculum. One of these is a collage created by the students titled "Air, Land, and Water," which is constructed of innumerable pictures cut from magazines. The other is a science "word wall" that is bordered with words describing the traditional steps of the scientific method and displays vocabulary words from the introductory lesson of the current science unit of study titled "Coming Attractions."

The students file into the room at the start of day, chatting and laughing, settling in for science the first thing on Monday morning. Conscious of the limited time she has available for science in order to accommodate an increased emphasis on mathematics and the 120 minutes per day required for literacy because of the recent No Child Left Behind legislation, as well as the lengthy list of science standards required by the mandated state curriculum (all of which will be assessed and published at the end of the year), Catherine glances at the clock, quickly requests the students' full attention and hastily begins.

Today's lesson begins with a class discussion about things the students did before coming to school that involved magnets. After no comments from the students, Catherine emphasizes some everyday uses of magnets —whiteboards are magnetic, door latches use magnets, some can openers have a magnet to pick up the lid, and so forth. The discussion continues with a short review of the ideas on the word wall, reinforcing information from the introductory lesson. Quickly and naturally, the topic turns to things that stick to magnets and the students' speculations that "magnets pick up all metals."

Suddenly, the speaker above the classroom door splutters to life. The principal asks teachers and students to "Pardon the interruption," then announces the school lunch menu for the day, and adds that there will be an assembly the following morning, previously unannounced. Catherine groans inwardly, noting that once again her science time has been truncated because of the lengthy interruption. Additionally, further adjustments to a carefully designed unit plan will again be necessary. What will she now need to abandon?

Catherine plunges back into her lesson, hastening to quiet the excited conversations triggered by the announcements. At this point, the lesson moves along quickly to allow students time to work with the materials. Catherine's goal, taken directly from her old science methods textbook, is that the students will discover that iron, nickel, and cobalt are magnetic. She emphasizes the importance of having the students really experiment, discovering for themselves.

Finally, with just 12 minutes left, Catherine explains the hands-on investigation in which the students will be engaged. Students are hastily assigned to work as partners. Their task is to use the materials they have been given to create groups of things that stick to a magnet and things that do not stick to a magnet. She prompts the students to determine what is common or the same amongst the things in each group and what is different between the two groups. As the children quickly access their materials from the science table and adjust for groups having an odd number of students, they begin work on their inquiry. It is obvious that they are familiar with the process of investigating with others. Meanwhile, Catherine circulates among the groups, asking and answering questions, making a quick evaluation of students' understanding, reinforcing new vocabulary, and clarifying or correcting misunderstandings on an individual basis. She constantly tries to involve students in the conversation, asking them to recall information from earlier science lessons, to explain what some things are called or made of, and to read the label on the boxes of paper clips and fasteners. Students eagerly talk with one another and their teacher about their options and experimental results, using the new vocabulary learned: bar magnet, donut-shaped magnet, horseshoe magnet, magnetic, etc. Other snatches of conversation within each group and between students and teacher indicate that experimenting and questioning is a large part of the way science is learned in the class:

- "Could we try using other things in the room—things that aren't in our bag?"
- "This is surprising—the U.S. nickel and the Canadian nickel act differently!"
- "This doesn't work, Miss Bateman. (pause) Well, it's not that it won't work, I guess. We must be doing something wrong. We'll keep experimenting."

The next portion of the lesson was to include a large-group discussion and closure that provided a demonstration of magnetic and nonmagnetic objects and a conversation wherein students would be asked to explain why things are magnetic and provide examples of magnetic objects around the classroom and at home. Although Catherine had hoped to have several groups share their observations, to create a two-group classification chart (magnetic and nonmagnetic), and to explain commonalities, time runs short. Students are asked to clean up, making sure each item is returned to the bag before they go to the gym for physical education. Once again, to Catherine's dismay, time does not permit the sharing and discussion she believes the students need in order to clarify and reinforce the concepts they have learned.

PROMISES OF INQUIRY IN
ELEMENTARY SCHOOLS AND CLASSROOMS

Teachers' Background Beliefs

Many elementary teachers believe that inquiry approaches present a developmentally appropriate, concrete, and less abstract mode of interactive learning that allows students to construct their knowledge about science and is compatible with elementary students' physical, intellectual, and emotional development. They frequently describe the inquiry as free play, messing around with objects and ideas, or discovery learning. Unfortunately, many teachers overemphasize the importance of sensory experiences, placing primary emphasis on activities and physical engagement leading to "activitymania." The emphasis is on the activities and not on the debate/argument around the experiences, evidence, and claims and the cognitive scaffolding required in the meaning-making process. Unlike Catherine, many elementary teachers start to believe that lack of successful learning could be overcome by another activity; little is done to support knowledge construction, integration of new ideas in learners' conceptual schema, and to connect experience and self-generated understanding with established science ideas. Collectively, these influences encourage many elementary teachers to endorse open inquiry (discovery) or free play approaches that are heavy on process and attitude and light on understanding at the expense of guided inquiry and learning cycle approaches (Lawson, Abraham, & Renner, 1989; Shymansky, Kyle, & Alford, 2003).

Science Literacy for All as Interacting Fundamental and Derived Senses

Inquiry science embraces a contemporary view of science literacy, a modified learning cycle, and interdisciplinary approaches to address both fundamental and derived senses of science literacy (Yore & Treagust, 2006). The learning cycle is usually divided into phases or stages. The first stage is to engage the learner in the topic. The second stage is to have the students explore the concept in a hands-on fashion to develop some ideas about that concept through the manipulation of materials. The third phase is to consolidate the concept using the students' emerging ideas and questions as the basics of the concept explanation. Finally, the last phase is to assess student understanding.

In addition, the teacher has incorporated a literacy component with a public assessment of knowledge claims into her science inquiry in terms of the rich oral discourse and debate in peer-pairs and small groups and in the development of technical vocabulary that parallel the construction of conceptual understanding found on the word wall and graphic displays (Blank, 2000). The engage–explore–consolidate–assess form of the learning cycle was apparent in her planning, but time constraints prevented the consolidation and assessment phases from occurring in this time block. The school's priorities and organization do not allow her to fully incorporate ideas from language arts and mathematics, and the fixed schedule of physical education does not allow her to capitalize on the opportunities resulting from the exploration and small group interactions.

Priorities, Strengths, and Multicultural Characteristics of the Elementary Classroom

Generalist elementary teachers, usually with backgrounds in language arts, have opportunities and potentialities to stress the cognitive symbiosis between the senses of science literacy—fundamental and derived. Explicit language arts instruction related to the fundamental sense of science literacy embedded in inquiry science units do much to enhance students' science discourse and science understanding. The research and professional literature is starting to provide compelling evidence for connecting oral discourse, argument, reading, writing, and multiple representations with science (Yore, 2003). The stories of El Centro, California (Klentschy & Molina-De La Torre, 2004), Seattle, Washington (Stokes, Mitchell, & Ramage, 2005), and Broward County, Florida (Romance & Vitale, 1992), are only a few of the successful large-scale programs in which consideration of the fundamental sense of science literacy led to significant gains in the derived sense of science literacy as well as performance in language literacy generally. Putting the literacy component back in science plays to the strength of the elementary generalist as 'a reading teacher' and provides a role for children's literature and information text in science.

Guided inquiry with embedded language tasks focused on learning the discourse of science and on constructing understanding have done much to improve classroom climate and address school-wide priorities in elementary schools. Children's literature can serve to engage children's prior knowledge and serve as springboards into inquiry (Shymansky, Yore, & Hand, 2000). Inquiry also levels the playing field by introducing a rich mix of activity, discourse, social collaboration, and opportunities for direct instruction (Klentschy & Molina-De La Torre, 2004; Lee, 2005). The recognition of prior knowledge and the sensitivity to multicultural backgrounds have also encouraged teachers to anchor formal science ideas in the students' home language (L1) to help them cross the border into the formal language of instruction (L2) and transit to the language of science (L3). Without doing this, schools disrespect students' culture and informal learning and do not access the rich, prior experience and knowledge students bring to the formal learning of science (Yore & Treagust, 2006).

BARRIERS TO INQUIRY SCIENCE IN ELEMENTARY SCHOOLS AND CLASSROOMS

Institutional Characteristics and Educational Climate: Time, Space, and Instructional Resources

Some literature suggests that specific institutional characteristics (e.g., level of administrative support, school climate, student response, available physical space or instructional materials, and academic time devoted to teaching science) have a significant impact on teachers' ability or inclination to teach science in certain ways (Lynch, 2000; Raizen & Michelsohn, 1994; Sandall, 2003; Schwartz, Abd-El-Khalick, & Lederman, 1999; Tilgner, 1990). Dickinson, Burns, Hagen, and Locker (1997) found that their efforts to change their science instruction was dependent, in part, upon their ability to collaborate and the support they received from their principal in enabling them to do so. This required an allocation of planning and development time, a resource that Catherine and many elementary teachers lack.

Hargreaves (1994) suggested that the context of teaching elementary school is "a complex, densely packed world where the sophisticated skills of the teacher must be directed to dealing with many things at the same time" (p. 104). Multiple goals and tasks continuously compete for attention and time. Indeed, the elementary school classroom has a sense of immediacy about it; and teachers often suggest that they need more time for what they are able and expected to achieve. Thus, for Catherine, as for many teachers, time confounds the implementation of inquiry (Jackson, 1968) requiring her to either truncate her lesson and forego consolidation and assessment or to postpone these essential aspects of the learning cycle until a later time. At the same time, her science instruction is clearly rushed; and like other elementary teachers, she struggles to find the time required to implement an inquiry-based science curriculum while teaching an overloaded school curriculum in a school day where institutional and classroom priorities seem to be constantly changing (Smith, 2002).

Additionally, other institutional requirements (e.g., use of the gym, students going to specialized instruction, school priorities to address at-risk status, specialty teachers coming into the classroom) serve to fragment the instructional time necessary for inquiry. Scheduling is often challenging and repeatedly disrupted, as Catherine's morning science lesson illustrates. Lesson schedules are often interrupted by daily announcements, extra-curricular activities, and other scheduling changes. Time demands also include the extra planning, consultation, and preparation needed to deliver inquiry experiences. Unless they receive specific and positive administrative support (Dickinson et al., 1997), elementary teachers responsible for the same grade level and topic do not have time to share ideas and collaborate in planning and developing inquiry units. Also, time to locate and organize materials is not always addressed by schools in terms of ordering and replacing materials in a central storage area or in curriculum kits. The demands of inquiry-based science, when added to the preparation for other content areas that require manipulative and supplemental resources, become overwhelming for the self-contained and isolated classroom teacher.

Elementary teachers also often believe they lack the physical space and/or the instructional materials necessary for inquiry (Raizen & Michelsohn, 1994; Sandall, 2003). Like Catherine, who teaches in a small, portable classroom without ready access to water, elementary classrooms are often ill equipped for science investigations. Unlike secondary teachers, whose classroom and storage space can be devoted to instruction and materials that enhance instruction for one academic subject, elementary teachers are classroom generalists, routinely teaching multiple subjects each day. Thus, their instructional space must be shared amongst the various subjects they teach and instructional materials spill from makeshift storage containers stacked under tables, atop counters, and in other odd spots around the classroom.

Although elementary teachers may like to implement inquiry-based science curricula, they are constrained by nonacademic considerations. Schools lack the curricula and instructional materials needed to teach inquiry because they lack the monetary resources necessary to acquire them (Sandall, 2003). Although investigation at the elementary level can be successfully accomplished using simple, everyday materials that can easily be purchased at local stores, time to access these materials and resources to purchase them are necessary. Commonly, teachers must resort to using personal funds for materials if they choose to implement simple investigations.

Science Education and Competing Goals

Interestingly, although the emphasis in science education at the national level focuses on a vision of inquiry-based instruction, some research suggests that the current focus on classroom investigation is largely silent for the average classroom teacher (Smith & Southerland,

2007). Many elementary teachers may be unfamiliar with or even unaware of the tools of reform (e.g., standards documents) that describe inquiry as a desirable instructional model in the classroom. Through conversations with teachers at the local level, Smith (2005) found that many Grades 3 and 6 teachers were unaware of the scope of the organized national effort to change the way science is taught. Overwhelmingly, teachers stated that they were completely unfamiliar with the *National Science Education Standards* (NRC, 1996) or any other nationally disseminated reform document or agenda. Moreover, they claimed no knowledge of any organized national efforts to help them think differently about science instruction. Local efforts, either through state or district teacher development workshops or programs such as the one they were attending, to encourage a more hands-on approach to science, as the teachers understood it, were acknowledged, although notions of an inquiry-based approach to instruction in connection with district or state expectations were only rarely mentioned. Any remote familiarity with inquiry was most often tied to experiences in university courses and, occasionally, connected to attendance at conferences sponsored by the National Science Teachers Association.

Additionally, if teachers are aware of national standards for science instruction that promote inquiry, there are five or six or more other standards documents (e.g., Ford, Yore, & Anthony, 1997; International Reading Association, 2004; International Society for Technology in Education, 2000; National Council of Teachers of Mathematics, 2000) begging for consideration and equal time. Smith and Southerland (2007) suggested that elementary teachers might not believe they have the time or the personal responsibility to familiarize themselves directly with each of the subject-specific standards documents. Instead, the participants in this study claimed to rely on local curriculum specialists or developers to align all required curricula with national or international standards, contending that they personally had only briefly interacted with the standards documents themselves. Furthermore, the current trend toward publicized teacher accountability systems in many countries also impacts school scheduling and the time devoted to science, a subject already traditionally neglected at the elementary level. In the United States, for example, recent NCLB legislation (2002) placed an increased emphasis on mathematics and literacy instruction at the expense of science, social studies, health, art, music, and other subjects that are not included in mandated testing or as evidence for AYP reports. Conversations with teachers indicate that some administrators have even banned science instruction from their schools in order to devote all instructional time to core subjects: reading and mathematics. Other schools and school districts, like Catherine's, have retained most academic subjects in the daily curriculum but have mandated specific time allotments for each subject, with mathematics and literacy receiving the bulk of the time. Still other school districts and local and state offices of education have responded to the more recent legislative mandate to include scores on end-of-level science assessments as part of the publicized accountability package.

In summary, elementary school teachers may believe that teaching science as inquiry enables them to focus their instruction on the dual senses of science literacy in developmentally appropriate ways. However, the institutional structures and other competing contextual forces that exist within their schools may be so overwhelming as to prevent many teachers from risking reform. Teachers have quickly and effectively picked up some phases of the modified learning cycle (engage and explore), and they have embraced authentic assessment carried over from their language arts programs—but it is not well applied and practiced in science. Teachers have been slow to implement effective consolidation and enhance their questioning and scaffolding of inquiry explorations and science understanding that should be the target of the consolidation phase (Gilbert, 1992; Martens, 1999; Otto, 1991; Penick, Crow, & Bonnstetter, 1996; Rowe, 1996). As Catherine illustrated in the vignette, a well-planned and well-prepared cycle of this inquiry approach can take more time than expected for a variety of reasons, requiring the consolidation and assessment phases to take place the next time the class meets for science or at the end of the day. Institutional barriers (such as time, space, and instructional resources), and high-stakes assessment may have a more profound impact on elementary school teachers' pedagogical decisions than anticipated.

Middle schools are the bridge between elementary and high schools. Their institutional structure reflects the unique blending of both. Middle school children often change classes and learn from teaches who are certified in a discipline. However, many middle schools have a team approach to teaching students so that teachers can work together to try to teach the whole child. In this next section, we will explore the opportunities and realities of integrating inquiry into a middle school science classroom.

INQUIRY IN MIDDLE SCHOOL CLASSROOMS

Middle schools are the bridge between elementary and secondary schools. Their institutional structure reflects the unique blending of both. Middle school children often change classes and learn from teaches who are certified in a discipline. However, many middle schools have a team approach to teaching students so that teachers can work together to try to teach the whole child. In this next section, we explore the opportunities and realities of integrating inquiry into a middle school science classroom.

Vignette

Is This Heaven? No, it's Middle School Science!

David teaches at a middle school in a large urban city. The school serves both a lower socioeconomic and middle-class community. Over the last few years, the school has seen a 20% increase of English language learners in its population. David teaches 5 classes a day of 30 to 35 students each. For many of his students, this is their first year with a dedicated class period for science. David has a liberal arts degree with a science specialization and has been teaching middle school science for 6 years. Today, David is being observed by a faculty member at the local university to determine if David might be a good cooperating teacher for science interns.

The walls of David's classroom are filled with words related to the concept of convection currents, such as heat, current, and expansion, along with pictures and definitions, and student drawings of scientists along with written biographies of scientists. The challenge of the week is posted on the board: How does heat affect the movement of fluids?

The room is buzzing with activity. While the room lacks sophisticated equipment, there are ample supplies for students to carry out investigations. Cupboards and shelves of everyday materials and simple scientific tools abound. There's a small library in the corner that consists of an Internet-linked computer, books, and magazines.

Groups of heterogeneously mixed students are sitting in clusters of desks. One group is investigating how hot and cold water moves by observing baby food jars of heated and chilled colored water placed in a tub of water. Another group has moved over to the library section where a pair sits at the computer and another pair is looking through books for information on convection currents. A third group appears stumped; David is squatting by their desks and asking them questions about their diagram related to their investigation.

Teacher:	*So what did you learn so far about convection currents?*
Student:	*I don't know. Nothing.*
Teacher:	*What did you observe when you placed the jars of hot and cold water in the tub?*
Student:	*We saw the water move. The hot, red water moved up and the cold, blue water moved down.*
Teacher:	*Why do you think that happened?*
Student:	*(gives blank stare)*
Teacher:	What did you learn in your reading and computer research?

Student:	*Well, we think it has something to do with convection, but what we found in the books only talked about air currents. It said that hot air expands up and cold air gets pushed down.*
Teacher:	*How can you apply this to what you saw here?*
Student:	*The water moved like convection in the air does.*
Teacher:	*Did you observe anything else?*
Student:	*Yes, eventually the water stopped moving and by then the colors were all mixed.*
Teacher:	*Why do you think that happened?*
Student:	*We are not sure. We think that maybe it has something to do with the hot water not being so hot after a while.*
Teacher:	*Hmmm, what would you need to know to be sure about that?*
Student:	*Well, I guess if the hot water stayed the same temperature the whole time.*
Teacher:	*Here are several thermometers. Why don't you put them around the tub and try this again. This time, collect data on the temperature of the water and see what happens. I will be back in a bit and we can discuss what you found.*

Five minutes before the period is to end, David gives the students a 5-minute warning. They immediately begin picking up their work, cleaning, and putting supplies away. They return to their desks, and David asks them what supplies they might need for tomorrow that they did not have today. Two groups are asked to share what they have learned thus far and what their plan for tomorrow includes. The bell rings and David dismisses them. Several stay behind to ask a question about their project. While the students are filing out, another teacher, Allen, is waiting in the hallway. Allen teaches in this classroom during David's prep periods. While David hates having to share his room and not being able to use it during his prep period, it is better than being a roving teacher. Just as the last student leaves, he remembers that he did not get back to the group set on the temperature collection task.

During David's prep period, the university visitor asks him how the class came to function so seamlessly. Students appeared to know what to do, they were busy learning, and they were all doing different investigations about convection currents. David replies that this sort of classroom does not happen overnight. Together, David and the students work toward open-inquiry activities. He shares a story about a colleague, Allen, who tried doing inquiry activities during the first weeks of school. Allen did not know the students or their abilities, and the students had not learned any of Allen's procedures, expectations, and classroom routines. The lesson failed miserably, and Allen vowed never to try inquiry activities in his science classroom again. David believes that the key to success with inquiry is to start slowly, to make small changes to an activity, practice the changes, and then add *another change. Eventually, laboratory activities can be more open ended; every single laboratory does not need to be, or should be, a full inquiry laboratory.*

The university professor walks away wondering if David, while successful, might be too comfortable teaching inquiry as this level and wonders if his students do any other kind of inquiry by the end of the year. He decides that David might be a good choice as a cooperating teacher to mentor a new intern.

Promises of Inquiry in Middle Schools and Classrooms

Middle schools, the integrative dominion of childhood and young adulthood and social-emotional development and disciplinary expertise, were to be utopia for science inquiry (Fenwick, 1987). Unlike elementary schools where science instruction is sporadic and teacher- or school-dependent, middle schools teach science daily and usually by someone who chose to be a science teacher. Like elementary schools, the focus on the whole child still exists. Unlike secondary schools where testing and college preparation pressures exist, middle schools are a place where children explore new content opportunities in a more supportive, integrated environment. Middle schools are supposed to be more nurturing than secondary schools, and content areas have the potential to be linked in meaningful ways as in elementary schools. Teams of teachers work with the same group of students, building a rich thematic curriculum that helps students understand how science and other disciplines interact. It is quite common at all levels in middle schools to believe that the teaching of reading and writing is the responsibility of all teachers. While writing and reading have traversed disciplinary boundaries, the possibilities of integration envisioned have not been fully realized for lack of attention to expository genres and argument common in science discourse in most language arts programs (Yore et al., 2003). David recognizes a natural fit between interactive-constructivist inquiry teaching and the traits of middle school students: curiosity, cognitive development, need for relevance, independence and interdependence, and emotional attributes (Jorgenson, Cleveland, & Vanosdall, 2004). Middle school students are receptive to collaborative learning activities with varying degrees of teacher, content, and student structure and to interdisciplinary, project-based approaches that address both the fundamental and derived senses of science literacy within the inquiry context.

Text and Graphic Adjuncts to Support Science Literacy for All

Word walls support vocabulary development; this instructional approach is encouraged by the middle school context and is accepted by most middle school students as being developmentally appropriate, which might not be true with secondary school students. Science has its own vocabulary with some words having particular meaning in the context of science, which is different than outside of science (e.g., wave, theory, genes—as opposed to jeans). Having both pictures and definitions is particularly helpful for English language learners to cross discourse boundaries (L1—home language, L2—instructional language, L3—scientific language) (Maalta, Dobb, & Ostlund, 2006). Middle school students often have previous experience with terms and vocabulary and, although they do not understand the full meaning of the term, they have a partial understanding or misconception about the term. The teacher can gain valuable insight into students' previous understanding by simply asking, *What do you know about this word?* or *What do you think it might mean?* In addition, it is often useful to not define vocabulary for students until they have had experience with the concept first (Barman & Kotar, 1989; Bybee, 1997). For example in the vignette, David could have waited to use the term "convection current" until the students observed the water movement in the tub—experience first, concept label second. In this case, students would have developed an understanding of the term themselves and the teacher is simply adding a new name (concept label) to what they already know. Furthermore, word walls can easily evolve into collaboratively developed concept maps illustrating the interpretive relationship amongst concepts.

Supports for Authentic Inquiry

Teachers are often overwhelmed by the prospect that their students will wish to explore an unlimited number of questions relating to the topic at hand (Bybee, 1997). Listing or recording student ideas as pending "questions of the week" provides David time to prepare and to assess the practicality of using some of the students' ideas as challenges. "Teachable moments" can be reactivated after reflection and planning; and by using the students' ideas, science instruction can become more relevant and authentic for students.

A material-rich environment is important (NRC, 1996). During their investigations, students need to manipulate materials in order to test out their ideas and explanations. Since middle school students are dealing with increasingly more abstract concepts in science, it is essential that they have materials with which to work out their ideas in a tangible way. These materials need not be expensive or complicated; often, bricks, pieces of board, plastic cups, and baby food jars make excellent tools. Storage space becomes a critical feature of an inquiry classroom.

An information-rich environment—print and digital—is important (AAAS, 1989). It is unrealistic to assume that students will be able to construct an understanding of scientific concepts on their own. Students will need to have print materials available to provide some content expertise to develop scientific understandings. An information-rich environment means more than having the adopted science textbook available. It can include Internet access, nonfiction books, magazines, the science sections in the newspaper, nature guidebooks, posters, digital videodiscs and videotapes, and related technologies. Students should use these resources when their investigations call for additional information to help explain or extrapolate the data they have already collected and to develop their fundamental sense of science literacy (21stcenturyskills.org). It is in these print materials that students will begin to distinguish between those questions best answered through an investigation or an information search. Science is not just in the laboratory. Real scientists build on information already gathered when developing their current experiments to push science forward (Yore, Florence, Pearson, & Weaver, 2006; Yore et al., 2004). Since middle school is where reading takes the leap from learning how to read to reading to learn, students can begin to use print material to further their understanding of a particular concept developed through investigation and discussion (Yore et al., 2003). While the full integration of science and literacy is a promise of inquiry, it is also a barrier as classrooms do not always have sufficient space for a dedicated science library, nor do they always have funding for each classroom to have its own collection.

Grouping to Support Knowledge Construction

Placing students in groups has several benefits, as David demonstrates. First, having students work in groups facilitates the disbursement and use of materials. As the experiments become more sophisticated at this level, they require more than one pair of hands or eyes to complete. In addition, sharing ideas and sharing data are part of authentic science. In middle school, peers become increasingly important in students' lives, replacing adults as the primary focus (Ryan, 2001). Having students in groups allows for peer assistance. It is unlikely that a classroom will have all students at the same ability level. Students in groups are able to assist one another rather than relying on the teacher as the sole authority over knowledge; however, this requires that students be placed in groups of mixed ability (Johnson & Johnson, 1989). In one group a higher functioning student may work with a lower functioning student or an English learner may work with students who have more advanced English skills.

Finally, students need the opportunity to discuss what they are learning. Students at the middle school level are able to discuss their ideas with a higher level of sophistication than elementary students. Often, they are able to develop a significant level of content understanding through their own conversations. When students share their ideas with each other, those ideas are clarified, reevaluated, and refined through the negotiation that comes with making their ideas public. This also happens through questioning from the teacher, but student-to-student dialogue is often more meaningful for student learning (Howe, 1996). However, simply placing students into groups does not ensure that they will cooperate or that productive discourse will occur. Giving them a task that requires cooperation or group effort will have a significant impact on student motivation and achievement (Slavin, 1987). For example, while working on experiments, one student may be placed in charge of materials, one in charge of recording data, and one in charge of communicating questions and findings. Another possibility is giving each group a separate piece of a larger puzzle. Each group is responsible to the whole class to complete its portion of the task.

Safe and Supportive Learning Environments

Creating a safe environment that encourages inquiry and interactions is essential (Ryan, 2001). Safe means free from physical and emotional harm. State or provincial guidelines, safety manuals, and selection of low-risk activities address physical harm. Students at the middle school often have anxiety about their self-image. This concern over self-image goes beyond how they look physically. Middle school students are often concerned about how they are seen in the social atmosphere of the school (e.g., are they smart, dumb, teacher's pet, or jock). This requires a great deal of effort on the part of the teacher to ensure that students feel safe to express and share their ideas about the content being covered in class. It cannot be assumed that the necessary social skills are there. It is essential that the teacher model how to make comments that are constructive rather than insulting to each other, that is, academic civility (Good & Brophy, 2002). It may also be useful to have students work together to negotiate a list of classroom rules related to open discussion. The debate of ideas is an essential part of inquiry, but one that is problematic in middle school without the teacher developing the necessary social skills in students.

Middle school students may require teacher questioning to push their thinking beyond a simple answer, restating data, or repeating what is stated in the textbook or data table (Martens, 1999). By this age, students often become savvy about how to answer teacher questions with limited personal or intellectual investment. Thus, a teacher cannot be discouraged when a student answers their probing question with "I don't know" or "nothing." Student engagement can be achieved by simply breaking down the question further to something that the student can answer. Often this is done through higher level, open-ended questions, such as, *What evidence do you have for this? How do you know? How would this apply to* (similar situation)? *What questions do you still have?* Since middle school students are more sophisticated about the unspoken procedures of the classroom, wait-time becomes a significant factor in student dialogue (Rowe, 1996). Middle school students may outwait the teacher, blankly looking back without volunteering any responses to a teacher's questions. Students often need processing time and can benefit from a minute or two to discuss at their table groups before answering a question. The teacher can rotate discussing the students' ideas in the safety of a small group, building student confidence for whole class discussion and sequence questions designed to share, organize, interpret, and generalize experiences.

BARRIERS TO INQUIRY IN MIDDLE SCHOOLS AND CLASSROOMS

Developmental Level of Middle School Students

Inquiry involves the blending of scientific knowledge and a scientific view of the world. However, it is unrealistic to think that students of all age levels would be able to participate in inquiry to the full extent implied in this definition. For middle school teachers, this means designing experiences for students that develop their ability to construct arguments and to see the relationship between evidence, claims, and an explanation (NRC, 1996). The use of language in the science classroom and a teacher's understanding of the nature of science are important. Teachers and students need to understand the difference between cookbook science laboratories and inquiry and the difference between school science and real science. Where appropriate, teachers should emphasize the nature of science and describe how the in-class activities are like and not like real science. When students get results that match their predictions, they have not *proven* their prediction in spite of what textbooks might say. Their results *support* their claim, and additional similar results would further increase their confidence. Teachers are starting to recognize the importance of the nature of science in their classrooms as science teacher education programs include explicit reference to the nature of science.

Doing inquiry in the classroom provides a unique opportunity to address the nature of science *in situ*.

Although middle school students have had experience conducting scientific investigations, they tend to depend on personal explanations for investigations rather than relying on evidence (NRC, 1996). They will focus on the evidence that supports their beliefs and disregard what contradicts them. It is important that teachers design activities that challenge students' preexisting beliefs and move them toward a scientific explanation, such as using the modified learning cycle (Bybee, 1997; Posner, Strike, Hewson, & Gertzog, 1982; Stepans, 2003). Students at this age are likely to have difficulty identifying variables in an experiment. They are also likely to have difficulty controlling for more than one variable in their investigations and understanding how different variables influence the results of an investigation (NRC, 1996). Keys and Bryan (2001) claimed the literature indicates that by the age of 11 students are capable of making observations, recording data, and identifying one variable. However, when faced with more complex data, such as multiple variables, making inferences based on evidence, or distinguishing between categorical or continuous variables, students experience greater difficulty and their performance plummets.

Limited Classroom Space and the Roving Teachers

Many middle schools have a shortage of space. In addition to portable classrooms, middle and secondary teachers often have to share their classrooms. While middle school teachers usually have a preparation period, they are often unable to use their classroom during that time block because another teacher is teaching there. David's vignette illustrates how this increases the difficulty of doing laboratory activities of any type—inquiry or traditional. The roving teacher usually pushes a cart around from one classroom to another. Jokingly referred to as doing science "a la carte," this teacher needs to quickly get from one room to another during the passing period. It is difficult for them to do much setup in their classrooms, as none of the classrooms are "theirs." If they are teaching physical science in a life science classroom, they may not have the materials they need. The teacher who regularly teaches in the classroom has the added difficulty of not being able to use the classroom during the preparation period. This means that laboratory materials need to be set up before or after school and quickly put away, or off to the side, before the roving teacher arrives.

Time Factors

As we saw at the elementary level, time is a barrier at the middle school level as well. While there is daily time set aside for science instruction, often there is insufficient time for inquiry or time becomes the convenient excuse to avoid inquiry. It is more time consuming to do inquiry activities than lecture or traditional laboratory activities (Windschitl, 2002). Like scientists, not all students work or succeed at the same rate—some students are likely to make false starts and need to begin again while other students will finish more quickly. It is difficult for teachers to fully implement their lesson plans as designed because of the time factor. In the vignette, David did not get back to students and there was not time for discussion based on student presentations. The assumption is that this teacher will pick up where things left off, but getting back to that group of students is likely to fall through the cracks if the teacher does not make note of that need. Students need the class discussions to help them make sense of what they experience in the activity—the consolidation phase of the learning cycle is critical.

Organization and Management

Procedures and routines are important classroom management issues related to inquiry teaching (Jones, 2000; Wong & Wong, 2004). Often in middle school, the teacher is responsible for more than one class section each day, which means there may be several set-up and clean-up times with only minutes between. While students are working through investigations, there should be points in the investigation where the teacher is able to make formative assessments about their progress. Teachers need to plan for these points so they can decide whether to allow students to continue or if additional information is needed before going further. Inquiry requires that students be allowed some degree of freedom to investigate and comprehend the world on their own. These divergent explorations and experiences can enrich later class discussions and consolidation.

Dividing the investigation is a useful technique (Johnson & Johnson, 1989; Slavin, 1987). It is often easier to have students share and pay attention when everyone has done different investigations. Rather than having every group conduct each experiment the exact same way, altering the question being investigated allows students to have a similar experience from which to talk to each other; the conversations will be richer when each group has something unique to add. The jigsaw approach closely approximates the distributed-expertise found in science research groups and international research networks (Florence & Yore, 2004). In these settings, parallel but different research activities are spread out.

All or Nothing Approach

New teachers often feel compelled to implement every new strategy they learn. Many times teachers try to do too much at once, which can result in less than desirable results. Some teachers simply quit at that point and decide the innovation is not worth the effort (Windschitl, 2002). We know this happens for teachers trying to change from a traditional, cookbook-type laboratory to inquiry. Trying to change too many variables in a classroom at once can be problematic. Change is a vector quantity composed of steps in the right direction—get the direction first and worry about the magnitude later. Teachers should consider making a series of small changes and consolidating progress to slowly move the class toward a more inquiry-based environment (Colburn, 1997, 2005).

Teachers may believe that inquiry promotes student thinking and conceptual understanding of science, but the philosophy behind inquiry teaching often conflicts with many teachers' cultural beliefs about the transmission of knowledge and instructional efficiency of teaching (Bryan & Abell, 1999; Weinburgh, 2003). The traditional Western philosophy that knowledge is transferred through language from teacher to student conflicts with the constructivist philosophy behind inquiry teaching that students create their own knowledge through their personal experiences (Scheurman, 1998). The teacher as dispenser of knowledge is difficult to overcome (Windschitl, 2002). Keys and Bryan (2001) found that the body of research implies high levels of content, pedagogical, and pedagogical content knowledge are necessary to successfully implement inquiry teaching, especially in terms of knowledge about the nature of science—something classroom generalists often lack in science.

Changes Beyond the Classroom

Initiating inquiry-based approaches to science teaching often involves changing the culture within the school and classroom from what is often expected by most administrators, teachers, and parents: quiet classrooms with students working independently. As teachers are faced with the standards movement and related high-stakes testing, inquiry-teaching methods may seem at odds with the political realities; but the 1980 meta-analyses indicate this is not necessarily the case (Shymansky et al., 2003). For example, administrators expect to see learning objectives and standards posted (a behavioralist strategy) when they enter a classroom. Some science investigations would be less powerful learning experiences for students if told in advance the standards to be learned. In these cases, it requires educating administrators to science teaching best practices. It does not eliminate the need for carefully planned instruction or standards-based instruction, but the way in which the standards are revealed to students may vary.

In summary, teachers are often overwhelmed with the difficult task of implementing the more interactive and unpredictable teaching methods associated with inquiry and constructivism. Implementing this type of learning involves sophisticated integration of pedagogical skills and deep content. Learning and understanding do not come to students simply by the doing of activities (Henriques, 1997; Nelson & Moscovici, 1998). They need the consolidation phase of the learning cycle. Even better, the students should be given opportunity to extend their understandings into new contexts or with new examples to help them make sense of what they have done and seen and to connect it with their prior knowledge and the established knowledge of science (Bybee, 1997). Doing inquiry requires more than merely memorizing content or listening to lectures. Students must use their cognitive strategies and knowledge from disciplines other than science to be successful. Language arts strategies are tapped as students read and write to learn about science. Providing a rich experiential and interdisciplinary context in a multicultural classroom levels the academic demands for all students, especially for English language learners (Amaral, Garrison, & Klentschy, 2002; Bravo & Garcia, 2004; Hampton & Rodriguez, 2001; Lee, 2005; Rosebery, Warren, & Conant, 2003; Settlage, Madsen, & Rustad, 2005). The concrete experiences they get through hands-on investigations help provide context on which to cross cultural, language, and worldview borders in order to construct meaningful understanding.

INQUIRY IN SECONDARY SCHOOL CLASSROOMS

Vignette

Eastern Ridge High School is located in a small city of about 50,000. The science department has 15 faculty members whose classrooms are mostly in different buildings separated from the main building by a busy street. The school offers academic and vocational courses, with opportunities for students to take university-level courses for credit. The majority of the students achieve well, attaining high SAT with 85% of the graduating students pursuing a postsecondary education. The students also test well in the state Regent's examination. This high stakes test determines whether a student graduates secondary school. Last year 16 students earned National Merit Scholarships. Eastern Ridge High School has been traditionally viewed as successfully serving its student population.

Located in close physical proximity to Mountain State University, this year the school started serving as a professional development school (PDS)—a school/university partnership in science teacher education with an emphasis on inquiry-based teaching. Five science teachers agreed to participate in the science PDS as mentors; each selected a student teacher (intern) to work with throughout the academic year. A component of the PDS is a weekly, after-school, university credit (optional) seminar led by a professor. The seminar focuses on teaching science as inquiry as articulated in the National Science Education Standards.

Darren and Jason, who teach biology in adjoining rooms in the West Building, and Adam, a physics teacher whose science room is in the East Building, are consistent participants in the seminar. Two other teachers attend less often; one, a biology teacher, is the school basketball coach. By mid-semester, he had begun after-school basketball practices. The other teacher, Amy, who teaches earth science in the east building and has a young child in day care, also serves as president of the teachers' union. The five PDS mentors and the professor have been meeting for several months.

It is 3:30 p.m. on a Wednesday afternoon in early December. Three of the teachers and the professor are gathered around a table making small talk. Amy rushes in: "Sorry I'm late! My intern is sick, and I had to set up my lab for tomorrow on mineral identification." One teacher (the basketball coach) is attending a meeting on how to better meet the State Regents' tests in the middle and elementary schools. The professor starts the session by asking the teachers to share their reflections on the previous week's science lessons. She asks, "Did you and your intern try out any new approaches, laboratories, or activities that you would consider centered in inquiry? Did you try to connect with inquiry-based teaching, as outlined in the NSES book?"

Jason immediately begins to describe how he and his intern changed a lab he had used successfully for several years.

I have this lab on diffusion, using potatoes and various concentrations of salt water. In one of my classes, I handed out the lab instructions and worksheets, and we went over the procedure as usual. In the other class, I just put out some materials and said, "Come up with a question and a procedure." You know, I wanted it to be open inquiry, like in the NSES book. In the inquiry class, it took most of the period for the students to come up with a question. They did not have a clue about what they should do. They became frustrated. The whole group complained, and one boy said to my intern, "Just tell us the answer!" We had to extend that lesson into another day for the inquiry class. At the end of the week, we gave the same test to both classes, and there did not seem to be any difference. The open inquiry just took much more time. I am up in the air, if it is more beneficial to spend extra time covering the same material in a different manner when the results are the same.

Adam joined in.

In my physics class, I am actually trying to change a lot of what I do in the classroom, especially in my labs. I count on my intern to have fresh new ideas. It gets me out of a rut, so to speak. I want to show you something. I brought with me this trebuchet. Some of the girls in my third period physics class have been meeting every Wednesday after school with my intern. They are building this for the middle school Renaissance Fair. These girls have learned a lot about calibration and forces. You should hear them talk about science. But something like this is tough to do in my regular physics classroom. Also, I am finding that my intern does not really understand all the aspects of inquiry either.

Amy entered in the conversation:

Inquiry is an awful lot of work. I am not sure I am willing to invest the time and energy to learn and implement new classroom strategies, particularly technology-based ones. I am pretty comfortable with my teaching right now. Besides, the state is requiring us to have students do three mandated labs. Preparing my students to carry these out takes up enough time in my class. Those state labs are my first priority. Last week the assistant principal observed my teaching. He told me one of the most important things in my teaching is to keep my students listening to me and out of the hallway. He was worried that we were using acids and other chemicals in my classroom, because of a possible lawsuit.

Darren quickly commiserated, "I agree. It is risky, you know. What if it fails? You and I know that a lecture is not going to fail, but an inquiry activity could really flop. Yet, I am not giving up on inquiry."

Jason interjected, "We don't meet often enough to talk about our teaching. The biology teachers do not have a common planning time. In addition, they even assigned a study hall to me during one of my prep periods this year."

Amy said,

Sometimes I feel out of the loop, because I am teaching in the other building. I am sorry, but I have never heard the term "inquiry" before this year. One of the things I said at last week's meeting was that I feel that inquiry is being pushed on us, as the only method of teaching. My feeling right now is that inquiry is an abstract idea, an unproven method. We are assuming kids can make connections by themselves, and many times they cannot. My ninth grade earth science students need to be able to do well on the Regents' test. Many of my kids are struggling with reading. It takes all semester, just going over all the questions from last year's test.

Adam said,

Well, I feel as though I was falling into the trap of being too didactic over the years. Moreover, I feel as though this experience has pushed me to re-institute a little more creativity with my students. One of my goals is that by the end of the year I will have a better understanding of what inquiry-based teaching is. The second goal would be to find materials that help me—computer-based simulations and things like that. I really do not have good access to inquiry-based materials.

Darren commented,

I admit that I do want to change. I want to be less teacher-directed. I am counting on my intern to help me try out some new things in my labs. I am trying to use my intern's creativity to make some changes in my own teaching.

Jason said,

My intern knows more about inquiry than I do. For me, the real problem is not enough time. It would be really nice if science teachers would get together and have more collaboration with Mountain State. To be perfectly honest, I am still kind of up in the air about inquiry, but at least we tried it this week.

The professor said to the group, "I would like to read a section here, from the NSES (NRC, 2000, p. xii): 'Inquiry is in part a state of mind, that of inquisitiveness.'" Further, she explained that, "Students need to learn the principles and concepts of science, acquire the reasoning and procedural skills of scientists, and understand the nature of science as a particular form of human endeavor." She asked: "Do you think it is necessary to form a consensus on what inquiry teaching would look like in your classrooms?"

PROMISES FOR INQUIRY IN SECONDARY SCHOOLS AND CLASSROOMS

Contemporary Science Literacy: Fundamental and Derived Senses

The vignette of these secondary school science teachers grappling with and figuring out what inquiry can mean to students in a traditionally successful secondary school illustrates several promises. Frequently, these promises are not as transparent to teachers, students, and the community as suggested in the literature. The realization of these promises involves revisiting the learning potential of inquiry science compared to traditional "chalk'n'talk" science and capitalizing on institutional strengths and resources to support inquiry-based teaching and learning. This process of rethinking science education requires consideration of the changing role of schools within the community, viewing students as young adults and citizens, and building cross-curricular learning communities where the diversity of students' culture, interests, and ability levels can be viewed as positive assets to enrich the learning environment. Furthermore, some of the promises are only opportune to schools with a pattern of success, like Eastern Ridge, on which to build further successes and to enlarge the circle of engagement to students not already involved in science.

One of the most important promises concerns the institutional need to develop in students a deep understanding of the big ideas in science and of the nature of science (Norris & Phillips, 2003; Yore & Treagust, 2006). Institutions need to strive to position students to become scientifically literate citizens and develop into life-long learners. Students should gain an appreciation of what scientists do with data in constructing explanations and models as well as a deep, meaningful understanding of the unifying concepts and big ideas of science. The girls participating in the after-school physics program at Eastern Ridge developed in-depth knowledge of physics concepts through an inquiry process of solving a problem. They also had opportunity to gain skills in manipulating variables, making sense of data, and an appreciation for the importance of creativity in science. Arguably, this inquiry experience provided these female students with rich opportunities to use and apply their knowledge of scientific concepts in more intellectually challenging ways than they encountered in their typical science classes.

Science is a way of knowing and thinking about the natural world, not just a mere collection of facts. The use of evidence-based explanations derived from the physical world separates science from other important ways of knowing based upon faith or interpretation of human generated texts. Inquiry-based approaches facilitate student development as scientifically literate critical thinkers and problem solvers, and promote scientific process skills and reasoning abilities, including formulating hypotheses and building evidence-based models and explanations (NRC, 1996, 2000). Too often, however, science teachers are faced with the perceived pressure to cover all of the required content that will appear on the year-end state test. This results in teachers placing too much emphasis on the "what we know about science" by presenting factual information and ignoring the "how we know" that embodies the nature of the scientific endeavor (Gallagher, 1991).

Secondary schools provide science laboratories, equipment, and intellectual support for authentic inquiry similar to scientists doing science. In the after-school club, students worked collaboratively on designing and testing a trebuchet, a device used in medieval times that is similar to a catapult. The students used protocols similar to ones used by scientists, yet modified given the available materials and level of student expertise. They volunteered to participate in the after-school club and were motivated to learn physics concepts as well as to use critical thinking in engineering the device and solving a design problem. It is these authentic contexts of making sense of naturally occurring events and constructing compelling arguments and explanations that justify the time, resources, and effort needed to set inquiry into action (NRC, 1999).

Connections With Community-Based Problems

Secondary schools are becoming more integrated and active participants in their communities (Crawford, 2000). There are many examples of community-based investigations, including water quality studies of local ponds and lakes. Another example involves studying local birds that come to school or home feeders. Students track the kinds of birds and maximum number of a species visiting a birdfeeder and enter their data on the Cornell Lab of Ornithology e-Bird Web site (http://www.ebird.org). In this way, students participate in monitoring their local environment as well as contribute data to a national, scientific database.

Such experiences contribute to the personal relevance of science and places science in a social context—an underemphasized standard of NSES (NRC, 1996). Secondary students often view school science as disconnected from reality, impractical, and a series of trivial academic tasks to be completed. Inquiry activities connected to the community encourage students to understand and apply the target concepts and processes resulting in meaningful learning and authentic science inquiry without known solutions, not just acquiring the needed marks for graduation, athletics eligibility, and college entrance.

The teachers at Eastern Ridge already enjoy strong community support and have the potential to expand their science curriculum to include inquiry projects that serve as powerful learning scenarios and ones that can raise community awareness about issues revolving around science and technology. The fact that Eastern Ridge has a well-established partnership with Mountain State University could further enhance such activities (The Holmes Group, 1990). By utilizing the university's science faculty and resources, the science teachers have the potential to develop inquiry projects that expose their students to the university's intellectual and physical resources while providing an authentic science research experience that has local significance.

Movement Toward Adulthood and Citizenship

Another promise of using an inquiry-based approach and constructivist frameworks involves relevancy to learners and their responsibility for their learning (Dewey, 1933). Many secondary school students may perceive they are on the academic fringes, especially in large schools with many high-achieving students (Tobias, 1990). Inquiry-based approaches may serve to engage students who are not in the upper level, tracked science classes and whom institutions may struggle to reach academically (Oakes & Lipton, 1998; Rosebery, Warren, & Conant, 1989). Inquiry also empowers and facilitates metacognition in all students. Thus, the need to be aware of the purposes, procedures, and ways of knowing and how to manage these cognitive strategies, processes, and procedures becomes paramount (Yore & Treagust, 2006).

Students who engage in metacognition—the awareness and self-regulation to gain insight into one's own learning and thinking processes—develop skills that contribute to life-long learning. Inquiry is in part a mental state of inquisitiveness (NRC, 2000). When students engage in inquiry, they may consider how scientists develop explanations of how the world works, based on data and creativity. Given the opportunity to develop their own understandings of scientific phenomena, students can begin to think about how they construct their own knowledge (Minstrell, 1989; White & Frederiksen, 1998).

Cross-Curricular Integration of Language, Science, Mathematics, and Social Studies

Investigations and solving science, technology, and societal problems are contextualized, authentic, multifaceted, and interdisciplinary. Science has become increasingly interdisciplinary, and school policy and practices have encouraged collaboration and integration of the disciplines to address realistic and complex issues. The vignette's inquiry-based project of building and testing a trebuchet connects technology and science and provides a context for students to learn important principles of physics. Later, these students combined knowledge of medieval times, food and culture, literature, and practices with learning physics. Interdisciplinary units and problem-based projects provide excellent opportunities for expanded integration of the content areas and to more fully develop the fundamental sense of science literacy involving habits of mind, cognitive and metacognitive abilities, critical thinking, scientific communication and information communication technologies found in scientific communities (Yore et al., 2003; Yore et al., 2006).

Classroom Environments Must Be Responsive to the Differentiated Needs of Science Learners

Federal and state or provincial laws have encouraged schools to address the needs of a much more diverse student population than ever before. Cultural, linguistic, and physical needs must be considered in planning and delivering instruction (Lee, 2005). Inquiry provides students with learning disabilities and physical disabilities and students who may learn best in small groups and peer discussions with opportunities to be active learners. Inquiry-based approaches provide greater opportunity for collaboration than traditional, teacher-centered approaches (Crawford, Krajcik, & Marx, 1999). The institutional constraint of having several class periods per day precludes teachers from taking time to have students work through problems at their own pace. Teachers often default to using primarily a lecture format to get through all the science content in the curriculum. Student-centered approaches offer an alternative setting for girls and students with a preference for other types of learning. Specific consideration of students' language, cultural beliefs, and traditional knowledge are a natural extension of the engagement of students and will reveal rich opportunities to anchor inquiry and to challenge many science, technology, and societal issues (Cognition & Technology Group at Vanderbilt, 1990).

BARRIERS TO INQUIRY IN
SECONDARY SCHOOLS AND SCIENCE CLASSROOMS

Overcoming the Culture of Perceived Success

The vignette paired prospective and practicing teachers in the class-room and situated teachers with university researchers and teacher educa-tors in a community of learners. This vignette highlights some of the institutional constraints that may dissuade a teacher from exploring and eventually implementing an inquiry-based approach. Teachers' views of science, experience with science inquiry, and beliefs about science learn-ing contribute to the resistance to change (Crawford, 2007).

One of the most difficult barriers is the general perception of what constitutes success in schools like Eastern Ridge with traditional strong records of sending students to postsecondary education and where 5-10% of the graduates pursue science-related careers. The belief that the system of science programs and instruction in this school district is not broken, so why are we trying to fix or reform it, is often the norm. What this argu-ment fails to take into consideration is how the current science curriculum and instructional practices in such schools serve only select populations of students, as opposed to promoting scientific literacy for all learners. Both "science literacy" and "all students" need to be clarified and accepted by the school and community. While the discipline of science is deeply rooted in the tradition of hands-on research and problem solving, school science, ironically, often revolves around content knowledge and rote memorization (Hazen, 1991). This overemphasis on rote learning of facts frequently results in an overuse of didactic teaching, which is contrary to the needs of so many students. This pedagogical approach does little to equip students with the fundamental sense of science literacy necessary to make informed judgments about science issues they will face throughout their lives (Norris & Phillips, 2003).

The end result is that many talented students who might possess problem-solving, higher-order reasoning, and creative thinking skills are turned away from science courses based on faulty assumptions and academic prejudices about who can succeed in science at the secondary school level. While some science learners can adapt their learning to accommodate a narrow, didactic pedagogical approach, others face immense challenges in trying to conceptualize the abstract and cursory presentations of science information that often predominate, even in successful schools like Eastern Ridge. Thus, many of the students who are tracked as future scientists and achieve high examination scores are those who have persisted in rote memorization of science courses, not so much because of the quality of their science education but rather in spite of it (Tillotson & Kluth, 2003).

Teachers, parents, students, and administrators alike are quick to equate high test scores with successful learning. Yet the reality is that many of these labeled-successful students leave secondary school lacking a deep, conceptual understanding of scientific concepts and are ill prepared to apply their knowledge of science as citizens or undergraduate students. At the heart of this barrier is the pressure placed upon teachers to cover a large volume of content material in preparation for a standardized examination at the end of the school year. These high stakes examination results are used in many jurisdictions to make decisions about teacher effectiveness, tenure decisions, and overall school quality. Faced with these constraints, many science teachers opt to avoid using an inquiry-based approach and, instead, choose to use a more didactic, lecture-based approach that allows for rapid coverage of the core content. In this classroom environment, rote learners excel while learners seldom have an opportunity to learn content in a fashion that capitalizes on their true academic potential (Tillotson & Kluth, 2003).

The Meaning of Inquiry Itself is Confusing

Teachers need to know what "it" is, if we expect them to design instruction that supports inquiry (Anderson, 2002; Keys & Bryan, 2001; Windschitl, 2004). Researchers and professional development providers need to be clear about what it means to teach using inquiry. Inquiry as a term has been complicated by multiple interpretations. Secondary school science teachers need to comprehend what researchers and professional development providers are talking about (Kang & Wallace, 2005). Inquiry has several components: teaching *through* (using inquiry as an approach to learn science subject matter), teaching *to do* (learning about the processes of carrying out inquiry), and teaching *about* inquiry (the human aspects of the nature of scientific inquiry) (NRC, 1996, 2000). Equally puzzling for some teachers is what exactly is meant by the "reform of science education." One institutional constraint is that many secondary schools do not offer appropriate professional development opportunities for science teachers to learn about and consider trying different approaches in the classroom. This is particularly problematic because many science teachers are strongly influenced by the experiences they encountered in university science courses, which were dominated by lectures, with a verification laboratory infused somewhere within the week of study (Yore, 2001); they viewed this as the primary model for developing their own teaching practices. Many current secondary school science teachers have not experienced constructivist-oriented inquiry teaching and learning; therefore, inquiry-focused professional development needs to provide experiences to practicing teachers that emphasize pedagogical-content knowledge—not just more science content knowledge. There are many professional development opportunities designed to help practicing teachers gain experience in this area.

Lack of Compelling Evidence on the Effectiveness of Inquiry Teaching

Teachers have their students' best interests at heart. In order to justify choosing an inquiry-based teaching approach, teachers need to know that an inquiry-based approach is better and more effective (Tretter & Jones, 2003). Many secondary school students go on to postsecondary institutions, do well on entrance examinations, and pass science courses taught in traditional ways. Some secondary school students go on to become career scientists. Inquiry-based teaching takes an extended period of time and added effort while covering less content topics. The inquiry advocate and practitioner must believe that "less can be more"—less coverage leads to more in-depth understanding. Thus, time is an important factor in choosing an inquiry-based approach over more didactic, teacher-centered approaches.

Practitioners may not have access to evidence that using an inquiry-based approach to teach science is better than a teacher-centered approach (Anderson, 2002; Marx, Blumenfeld, Krajcik, Blunk, Crawford,

& Meyer, 1994). Successful secondary school science teachers need to have a compelling reason to change their orientation to teaching science. Institutional constraints include primarily assessing students using high-stakes testing methods, which provide only one kind of evidence of science teaching effectiveness. Traditional assessments do not demonstrate the extent of what students may learn through inquiry (Duschl & Gitomer, 1998). Institutional barriers include supporting the use of traditional assessments that focus mainly on memorized information and do not measure students' abilities to solve problems and think critically. High-stakes testing programs may not reward teachers for developing students' deep understanding or appreciation of science. Teacher and student accountability in many areas is based solely on test scores that stress traditional teaching and learning. Test score accountability is seemingly all that matters to parents, administrators, and layperson school boards; and these stakeholder groups are not easily convinced of the merits of inquiry.

Self-Efficacy in the New Roles of the Secondary School Inquiry Science Classroom

Secondary school science teachers, both practicing and prospective, may not know how to plan for and teach science as inquiry (Keys & Bryan, 2001). Practicing teachers may desire to change their teaching, but they may not know how to shift from the role of authority figure and transmitter of knowledge to the role of facilitator and mentor (Tobin, Tippins, & Gallard, 1994). Institutional constraints may prevent teachers from co-planning, sharing new teaching strategies, and peer support. Prospective and beginning science teachers often lack confidence in their science content knowledge, and inquiry-based classes often generate student questions that require a deeper conceptual knowledge. Furthermore, prospective teachers often work with cooperating teachers who use traditional ways to teach science versus inquiry-based approaches, leaving them with few opportunities to witness models of teaching science as inquiry in their field experiences.

Change can be hard, and inquiry teaching is not easy; it is difficult and complex (Crawford, 2000). Teachers who have tried it find that planning for and managing inquiry-based instruction are challenging endeavors (Marx et al., 1994). For example, how does a teacher help students work collaboratively in groups on long-term problems? How does a teacher manage many students working on different projects at the same time? Furthermore, there is a lack of innovative curriculum materials specific to inquiry-based instruction. Few secondary school textbooks support inquiry-based approaches in classrooms. Colburn (1997) provided suggestions for the gradual transition to inquiry teaching.

A prevailing myth among many teachers is that secondary school science's primary purpose is to prepare students for postsecondary science where lecture-based teaching methods predominate (Tobin & McRobbie, 1996; Yore, 2001). While the goal of preparing students for the next academic level is not without merit, an overemphasis on postsecondary preparation can cause secondary school science teachers to experience academic tunnel vision, neglecting a large majority of students (Tillotson & Kluth, 2003). What is lost in this endeavor is meaningful, practical, science learning that empowers all students to become better, problem-solvers, develop better reasoning skills, and make more informed decisions about scientific issues (Fradd & Lee, 1999; Yager, 1991). The notion that, in order to be successful in college, secondary school students need rigorous, content-rich, science courses was challenged by Leyden (1984) who used secondary school drop-out rates, college attendance figures, graduation rates, and justice department data to reach the sobering conclusion that,

> One thing is for certain—8 years after you teach those [secondary school] freshman, there is a good chance that more of them will have been in jail or state prison than the 1.2% who will have a degree in science. (p. 28)

Secondary School Environment Discourages the Use of Inquiry-Based Approaches

There are institutional constraints that interfere with the promotion of inquiry science. The traditional structure of a secondary school day may not allow for extended periods of time where students can carry out investigations, engage in fieldwork, or gather data. A class schedule of nine, 45-minute periods per day precludes flexibility and the opportunity to team-teach multidisciplinary units of instruction. More often than not, in larger science departments, there is almost a pressure to conform and for all science teachers to be at the same point and the same place in the curriculum (Tillotson & Olmstead, 1998). This tendency toward uniformity stifles attempts to create inquiry experiences that likely result in students being in different stages of learning and project completion at different times. There also may be resistance from parents and school administrators, who themselves may not have experienced or understand inquiry-oriented approaches to learning and teaching. Curricular constraints in a school district, coupled with state or provincial curriculum mandates, may make it difficult to reduce the number of science topics covered during the secondary school year in order to focus on fewer topics but in greater depth. The most expedient way to expose students to all of the material contained in the curriculum guide is through lecturing, and drill-and-practice exercise. In doing so, science teachers rely heavily on the textbook as their sole source of curriculum (Lorsbach & Tobin, 1992). Reaching the end of a textbook chapter or assigning repeated worksheets does little for the students who are struggling to adapt their learning to this linear, didactic approach.

Students may not embrace the new roles required by inquiry learning (Duggan, Johnson, & Gott, 1996). Institutional constraints include the predominance of lecture-driven, didactic teaching as the norm throughout secondary school. Students have learned their roles well and are often resistant to inquiry-based ways of learning science; they may have experienced eight or more years of simply receiving information from their teachers. It takes effort to shift from the role of passive learner to that of an active one (Brooks & Brooks, 1999). Students who are most successful in traditional science classrooms (i.e., students in advanced courses) may be the most uncomfortable and dissatisfied with nontraditional, inquiry classroom environments. Secondary students who score well on performance measures and less successful students may not want to commit the extra effort and cognition required for making sense and constructing understanding.

The physical layout of secondary schools can also serve as barrier to inquiry in science classrooms. Schools similar to the one in the vignette are typical where science teachers in different buildings within large schools may struggle to find time to collaborate on science curriculum development, interdisciplinary teaching, or joint professional development programs. In many rural school districts, the issue is not that the science teachers are spread out across so many buildings; rather, there may be only one or two science teachers for all 7-12 grades, which makes it difficult to consider implementing inquiry when faced with multiple science subjects to teach and multiple sets of core curriculum guides and examinations with which to contend.

Overcrowding in science classrooms has become an increasing barrier to inquiry-based instruction and student-centered learning. Finding ways to provide active and engaging experiences for individual students in classrooms with 25 or more students is a daunting challenge. In addition to basic safety concerns, science teachers often struggle to effectively provide resources and support to students associated with authentic inquiry projects. In classrooms where classroom management is an issue, many teachers revert to more traditional, lecture-based instructional methods as they have greater control while all students work on the same task. Many science teachers are not prepared for the organized chaos that often predominates in active, inquiry-oriented classrooms where not all students are working on the same learning activities at the same time (Tillotson & Kluth, 2003). An experienced science teacher knows how to determine if the level of chaos in the classroom is productive or out of hand. Structures can help minimize unproductive chaos. Clear project expectations, established checkpoints where students need to review their progress with the teacher, and practice routines for transition from project work to whole class activities are just a few ideas.

Laboratory Safety

The relationships among learning, prior knowledge, teaching, laboratory experiences, and improved science literacy (fundamental and derived senses) are complex and not well defined or associated with large-scale test results (NRC, 2006). It is generally believed in the science teaching and research communities that constructivist approaches require classroom-laboratory spaces that are flexible, safe environments. This allows for easy and quick transition between discourse, knowledge construction, and exploratory activities; and that provide opportunities for student groups working on a variety of experiences under the supervision of a single teacher. Schools need to plan and provide the financial support to design, build, equip, and maintain such classroom-laboratory facilities. Between 20-51% of the schools responding had inadequate science laboratories, and the pattern of responses indicates an association between the school's socioeconomic status and the adequacy of their laboratory instruction space.

Concern about safety issues and litigation has been a deterrent to including some laboratory activities and open-ended inquiry projects. State departments distribute increasingly longer lists of hazardous materials, thicker safety manuals, and occupational working conditions. The National Science Teachers Association (nsta.org/positionstatement &psid=32) has provided basic guidelines regarding activity selection, safety procedures, insurance, reasonable judgment and supervision, professional development, and liability to mitigate concerns about injury, risk, and litigation for laboratory activities and field trips. Federal, state, and provincial workplace safety and occupational health organizations also provide resources and professional development activities to address laboratory safety, healthy practices, and the safe handling and storage of materials (labsafety.org; nsela.org; osha.gov). Clearly, the well-prepared mind is the best safety feature possible.

Technology May Not Be Readily Accessible to Support Students in Learning About Inquiry

Although more and more schools are acquiring computers and related technologies, in reality, teachers may find it difficult to schedule their classes in the computer laboratories. Teachers may have the knowledge and desire to integrate technology in their science instruction, but they may only have access to old computer technology gained from donations from parents and businesses. The school district may provide teachers with limited funds for purchasing new computer software. A lack of site licenses may prevent teachers from installing software on a set of computers. Other institutional barriers related to technology-based inquiry include administrators who may be fearful of teachers allowing students to fully utilize the Internet in using web searches and creating web-based pages.

Wealthy or resource-rich schools often have well-equipped science classrooms with ample laboratory equipment and resources to successfully implement an inquiry-based science program. Many high-needs rural and urban schools, however, do not enjoy these same advantages; they lack any type of budget for science equipment and supplies. The end result is fewer inquiry experiences for students, more teacher-led demonstrations, fewer authentic research experiences, and more confirmation or recipe-type laboratory activities. Inquiry-based science projects often require equipment and supplies that may extend beyond those available in many science stockrooms. While wealthier school districts may be able to provide the resources necessary to sustain an inquiry-based science program, poor school districts are less able to accommodate such needs, further perpetuating the disparities between high- and low-income school districts. Many science teachers in low-income schools work valiantly to provide resources for inquiry-based instruction and access to expert knowledge by maintaining connections with their college colleagues and professors.

In summary, secondary school science teachers may have adequate content knowledge and a philosophy that supports teaching science as inquiry, yet their pedagogical content knowledge and institutional barriers may be overwhelming to fully utilize the promises that exist. Institutional barriers—such as high-stakes testing, school performance in statewide rankings, and public image—may have a larger impact on science teachers than other teachers. Finally, there are few, if any, incentives for secondary school science teachers to enact inquiry. These barriers need to be addressed before wide-scale changes can be made in the majority of secondary school science classrooms.

EXAMINING THE EFFECT OF THE CONTEXT

As mentioned at the outset of this section, the context in which teachers make decisions about the use of inquiry is complex and extends far beyond the bricks and mortar of a school. School culture, grade-level norms, politics, and people's (teachers, administrators, parents, students') beliefs about science, science teaching, and science literacy have at least as much impact on a teacher's ability to implement inquiry teaching and learning as the physical space in which they work. Although much of the science education literature has focused on the influence of a teacher's beliefs and knowledge in their practice of inquiry, far less research has been conducted focusing on the influence of other institutional factors, an omission that this chapter suggests is a serious one.

Much of the foundation for this chapter has been based on research from North America; but most of these claims are applicable on an international basis (Abd-el-Khalick et al., 2004; Songer, Lee, & McDonald, 2002). Our synthesis of the work on the contextual influences on inquiry suggest that there are several points that cut across grade levels that beg further attention as we struggle to offer better support for teachers. As mentioned at the outset of this section, there are three sources of structure that we understand to influence the success of inquiry teaching/learning: students' cognitive influences (learner structure), content influences (content structure), and contextual influences (teacher structure, institutional structure, curricular priorities, timetable, school environment and classroom climate, instructional resources). As we look across the three essays in this section, the following influences seem to hold the greatest sway in terms of inquiry-based teaching.

Clearly, teachers' understandings of and skills in moving toward inquiry are fundamental features that must be addressed if inquiry-based teaching is to become more common. (This is a feature that will be discussed in more detail in the final section on teachers in this book.) As important, teachers' notions of teaching and learning as well as their views of science play significant roles in influencing their personal decision making.

It is becoming clear that teachers must become adept at differentiated instruction in order to address the needs of the various learners in their classrooms. Thus, the manner in which inquiry-based teaching is enacted will and should depend heavily on the nature of the learners in the classroom.

The physical makeup of the classroom and school play huge, yet theoretically underappreciated, roles in shaping the nature of instruction. The layout of the classroom, access to water/gas, the area in which students are able to move in order to have activities can and do heavily influence teachers' decision making.

Likewise, the availability of materials is a vital piece of the puzzle for inquiry, and one whose salience increased as grade level increases, as what is useful in the early grades can often be found at the local hardware transforms into expensive and hard to acquire as the grade level increases.

Just as the nature of the equipment changes across grade level, so do the cultural expectations. So while inquiry-based teaching in some form may be readily embraced in elementary and middle school classrooms, the strong content coverage component expected of secondary schools may make this approach quite difficult for many secondary school teachers to attempt.

Schools are complex places and to focus on the question of inquiry by only examining teachers or their students ignores much of this complexity. While a sole focus on individual classrooms may allow for a finer grained focus, the knowledge it produces is oversimplified. As demonstrated in our section, the question as to the fate of inquiry-based teaching is determined by more than a teachers inclination or abilities (although those are powerful forces). The fate of inquiry in our classrooms is also determined by schools and their varied stakeholders. As we work with teachers to consider inquiry, we must help them make sense of these varied influences and weigh what is best for their students at that time given the resources at hand or those that could be made available. We are not suggesting that teachers are "trapped" into teaching in a particular way based on their teaching context. Instead, we are suggesting that for teachers to make informed instructional decisions, they not only need a more sophisticated understanding of science and science teaching and learning, but also a more robust understanding of the broader context of their work.

ACKNOWLEDGMENTS

The authors of this section would like to acknowledge the contributions of Shari Yore, SAY Professional Services, for all her efforts in managing and editing the various versions of the manuscripts and supporting authors in their revision processes. Authors have asked that she be explicitly mentioned for her professional and helpful editorial comments on format, style, references, and internal consistency. Furthermore, we would like to thank Dr. Alan Colburn, California State University, Long Beach for his suggestions during the development of this section.

REFERENCES

Abd-el-Khalick, F., Boujaoude, S., Duschl, R., Lederman, N. G., Mamlok-Naaman, R., Hofstein, A., et al. (2004). Inquiry in science education: International perspectives. *Science Education, 88,* 397-419.

Amaral, O., Garrison, L., & Klentschy, M. (2002). Helping English language learners increase achievement through inquiry-based science instruction. *Bilingual Research Journal, 26,* 213-239.

American Association for the Advancement of Science. (1989). *Science for all Americans: A project 2061 report.* Washington, DC: Author.

Anderson, R. (2002). Reforming science teaching. What research says about inquiry? *Journal of Science Teacher Education, 13,* 1-12.

Barman, C., & Kotar, M. (1989). Teaching teachers: The learning cycle. *Science and Children, 26*(7), 30-32.

Blank, L. M. (2000). A metacognitive learning cycle: A better warranty for student understanding? *Science Education, 84,* 486-506.

Bravo, M. A., & Garcia, E. E. (2004, April). *Learning to write like scientists: English language learners' science inquiry and writing understandings in responsive learning contexts.* Paper presented at the annual meeting of American Educational Research Association, San Diego, CA.

Brooks, J., & Brooks, M. (1999). *In search of understanding: The case for constructivist classrooms.* Arlington, VA: Association for Supervision and Curriculum Development.

Bryan, L., & Abell, S. (1999). Development of professional knowledge in learning to teach elementary science. *Journal of Research in Science Teaching, 36,* 121-139.

Bullough, R. V., & Baughman, K. (1997). *"First-year teacher" eight years later: An inquiry into teacher development.* New York: Teachers College Press.

Bybee, R. (1997). *Achieving scientific literacy: From purposes to practices.* Portsmouth, NH: Heinmann.

Cognition and Technology Group at Vanderbilt. (1990). Anchored instruction and its relationship to situated cognition. *Educational Researcher, 19,* 2-10.

Colburn, A. (1997). How to make lab activities more open ended. *CSTA Journal, Fall,* 4-6. Retrieved July 12, 2007, from http://www.exploratorium.edu/ifi/resources/workshops/lab_activities.html

Colburn, A. (1998). *Constructivism and science teaching.* Bloomington, IN: Phi Delta Kappan Educational Foundation.

Colburn, A. (2005, October). *Solving the mysteries of CSI: Constructivism, science and inquiry.* Paper presented at the California Science Education Conference, Palm Springs, CA.

Crawford, B. A. (2000). Embracing the essence of inquiry: New roles for science teachers. *Journal of Research in Science Teaching, 37,* 916-937.

Crawford, B. A. (2007). Learning to teach science as inquiry in the rough and tumble of practice. *Journal of Research in Science Teaching, 44*(4), 614-642.

Crawford, B. A., Krajcik, J. S., & Marx, R. W. (1999). Elements of a community of learners in a middle school science classroom. *Science Education, 83,* 701-723.

Dewey, J. (1933). *How we think.* Lexington, MA: C. C. Heath.

Dickinson, V. L., Burns, J., Hagen, E. R., & Locker, K. M. (1997). Becoming better primary science teachers: A description of our journey. *Journal of Science Teacher Education, 8*(4), 295-311.

Duggan, S., Johnson, P., & Gott, R. (1996). A critical point in investigative work: Defining variables. *Journal of Research in Science Teaching, 33,* 461-474.

Duschl, R., & Gitomer, D. H. (1998). Strategies and challenges in changing the focus of assessment and instruction in science classrooms. *Educational Assessment, 4,* 37-73.

Fenwick, J. J. (1987). *Caught in the middle: Educational reform for young adolescents in California public school* (Report of the Superintendent's Middle Grade Task Force). Sacramento, CA: California State Department of Education.

Firestone, W. A., & Louis, K. S. (1999). Schools as cultures. In J. Murphy & K. S. Louis (Eds.), *Handbook of research on educational administration* (pp. 297-322). San Francisco: Jossey-Bass.

Florence, M. K., & Yore, L. D. (2004). Learning to write like a scientist: Coauthoring as an enculturation task. *Journal of Research in Science Teaching, 41,* 637-668.

Fradd, S. H., & Lee, O. (1999). Teachers' roles in promoting science inquiry with students from diverse language backgrounds. *Educational Researcher, 28,* 14-42.

Ford, C. L., Yore, L. D., & Anthony, R. J. (1997). *Reforms, visions, and standards: A cross-curricular view from an elementary school perspective.* East Lansing, MI: National Center for Research on Teacher Learning. (ERIC Document Reproduction Service No. ED406168)

Fullan, M. G., & Stiegelbauer, S. (1991). *The new meaning of educational change.* New York: Teachers College Press.

Gallagher, J. J. (1991). Prospective and practicing secondary school science teachers' knowledge and beliefs about the philosophy of science. *Science Education, 75,* 121-133.

Gilbert, S. W. (1992). Systematic questioning. *Science Teacher, 59*(3), 41-46.

Good, T. L., & Brophy, J. E. (2002). *Looking in classrooms* (8th ed.). Boston: Allyn & Bacon.

Good, R. G., Shymansky, J. A., & Yore, L. D. (1999). Censorship in science and science education. In E. H. Brinkley (Ed.), *Caught off guard: Teachers rethinking censorship and controversy* (pp. 101-121). New York: Allyn & Bacon.

Gregoire, M. (2003). Is it a challenge or a threat? A dual-process model of teachers' cognition and appraisal processes during conceptual change. *Educational Psychology Review, 15*(2), 147-179.

Hampton, E., & Rodriguez, R. (2001). Inquiry science in bilingual classrooms. *Bilingual Research Journal, 25,* 461-478.

Hand, B. M., Prain, V., & Yore, L. D. (2001). Sequential writing tasks' influence on science learning. In P. Tynjälä, L. Mason, & K. Lonka (Eds.), *Writing as a learning tool: Integrating theory and practice* (pp. 105-129). Dordrecht, the Netherlands: Kluwer.

Hargreaves, A. (1994). *Changing teachers, changing times: Teachers' work and culture in the postmodern age.* New York: Teachers College Press.

Hazen, R. M. (1991). Why my kids hate science. *Newsweek, 117*(8), 7.

Henriques, L. (1997). *A study to define and verify a model of interactive-constructive elementary school science teaching.* Unpublished doctoral dissertation, University of Iowa, Iowa City, IA.

The Holmes Group. (1990). *Tomorrow's teachers: A report of the Holmes Group.* East Lansing, MI: Author.

Howe, A. (1996). Development of science concepts within a Vygotskian framework. *Science Education, 80,* 35-51.

International Reading Association. (2004). *Standards for reading professionals— Revised 2003.* Newark, DE: Author.

International Society for Technology in Education. (2000). *National educational technology standards for teachers.* Eugene, OR: Author.

Jackson, P. W. (1968). *Life in classrooms.* New York: Holt, Rinehart & Winston.

Jones, D. (1997). A conceptual framework for studying the relevance of context to mathematics teachers' change. In E. Fennema & B. S. Nelson (Eds.), *Mathematics teachers in transition* (pp. 131-154). Mahwah, NJ: Erlbaum.

Jones, F. (2000). *Tools for teaching.* Santa Cruz, CA: Fredric H. Jones & Associates.

Johnson, C. C. (2007). Whole-school collaborative sustained professional development and science teacher change: Signs of progress. *Journal of Science Teacher Education, 18*(4), TBA.

Johnson, D. W., & Johnson, R. T. (1989). *Cooperation and competition: Theory and research.* Edina, MN: Interaction Books.

Jorgenson, O., Cleveland, J., & Vanosdall, R. (2004). *Doing good science in middle school: A practical guide to inquiry-based instruction.* Arlington, VA: National Science Teachers Association Press.

Kang, N-H., & Wallace, C. S. (2005). Secondary science teachers' use of laboratory activities: Linking epistemological beliefs, goals, and practices. *Science Education, 89,* 140-165.

Keys, C. W., & Bryan, L. (2001). Co-constructing inquiry-based science with teachers: Essential research for lasting reform. *Journal of Research in Science Teaching, 38,* 631-645.

Klentschy, M. P., & Molina-De La Torre, E. (2004). Students' science notebooks and the inquiry process. In E. W. Saul (Ed.), *Crossing borders in literacy and science instruction: Perspectives on theory and practice* (pp. 340-354). Newark, DE: International Reading Association.

Lawson, A. E., Abraham, M. R., & Renner, J. W. (1989). *A theory of instruction: Using the learning cycle to teach science concepts and thinking skill* (NARST Monograph No. 1). Syracuse University, Syracuse, NY: National Association for Research in Science Teaching.

Lee, O. (2005). Science education with English language learners: Synthesis and research agenda. *Review of Educational Research, 75,* 491-530.

Leyden, M. (1984). You graduate more criminals than you do scientists. *The Science Teacher, 51*(3), 26-30.

Lorsbach, A. W., & Tobin, K. (1992). Constructivism as a referent for science teaching. In F. Lorenz, K. Cochran, J. Krajcik, & P. Simpson (Eds.), *Research matters ... to the science teacher* (NARST Monograph No. 5). Kansas State University, Manhattan, KS: National Association for Research in Science Teaching.

Lynch, S. (2000). *Equity and science education reform.* Mahwah, NJ: Erlbaum.

Maalta, D., Dobb, F., & Ostlund, K. (2006). Strategies for teaching science to English learners. In A. Fathman & D. Crowther (Eds.), *Science for English language learners: K-12 classroom strategies* (pp. 37-59). Arlington, VA: National Science Teachers Association Press.

Martens, M. L. (1999). Productive questions: Tools for supporting constructivist learning. *Science and Children, 36*(8), 24-27 & 53.

Marx, R. W., Blumenfeld, P. C., Krajcik, J. S., Blunk, M., Crawford, B. A., & Meyer, K. M. (1994). Enacting project-based science: Experiences of four middle grade teachers. *Elementary School Journal, 94,* 517-538.

Minstrell, J. (1989). Teaching science for understanding. In L. B. Resnick & L. E. Klopfer (Eds.), *Toward the thinking curriculum: Current cognitive research* (pp. 129-149). Alexandria, VA: Association for Supervision and Curriculum Development.

Minstrell, J., & van Zee, E. (Eds.). (2000). *Teaching in the inquiry-based science classroom.* Washington, DC: American Association for the Advancement of Science.

National Council of Teachers of Mathematics. (2000). *Principles and standards for school mathematics.* Reston, VA: Author.

National Research Council. (1996). *National Science Education Standards.* Washington, DC: The National Academies Press.

National Research Council. (1999). How people learn: Brain, mind, experience, and school. Committee on Developments in the Science of Learning. In J. D. Bransford, A. L. Brown, & R. R. Cocking (Eds.), *Commission on Behavioral and Social Sciences and Education.* Washington, DC: The National Academies Press.

National Research Council. (2000). *Inquiry and the National Science Education Standards: A guide for teaching and learning.* Washington, DC: The National Academies Press.

National Research Council. (2006). America's lab report: Investigations in high school science. Committee on High School Science Laboratories: Role and Vision. In S. R. Singer, M. L. Hilton, & H. A. Schweingruber (Eds.), *Board on Science Education, Center for Education. Division of Behavioral and Social Sciences and Education.* Washington, DC: The National Academies Press.

Nelson, T. H., & Moscovici, H. (1998). Shifting from activitymania to inquiry. *Science and Children, 35*(4), 14-17.

No Child Left Behind Act of 2001, Pub. L. No. 107-110, 115 Stat. 1425-2093 (2002).

Norris, S. P., & Phillips, L. M. (2003). How literacy in its fundamental sense is central to scientific literacy. *Science Education, 87*(2), 224-240.

Oakes, J., & Lipton, M. (1998). *Teaching to change the world.* New York: McGraw Hill.

Otto, P. B. (1991). Finding an answer in questioning strategies. *Science and Children, 28*(7), 44-47.

Penick, J. E., Crow, L. W., & Bonnstetter, R. J. (1996). Questions are the answers. *Science Teacher, 63*(1), 26-29.

Posner, G. J., Strike, K. A., Hewson, P. W., & Gertzog, W. A. (1982). Accommodation of a scientific conception: Towards a theory of conceptual change. *Science Education, 66,* 211-277.

Raizen, S. A., & Michelsohn, A. M. (1994). *The future of science in elementary schools: Educating prospective teachers.* San Francisco: Jossey-Bass.

Romance, N. R., & Vitale, M. R. (1992). A curriculum strategy that expands time for in-depth elementary science instruction by using science-based reading strategies: Effects of a year-long study in grade four. *Journal of Research in Science Teaching, 29,* 545-554.

Rosebery, A. S., Warren, B., & Conant, F. R. (1989). *Cheche konnon: Science and literacy in language minority classrooms* (BBN Technical Report No. 7305). Cambridge, MA: BBN Laboratories.

Rosebery, A. S., Warren, B., & Conant, F. R. (2003). Appropriating scientific discourse: Fingins from language minority classrooms. *California Journal of Science Education, 2,* 69-121.

Rowe, M. B. (1996). Science, silence, and sanctions. *Science and Children, 34*(1), 35-38.

Rudolph, J. L. (2005). Inquiry, instrumentalist, and the public understanding of science. *Science Education, 89,* 803-821.

Ryan, A. M. (2001). The peer group as a context for the development of young adolescent motivation and achievement. *Child Development, 72,* 1135-1150.

Sandall, B. R. (2003). Elementary science: Where are we now? *Journal of Elementary Science Education, 15*(2), 13-30.

Sarason, S. B. (1996). *Revisiting "The culture of the school and the problem of change."* New York: Teachers College Press.

Scheurman, G. (1998). From behaviorist to constructivist teaching. *Social Education, 62,* 6-9.

Schwartz, R. S., Abd-El-Khalick, R., & Lederman, N. G. (1999, January). *An explanatory study of the "effectiveness" of elementary science specialists.* Paper presented at the annual meeting of the Association for the Education of Teachers of Science, Austin, TX.

Settlage, J., Madsen, A., & Rustad, K. (2005). Inquiry science, sheltered instruction, and English language learners: Conflicting pedagogies in highly diverse classrooms. *Issues in Teacher Education, 13*(2), 35-57.

Shymansky, J. A., Kyle, W. C., Jr., & Alford, J. M. (2003). The effects of new science curricula on student performance. *Journal of Research in Science Teaching, 40(Supplement),* 568-585.

Shymansky, J. A., Yore, L. D., & Hand, B. M. (2000). Empowering families in hands-on science programs. *School Science and Mathematics, 100,* 48-56.

Slavin, R. E. (1987). Cooperative learning and the cooperative school. *Educational Leadership, 45,* 7-13.

Smith, L. K. (2002). *Reconceptualizing context from a situated perspective: Teacher beliefs and the activity of teaching within the context of reform.* Unpublished doctoral dissertation, University of Utah, Salt Lake City, UT.

Smith, L. K. (2005). *A description of elementary teachers' familiarity with the National Science Education Standards.* Uunpublished manuscript.

Smith, L. K., & Southerland, S. A. (2007). Reforming practice or modifying reforms?: Elementary teachers' response to the tools of reform. *Journal of Research in Science Teaching, 44,* 396-423.

Songer, N. B., Lee, H-S., & McDonald, S. (2002). Research toward an expanded understanding of inquiry science beyond one idealized standard. *Science Education, 87,* 490-516.

Stepans, J. (2003). *Targeting students' science misconceptions: Physical science concepts using the conceptual change model.* Riverview, FL: The Idea Factory.

Stokes, L., Mitchell, H., & Ramage, K. (2005). *Learning to teach science with writing: Implementation of the Seattle elementary expository writing and science notebooks program in typical classrooms.* Los Angeles, CA: Inverness Research Associates.

Tilgner, P. J. (1990). Avoiding science in the elementary school. *Science Education, 74,* 421-431.

Tillotson, J. W., & Kluth, P. (2003). Auto mechanics in the physics lab: Science education for all. In P. Kluth, D. Straut, & D. Biklen (Eds.), *Access to academics* (pp. 133-154). Mahwah, NJ: Erlbaum.

Tillotson, J. W., & Olmstead, S. (1998). Investigating the impact of a state-mandated science curriculum on teachers' beliefs and decision-making. In J. B. Robinson & R. E. Yager (Eds.), *Translating and using research for improving teacher education in science and mathematics* (pp. 83-89). Iowa City, IA: Chautauqua ISTEP Research Project, OERI, US Department of Education.

Tobias, S. (1990). *They're not dumb. They're different. Stalking the second tier.* Tucson, AZ: Research Corporation.

Tobin, K., & McRobbie, C. J. (1996). Cultural myths as constraints to the enacted science curriculum. *Science Education, 80,* 223-241.

Tobin, K., Tippins, D. J., & Gallard, A. J. (1994). Research on instructional strategies for science teaching. In D. L. Gabel (Ed.), *Handbook of research on science teaching and learning* (pp. 45-93). New York: Macmillan.

Tretter, T. R., & Jones, M. G. (2003). Relationships between inquiry-based teaching and physical science standardized test score. *School Science and Mathematics, 103,* 345-350.

Weinburgh, M. (2003). Confronting and changing middle school teachers' perceptions of scientific methodology. *School Science and Mathematics, 102,* 222-232.

White, B. Y., & Frederiksen, J. R. (1998). Inquiry, modeling and metacognition: Making science accessible to all students. *Cognition and Instruction, 16,* 3-118.

Windschitl, M. (2002). Framing constructivism in practice as the negotiation of dilemmas: An analysis of the conceptual, pedagogical, cultural, and political challenges facing teachers. *Review of Educational Research, 72,* 131-175.

Windschitl, M. (2004). Folk theories of "inquiry": How preservice teachers reproduce the discourse and practices of an atheoretical scientific method. *Journal of Research in Science Teaching, 41,* 481-512.

Wong, H., & Wong, R. (2004). *How to be an effective teacher: The first days of school.* Mountain View, CA: Harry K. Wong.

Yager, R. E. (1991). The constructivist learning model. *The Science Teacher, 58*(6), 52-57.

Yerrick, R., Parke, H., & Nugent, J. (1997). Struggling to promote deeply rooted change: The "filtering effect" of teachers' beliefs on understanding transformational views of teaching science. *Science Education, 81,* 137-159.

Yore, L. D. (2001). What is meant by constructivist science teaching and will the science education community stay the course for meaningful reform? *Electronic Journal of Science Education, 5*(4). Online journal: http://wolfweb.unr.edu/ homepage/crowther/ejse/yore.html

Yore, L. D., Bisanz, G. L., & Hand, B. M. (2003). Examining the literacy component of science literacy: 25 years of language and science research. *International Journal of Science Education, 25,* 689-725.

Yore, L. D., Florence, M. K., Pearson, T. W., & Weaver, A. J. (2006). Written discourse in scientific communities: A conversation with two scientists about their views of science, use of language, role of writing in doing science, and compatibility between their epistemic views and language. *International Journal of Science Education, 28,* 109-141.

Yore, L. D., Hand, B. M., & Florence, M. K. (2004). Scientists' views of science, models of writing, and science writing practices. *Journal of Research in Science Teaching, 41,* 338-369.

Yore, L. D., & Treagust, D. F. (2006). Current realities and future possibilities: Language and science literacy—empowering research and informing instruction. *International Journal of Science Education, 28,* 291-314.

SECTION III

ACCOMMODATING STUDENT
DIVERSITY WITHIN INQUIRY

Liza Finkel, Kathleen Greene, and Jose Rios

EDITORS' NOTE

Describing Section III's use of
Inquiry in the Classroom

Building from both the first section on students' knowledge and inquiry and the second section on the role of contextual factors, this section shows the complex, sometimes synergistic and sometimes antagonistic relationship between classroom inquiry and a number of salient dimensions in our classroom hyperspace for inquiry. This section allows us to see how teachers' expectations for students combined with the skill and knowledge level for students influence the kinds of inquiry enacted as well as the topic of inquiry to be enacted. Less obviously, but as importantly, this section illuminates how the goals for inquiry interact with the contextual factor of assessment to shape the ways in which inquiry is enacted. Indeed, because the inquiry described in the vignette was in addition to and apart from the typical curriculum and because the goals for inquiry were not the construction of specific content knowledge, these dimensions interacted to allow for a Level 3/open inquiry.

This section also begs the question of authenticity and student learning. Chinn and Malhotra (2002) suggest that science educators should seek to include authentic tasks in the science classroom if inquiries are to engender knowledge about inquiry as well as ability to inquire, something

Inquiry in the Classroom: Realities and Opportunities, pp. 91–139
Copyright © 2008 by Information Age Publishing

a simple task does not allow for. However in this section we see what would probably be overly simplistic experimental designs, but these simple designs may have been required given the nature of the research questions posed—research questions that gain new importance as the notion of student relevance is considered. This section causes us to question the wholesale rejection of simple tasks as we try to engage students both in inquiry and in the broader project of science through questions drawn from their everyday experiences.

GOALS FOR INQUIRY

While each of the three goals (learning about inquiry, learning to inquire, and learning to construct scientific knowledge) are mentioned in the outset of the section, it is clear that the goals of most valued in this discussion is **learning to inquire** and **learning about inquiry**. What is of particular interest here is that this goal of learning about inquiry must be seen in an expanded form, as this sections revolves around the notion that the very enterprise of science itself and so what counts as "scientific" is in sore need of revision if we are to increase the participation and influence of nontraditional students. One addition goal that bears discussion revolves around **inquiry for the construction of scientific knowledge**. Because inquiry was seen as an "add on," it was loosened from traditional content expectations—allowing the teachers to focus on questions drawn from and relevant to students' lives, what Roth and Baron (2004) refer to as "citizen science."

Means of Enactment of Inquiry

The means of enactment of inquiry (in this case a supported open/ Level 3 in which students pose the questions and design the research) make sense and are allowed for given the very specific goals of this inquiry—learning to inquiry and learning about inquiry (as well as engaging students via scientific sense making). Some parts of the discussion echoes back to Section I, in that the enactment of inquiry has to be mindful of student skill level. While student ability/skill level needs to be recognized and used to make instructional decision, teachers also need to be mindful that inquiry is a transformative experience, increasing students' knowledge of inquiry and ability to inquire. Thus, to fail to challenge students by more and more difficult and authentic task while it may allow for immediate success may serve to stifle student growth.

VIGNETTE

Located on a quiet corner lined by mature trees, Merrill School is one of the 12 public elementary schools in Beloit, Wisconsin, a small to midsized city in the upper Midwestern United States. Beloit has been characterized as postindustrial, meaning there used to be quite a bit of industry here, but there isn't much any more. Poverty and unemployment are higher here than state and national averages. While 3 of the 12 elementary schools are noted for the prevailing level of poverty among their students, it is Merrill School that has the highest percentage of students eligible for free and reduced lunch. It also, historically, has the city's lowest test scores in all areas.

Merrill School is located in an area of town known as "the hood," but in most ways it is indistinguishable from the rest of Beloit. Families live in one- and two-story homes on quiet streets, where children ride their bikes and adults visit on front porches. But there is more rental property here, shorter occupancy rates and bouts of violence more frequent than in wealthier neighborhoods. In reporting criminal activity, the local newspaper identifies the neighborhood only when it involves the Merrill neighborhood, which has certainly contributed to a reputation for being dangerous. The teachers at the school usually live in other areas, but they report feeling safe working here, even without special security measures.

The K-fifth grade school has a population that is predominantly "non-white." There has been a recent increase in Hispanic (mostly Mexican) students attending the school. There is a high level of transience, as well, with a steady stream of students entering and leaving the school throughout the year.

The school is a well-built, well-maintained, two story yellow brick building on a large, grassy, treed lot with a large recess area. There are no metal detectors at the front door, although, as with all the schools in the city, entrance is controlled by the secretary, who "buzzes in" visitors. The Merrill teaching staff is relatively stable. Tim and Carolyn, the two main teachers of the highest grade(s) in the school, currently combined fourth and fifth grade classrooms, have taught at Merrill for dozens of years combined. Both are "locals." Tim, the younger of the two teachers, grew up in the suburbs of the city, just south of the nearby state line, attended and graduated from Beloit College, a local 4-year private liberal college, and has been teaching at Merrill ever since. Tim teaches science and mathematics, while Carol teaches language and social studies for both classrooms.

For the last 10 years, Tim and Kathy, an education professor at Beloit College, have collaborated on a program that brings their students together for a 2-hour session each week during the fall semester. The preservice teachers are enrolled in Education 271, A Problem-Solving Approach to Teaching and Learning Science and Mathematics. The collaborative program has evolved over the years. Early on, the preservice teachers would spend most of the shared sessions guiding the elementary students in their completion of short test-book labs and written exercises, with a few sessions set aside for the preservice teachers to guide the elementary students through learning centers they (the preservice teachers) had designed, either individually or in pairs. Gradually, the preservice teachers have come to lead the students in multiweek projects sketched out by Kathy, and collaboratively developed, evaluated, and adjusted along the way by the entire group (the preservice students, Kathy, Tim, Carolyn, and the elementary students). The elementary classes have 20 to 25 students each, and the number of preservice teachers ranges from 8 to 21.

The Beloit schools are increasingly driven by notions of competency, accountability and learning standards. Beloit College, however, has a history of liberal education; its education department has a reputation for preparing its graduates to be innovative teachers who think for themselves. Kathy teaches and works to promote the idea that knowledge is created by, within and among learners rather than deposited there by teachers and texts. In other words, Kathy considers herself to be a constructivist teacher who works to prepare her students to teach likewise.

The Beloit School District's recent curriculum adoptions represent a familiar but largely unworkable compromise between two different elements—a response to the increasing pressure to raise test scores and meet standards on the one hand, and a desire to provide children with active and engaging learning opportunities on the other hand. Almost certainly more because of the latter than the former, all of the elementary schools welcome Beloit College preservice teachers, but Merrill School has been remarkably hospitable to the preservice teachers over the years. According to the Merrill teachers and other district staff, the children at Merrill School can use all of the positive academic attention they can get, and they view the ongoing collaboration between Tim and Kathy as generating that positive attention.

During the past fall, the fourth and fifth graders at Merrill School have worked every Thursday with the preservice teachers in the elementary science and math methods course described above. They engaged in various learning activities. The first quarter was spent on graphing exercises, model building, a 5-week quilt project, and math learning centers. The second quarter began with simple science laboratory experiments, and six of the final seven Thursdays were devoted to student-designed investigations.

As the section of the class on student-designed investigation began, the children had a discussion about science. Although they knew that science involved experiments, their comments revealed a lack of the fundamentals of scientific investigations. Kathy introduced students to the process they would follow:

Scientists need to figure out what they want to find out, and we are going to do that, too. We are about to begin our six-week investigations. That probably seems like a long time, but there's a lot we need to do, starting with deciding what we are interested in investigating. So, this week, groups of three or four of you will work with two of the college students to brainstorm some ideas for your small group to investigate. For today, you'll just be thinking of questions that you're interested in.

Now, one of the things that is really important for scientists to do is to keep complete and accurate records. Each of you has been given a scientist's laboratory notebook (examination blue book). In that notebook, you should write down everything that your group decides and everything that you do.

And, just as a preview of the whole six weeks, this week, Week 1, we'll be brainstorming ideas. Next week, Week 2, we'll talk about what makes a "good" question, and each group will choose one good question to investigate from the list you make this week. In Week 3 you'll design the investigation procedure (experiment) figuring out what to do and what you'll need in order to do it. The fourth week you'll actually do the experiment, taking excellent notes along the way. The fifth week you'll review your notes, and figure out what your results are—what you have found out, what you have learned.

Then, what's left for the last week? Scientists have to convince other scientists that what they have figured out makes sense, and they do that in various ways. One of the ways is to present their research at conferences. So, the sixth and final week of our investigations will be the Annual Merrill Scientific Research Conference. Each group will present their research using a PowerPoint presentation and a poster.

The preservice teachers take turns introducing subsequent weeks to the whole class. To introduce Week 2, a preservice teacher led the class in discussing how scientists choose which research questions to pursue. Students decide it is sensible to eliminate questions that would be difficult or impossible to research (lacking equipment, space, time, appropriate permissions or materials). They also decide it is reasonable to eliminate questions the answers to which could easily be "looked up" somewhere, because where's the fun in that? They often spend some time on the internet, searching for information about their possible questions. The bulk of the work of Week 2 is the small groups' deliberations to choose from among the list of research questions they brainstormed during week 1, applying the criteria they developed in the previous discussion.

In recent years, some of the questions selected have included:

- If paper is made from the pulp of wood, can it also be made from the pulp of oranges?
- What brand of soap smells the best?
- If you jump straight up three times in a row, which time do you jump the highest?
- Do crystals form faster in cold or hot water?
- What is the best recipe for making a model volcano erupt?

The following week, Week 3, is the time for design. The introduction to Week 3 is a discussion about the differences between an experiment that someone "makes up" to answer a certain research question and one that is already in their science books. Mostly it is a discussion about all the decisions that need to be made. So, the bulk of Week 3's work, now that the groups have settled on their question, is for the students in each group to design the experimental protocol they will follow to answer their question. They decide which equipment and materials they need to assemble, and where and how to locate them. They also construct the procedures they plan to follow the next week, and try to figure out whether what they are going to do will help them to answer their question. The preservice teachers and the student groups themselves consult extensively with Tim and Kathy this week, as they do every week.

Week 4 is the students' favorite week up to this point. They are eager to "do" their experiments. The teachers' first task this week is to slow the children down enough to help them think through their planned procedures to predict what kinds and amounts of information they will get and how they will record all of it. The groups also need to assign roles to the members of the group so everyone is involved. Eventually they realize the need to maximize the accuracy, precision, and replicability of their results (these concepts are explored before the vocabulary is attached to them). The children are excited to "run" their experiments and take their data, sometimes spreading to other parts of the school, depending on the nature of the experiments.

Week 5 is when the groups try to make sense of their data. What do the data "tell" them? Are they further along in answering their question? Are there other things they need or want to do, now that they have run their experiments, or are they satisfied with what they have done? Does the experiment need to be changed? Or possibly, does the question itself need to be changed, and, if so, is there time to do it all over? What, after all this, do they know? How confidently can they state the connections among what they wanted to know, what they did, what they observed, what they recorded, and what (they think) they know? How can they present all of this in such a way that their peers (and teachers) will be persuaded to agree with them? The discussion that precedes Week 5 covers all of these topics, as well as setting out the guidelines and requirements for the presentations the following week. The students' work this week is to analyze their data and prepare for the presentations, sketching out their posters and PowerPoint slides.

Although the students love Week 4, and actually "doing" the experiments, it is the presentations of Week 6 that they take most seriously. They spend much of the previous week (in science and language arts classes) working with Tim to complete their posters, refine their PowerPoint slides, and divide up the speaking so that every student has a meaningful part in the presentations. Before the presentations actually begin, the small groups rehearse what they will say and do.

For the actual presentations, usually one of the preservice teachers acts as "mistress or master of ceremonies," a task made relatively easy, because the students are always well prepared and uncharacteristically attentive for the presentations. Of course, group styles vary greatly, as some groups engage the rest of the class in seeing what they saw, and others do more straightforward "telling." But, the classroom atmosphere this week is one of serious purpose. Students listen closely to each group present its research, and ask questions and give feedback (using the praise-question-polish model) that demonstrates their understanding and concentration.

Following the presentations, the science investigation unit concludes with a simple celebratory reception for the scientists and their mentors.

INQUIRY-BASED INSTRUCTION AND DIVERSE LEARNERS

Liza Finkel

As important as overall national achievement is, the status and achievement of underrepresented groups of students is of even greater concern...[we must] ensure that all students, even those who are culturally and linguistically diverse, develop scientific and technological literacy to be effective participants and contributors to society. (Lee, Fradd, & Sutman, 1995)

Many who champion the use of inquiry-based science instruction as a way to improve the overall quality of science teaching and student learning have argued that this approach is best because it allows students the opportunity to both experience science as it is practiced and to construct scientific understandings in the process of doing science (e.g., American Association for the Advancement of Science [AAAS], 1989, 1993; National Research Council [NRC], 1996). In contrast, others express concern that using inquiry in the classroom is problematic because it is derived from a traditional model of science, a way of thinking that emerges from Western European male traditions. If the goal of inquiry-based science instruction is to help all students become scientifically literate, the needs of all students have to be acknowledged and the tension of bridging possible social and cultural gaps must be addressed. This section will investigate multicultural and gender challenges and opportunities as teachers use inquiry as a pedagogical approach.

Assumptions and Definitions

Proponents of inquiry-based instruction have argued that inquiry-based science is an instructional approach that will be accessible to most students in ways that more traditional models of science instruction are not (Warren, Ballenger, Ogonowski, Rosebery, & Hudicourt-Barnes, 2001, p. 529). For example, the widely cited and influential (on the research community if not on individual classrooms) 1996 *National Science Education Standards* (NRC, 1996) are based on a set of principles that include the following: "science is for all students," "learning science is an active process," and "school science reflects the intellectual and cultural traditions that characterize the practice of contemporary science" (NRC,

1996, p. 19). The document goes on to expand on the notion of making science accessible to all students as follows:

> Science is for all students. This principle is one of equity and excellence. Science in our schools must be for all students: All students, regardless of age, sex, cultural or ethnic background, disabilities, aspirations, or interest or motivation in science, should have the ability to attain high levels of scientific literacy. (NRC, 1996, p. 20)

A similar view is presented in the American Association for the Advancement of Science's policy initiative *Project 2061* (1989):

> When democratic realities, national needs, and democratic values are taken into account, it becomes clear that the nation can no longer ignore the science education of any student. Race, language, sex, or economic circumstances must no longer be permitted to be factors in determining who does and who does not receive a good education in science, mathematics and technology. (AAAS, 1989, p. 214)

In addition to making it clear that science should be something that all students can and should learn, these documents also explain that school science should reflect the intellectual traditions that characterize the practice of "contemporary science."

> To develop a rich knowledge of science and the natural world, students must become familiar with modes of scientific inquiry, rules of evidence, ways of formulating questions, and ways of proposing explanations...the Standards recognize that many individuals have contributed to the traditions of science and that, in historical perspective, science has been practiced in many different cultures. (NRC, 1996, p. 21)

The assumption that inquiry-based science is more accessible to wider groups of students than more traditional models of science instruction, and that the goals of inquiry-based science as described in the documents cited above (as well as in the National Science Teachers Association standards published in 1988) are those that should lead science education reform, has been questioned by a number of researchers (e.g., Barton, 2003; Eisenhart, Finkel, & Marion, 1996; Lee, 1997; Lee & Fradd, 1998; Warren et al., 1997), particularly with regard to girls (Eisenhart & Finkel, 1998), students from diverse cultures and languages (Lee, 1997; Lee & Fradd, 1998), and urban youth living in poverty (Barton, 2003). Eisenhart, Finkel, and Marion (1996) for example, argue that, while the pedagogical approach (inquiry) promoted in these proposals is promising, the actual goals of these reforms are too narrow to provide opportunities for the diverse student body they are designed to reach.

They question the notion that just a better pedagogical approach and sensitivity to student differences will permit all students access to science knowledge (p. 273). Barton (2003) and others (e.g., Lee & Fradd, 1998; Rodriguez, 1997) point out that we tend to see nonmajority students as missing something that instruction must provide and argue that we must rid ourselves of the view that these students are somehow "deficient" if we are to develop an approach to science instruction that is truly inclusive. As these critiques of inquiry-based science make clear, it is not enough to change the way that science is taught if we do not also think about the model of science that we are promoting and about the specific interests, knowledge and abilities of the different students we teach.

Although people have defined inquiry-based science in numerous ways, for the purpose of this section we define it as science teaching that provides students with the opportunity to experience all aspects of the scientific process. Our definition does not differ in many ways from the definition provided by others (e.g., NRC, 1996; Petersen & Jungck, 1998). As we see it, this process includes identifying a problem, asking scientific questions, designing an investigation, collecting and analyzing data and communicating final results and implications to a larger audience.

Necessary Conditions for Success

As a result of classroom-based research in this area, several conditions are thought to be necessary for this approach to work. First, researchers have suggested that the problems investigated in science classes must be authentic. By authentic, these researchers mean that the investigation be embedded in a real world context (Crawford, 2000; Eisenhart & Finkel, 1998; Moss, Abrams, & Robb, 2001). Second, the problem needs to provide a variety of entry points from which students and teachers can develop modes of inquiry (Lemke, 2001). This implies that problems studied in inquiry-based classrooms must be content-rich in the sense that they include a range of scientific concepts and ideas that provide students and teachers with multiple ways to approach teaching and learning. Third, the problems chosen should allow students to pursue a range of questions that interest them (Martin & Brouwer, 1993; Peterson & Jungck, 1988). Finally, enough time must be given to the students to allow them to fully investigate the problem being studied.

Research on inquiry-based classrooms suggests, however, that these conditions are rarely met (Crawford, 2000). In most classrooms where this model has been attempted, the problems investigated by students are selected by the teacher and perceived as contrived by students (Moss et al., 1998). In addition, classroom constraints (such as short class periods, limited access to buses or natural areas, and few funds for equipment) limit the actual problems that can be studied as well as the amount of time allotted for investigations. Researchers have also noted that students may not be learning as much content as was originally hoped (Berry, Mulhall, Loughran, & Gunstone, 1999; Edmondson & Novak, 1993; Hart, Mulhall, Loughran, & Gunstone, 2000).

We feel that there is more to making science accessible to diverse learners than creating inviting and engaging classrooms where all students can learn, though that is certainly a necessary first step. The more challenging goal is to help diverse learners develop the skills and dispositions needed to be interested in and able to participate in (and change) science practice (both in their everyday lives and as scientists). In order to ensure that inquiry-based instruction is implemented in ways that are both thoughtful and empowering, it is essential that we examine the beliefs about science, students and instruction that underlie our teaching.

The vignette with which we begin this section illustrates the way that one of us has worked with a classroom teacher to implement an inquiry-based approach to science teaching that avoids some of the concerns raised above, and that is empowering for both students and teachers. In the classroom we describe, students choose their own questions (with support from their teachers) and are given time to investigate them in ways that allow for meaningful exploration of both science content and personal experiences with scientific phenomena. In the remainder of this section we will explore the beliefs that underlie this vision of science teaching to in order to understand the ways that inquiry-based instruction might be made more welcoming to diverse groups of students.

QUESTIONS ABOUT SCIENCE, STUDENTS, AND INSTRUCTION

As a way to initiate this discussion, I would like to review some of the questions about the nature of science, students, and instruction that have been raised relative to inquiry-based science teaching. First, what questions have been raised about the nature of science? Second, what questions have been raised about students' interests, abilities and aspirations? And, third, what questions have been raised about the process of instruction in inquiry-based science classrooms? While these questions are not uniquely appropriate to situations involving diverse groups of students, considering them in this context will, we hope, provide some new insights into how to best meet the needs of all students in inquiry-based science classrooms.

Questions About the Nature of Science

As mentioned earlier, most calls for an inquiry-based pedagogy are based on Western science ideals:

> In *Science for All Americans* (AAAS, 1989), Western science counts as science, and therefore, scientific literacy is defined in terms of Western science. *National Science Education Standards* (NRC, 1996), although recognizing the contribution of other cultures, also defines Western science as the proper domain of science (pp. 201, 204). While these national documents generally define science in the Western science tradition, alternative views have been advocated by scholars in emerging areas of multicultural education, feminism, and sociology and philosophy of science. (Lee, 1997, p. 220)

A number of scholars, while supporting inquiry-based science as a pedagogical approach, dispute the notion that the view of science underlying these calls for science education reform is the only, or the best, view to represent in school science. A feminist view of this critique is elucidated by Eisenhart, Finkel, and Marion (1996):

> Over a decade ago, Evelyn Fox Keller (1985) argued that feminist and minority critiques of science could be arranged on a four-point continuum from liberal to radical. The liberal critique suggests that women and minorities are underrepresented in science because they have not been treated in the same encouraging way as men ... a second, more radical level of critique suggests that the predominance of men in the sciences has led to a bias in the choice and definition of the problems scientists have addressed. (p. 273)

Keller's most radical critique "is a challenge to the truth and warrant of the conclusions of natural science on the grounds that they reflect a preference for objectivist, rationalistic, and detached justifications more often associated with men than women" (Eisenhart, Finkel, & Marion, 1996, p. 274), and Keller cites as examples the writings of female scientists like Barbara McClintock who developed an almost-personal connection with the plants she studied in her groundbreaking work on corn plant genetics, describing her understanding as "a feeling for the organism" (Keller, 1983, pp. 197-98).

Another critique of the views of science underlying calls for inquiry-based science is presented by Beth Warren et al. (2001), who focus on the differences between what they refer to as *scientific* and *everyday* sense-making:

> The term *scientific* is commonly used to denote a sphere of human activity characterized by special qualities: rationality, precision, formality, detachment, and objectivity. This view is broadly held in society at large, in

schools, and even by some scientists themselves. The term *everyday* is commonly used to denote another, opposing set of qualities: improvisation, ambiguity, informality, engagement, and subjectivity. (Warren et al., 2001, p. 530, italics in original)

In the context of science education then, scientific sense-making is steeped in the language, habits and ways of working of scientists, while everyday sense-making derives from the "ideas and ways of talking and knowing that children of diverse communities bring to science" (Warren et al., 2001, p. 546). Warren and her colleagues argue that:

> What children from low-income, linguistic, racial, and ethnic minority communities do as they make sense of the world – although perhaps different in some respects from what European American children are socialized to do – is in fact intellectually rigorous and generatively connected with academic disciplinary knowledge and practice. (cf. Lee, 1998) (cited in text) (Warren et al., p. 546)

These scholars believe that the emphasis on one view of science, particularly a view that has, in practice, limited the participation of many women and non-White minorities, may contribute to the failure of inquiry-based science education reforms:

> Given the existing low level of student interest in academic work and the findings of feminists and others about the biases inherent in conventional science, efforts to involve more people, especially women and minorities, in science may fail precisely because conventional science and modes of practicing it are stressed in school. (Eisenhart, Finkel, & Marion, 1996 p. 274)

Scholars have also made some suggestions about how to address the concerns raised about the monocultural view of science represented by most calls for science education reform. Lee (2003) argues that:

> Students should have access and opportunities to learn the high-status knowledge of mainstream science as it is practiced in the science community, taught in school science, and presented in national standards documents (American Association for the Advancement of Science, 1989, 1993; National Research Council, 1996). At the same time, alternative ways of knowing should be recognized and valued. This balanced orientation emphasizes academic achievement as well as cultural identity. It leads students to acquire the language of science as well as their home languages, to understand the culture of science as well as their own cultures, and to behave competently across social contexts. (p. 467)

Stanley and Brickhouse (2001), in an article discussing the need for a multicultural science education, suggest that:

Rather than merely showing students that IK [indigenous knowledge] and TEK [traditional ecological knowledge] are different from WMS [Western modern science] (and possibly suggesting they were inferior), our approach would be to show students how these different views of science are firmly rooted in certain cultural assumptions that influence how they go about formulating and solving problems of significance. Furthermore, rather than teach a particular view of science or pretend as though the nature of what we were teaching was uncontroversial, we would then teach students about the controversy over what is to be included in the science curriculum and how such decisions might be made. (p. 47)

It is our contention that if we are to make inquiry-based science instruction accessible to diverse groups of students we must address the question of what views of science underlie our teaching. We must also help students become aware of (and potentially able to engage in) the controversies that surround the nature of science as we help them develop the skills needed to draw conclusions about the natural world. In addition, we believe that if students are to become more engaged by school-based science instruction, the inquiry in which they engage must be meaningfully connected to their interests and concerns and have the potential to empower them both in and outside of school (Eisenhart & Finkel, 1998; Eisenhart, Finkel, & Marion, 1996).

Questions About Students

Another set of questions that have been raised in reference to implementing inquiry-based science instruction in ways that will meet the needs of a diverse student body has to do with students. In particular, scholars have asked questions about what students know about the natural world, science, scientific knowledge, and the scientific process when they arrive in our classrooms, as well as about the assumptions we make about students' knowledge, interests, and abilities based on their language skills or cultural or family backgrounds.

Many of these researchers have focused on the needs of students for whom English is not their first language, and for whom the culture from which Western science emerges is not their first, or home, culture. Two different kinds of concerns are raised about the needs of these students: First, that our judgments about these students may be colored by their difficulty or facility with technical scientific language, and second, that students from diverse cultures may also face conflicts between their cultural values and those of school and science. Lee, Fradd, and Sutman (1995), for example, point out that we may be making mistaken assumptions about students' understanding of science based on their abilities or difficulties with spoken or written English:

> Students who are not able to apply precise science vocabulary, and who express their ideas in indirect and unclear terms, give the impression that they do not have the knowledge when in fact the knowledge is present. On the other hand, students who possess the vocabulary might be perceived to have science knowledge even though they do not actually understand the terms. (Lee, Fradd, & Sutman, 1995, p. 809)

In a later editorial, Lee et al. also points out that:

> Students from diverse cultures and languages are faced with multiple requirements in learning science. In addition to developing scientific knowledge and habits of mind, they also have to learn the discourse and interactional patterns of the mainstream culture. When these students' language and cultural practices are in conflict with scientific practices, when they are forced to choose between the two worlds, or when they are told to ignore their cultural values, the students may avoid learning science. This may be a main reason why science is alien to these students and they, in turn, resist learning science. (Lee, 1997, p. 221)

Both of these potential barriers may help to explain why teaching inquiry-based science in classrooms with diverse groups of students is not a panacea that will easily solve all the problems inherent in helping all students achieve scientific literacy.

Warren et al. (2001) point out that differing traditions with regard to our understanding of the relationship between the knowledge students bring with them to school and the more formal knowledge of science have emerged, and that these different traditions lead to different assumptions about what students can learn and how best to teach them:

> In one tradition, everyday experience and ways of talking and knowing are seen as discontinuous with those of science and as barriers to robust learning. This tradition assumes ... that children's everyday ideas and ways of knowing and talking are largely different from and incompatible with those of science.... [In this view] differences in the social, cognitive and linguistic practices of particular linguistic or ethnic minority groups from those of the "mainstream" are conceptualized as potential barriers to learning science, as outside those characteristic of science. A second tradition of inquiry in science education takes a different view. It focuses on understanding the productive conceptual, metarepresentational, linguistic, experiential, and epistemological resources students have for advancing their understanding of scientific ideas.... This work does not assume a simple isomorphism between what children do and what scientists do; rather, it view the relationship as complex and taking a variety of forms:

similarity, different, complementarity and generalization. (Warren et al., 2001, pp. 530-31)

Barton (2003) in her work with urban youth living in poverty argues that these proposals "view the needs of high-poverty, urban youth, non-English-language-background youth, minority students, and girls through [a] deficit model" (p. 26) that assumes that students in these groups, who may not come to school with knowledge of the culture of Western science, need extra help to catch up with their peers, which she claims further, "implies that minority students and females need to work and act like their White male counterparts, not that either science or instruction will be modified to accommodate them" (p. 26).

We feel that it is essential for educators implementing inquiry-based science to be aware of the different challenges that students may face in learning science content and participating in scientific inquiry, whether these challenges come from differences in language development or ability, or from cultural variations. Building in time for discussion and debate, alternative methods for expression, and an appreciation for the different ways students may have for understanding and explaining the world are necessary if we are to be successful with diverse groups of students.

Questions About Instruction

Questions about instruction also need to be acknowledged and addressed if we are to develop models of inquiry-based instruction that are welcoming and accessible to all students. Scholars who have been critical of assumptions about the nature of science included in calls for science education reform such as those discussed above have also had suggestions about how to change or focus scientific inquiry in the classroom to make it more accessible to diverse groups of learners. Eisenhart, Finkel, and Marion (1996), for example, argue that we should refocus the goals of science instruction on a broader vision of what it means to know science. They suggest that our instruction should have as its goal that students learn what they describe as "socially responsible science use." (p. 283). This view of science instruction entails helping students develop an: "(a) understanding of how science-related actions impact the individuals who engage in them; (b) understanding the impact of decisions on others; (c) understanding the relevant science content and methods; and (d) understanding the advantages and limitations of a scientific approach" (p. 284).

Other scholars have focused less on changing the goals of science instruction and more on the instructional process itself. In this vein, Okhee Lee and her colleagues have pointed out that:

> Although scientific inquiry is a challenge for most students (Minstrell & van Zee, 2000), it presents additional challenges for students from cultures that do not encourage them to engage in inquiry practices of asking questions, designing and implementing investigations, and finding answers on their own (Arellano, Barcenal, Bilbao, Castellano, Nichols, & Tippins, 2001; Jegede & Okebukola, 1992; McKinley, Waiti, & Bell, 1992; Solano-Flores & Nelson-Barber, 2001). (Lee, 2003, p. 466)

They have argued for the development of a model of instruction that they call "instructional congruence" that "combines students' cultures with academic disciplines" and that "recogni[zes] that interactional patterns within a language and culture group, although culturally congruent, may sometimes be incompatible with the academic content to be learned" (Lee & Fradd, 1996, p. 275), claiming that such an approach is useful because:

> Scientific practices to encourage empirical standards, logical arguments, skepticism, questioning, criticism, and rules of evidence may be incongruent with cultural interactions that favor cooperation, social and emotional support, and consensus building. Scientific practices to promote critical and independent thinking may also be inconsistent with cultural interactions in which information is given to learners by the authority of a teacher or a textbook. (Lee, 1997, p. 221)

Warren et al. (2001) take a somewhat different approach as a result of their work with Haitian American and Latino students in science classes, and argue that we need:

> to understand children's diverse sense-making practices as an intellectual resource in science learning and teaching...In our view, too little attention has been paid by researchers and teachers alike to the potentially profound continuities between everyday and scientific ways of knowing and talking, and this to the pedagogical possibilities that may be derived from such an analysis, especially for typically marginalized children. (p. 546)

These authors argue that unless we fully appreciate the ideas and forms of expression that children bring to the classroom, we will continue to see limited participation from these children in science classes (Warren et al., p. 547), and suggest that "we need to take seriously the intellectual power and complexity in the ways with words children, and all of us, use every day."

We believe that if we are to find ways to include all students in inquiry-based science classrooms that we must rethink both the goals and the processes of inquiry-based science instruction. We must appreciate both the similarities and differences in the ways that students perceive and explain the world around them, and we must instruct in ways that empower all of our students. In the following two chapters, we will look in particular at ways to include girls and diverse student populations in scientific inquiry.

GENDER AND INQUIRY IN THE CLASSROOM: CONTEXTS AND CONTESTS

Kathleen Greene

The three areas Liza Finkel presents in the introduction to Section III—the nature of science, beliefs about students, and the process of instruction—are all highly relevant to issues of gender in science education. First, in terms of the nature of science, historically there have been widespread beliefs that science is (best) done by men, that science is (supposed to be) objective, super-rational, reductionist, solitary and impersonal, an image of science dating back at least to Francis Bacon:

> Bacon's influence on molding science in the image of men and masculinity was considerable and long-lived—with us, in fact to this day.... Bacon elaborated the metaphors of science in sexual and gendered terms, with science as male and nature as female ... man as a thinker epitomized objectivity, rationality, culture, and control...the exclusion of women from the practice of science and the consequent male, patriarchal structuring of science is reflected in the concerns, concepts, metaphors, assumptions, and language of science. (Bleier, 1988, p. 6)

Second, in terms of teachers' (and society's) beliefs about students, girls are often considered (and, not surprisingly, consider themselves) to be less capable than boys in mathematics and science.

> Girls have been discouraged from developing their interest in [science and math] lest they be considered unfeminine and, thus, socially unacceptable. The personal conflicts so generated steered many women away from math and science and undermined the self-confidence of numerous others. (Namenwirth, 1988, p. 19)

And finally, in terms of science instruction, female students are considered to be and, as a result of socialization, often are less aggressive, less risk-taking, and more compliant than their male peers:

Our social system has sought to divide human qualities between men and women, instructing boys that they are naturally intelligent, logical, objective, active, independent, forceful, risk-taking, and courageous. The qualities encouraged in girls have been a different set: sensitivity, emotional responsiveness, obedience, kindness, dependence, timidity, self-doubt, and self-sacrifice. (Namenwirth, 1988, p. 19)

The science investigation unit described in the vignette, which provides the analytical focus of this chapter, is designed to be a science learning environment that is inclusive rather than prejudicial, enriching rather than remedial—for all of the students and teachers involved. In this chapter, I build on ideas generated by feminist critiques of science and feminist pedagogy to explore the impact of inquiry science education on girls and women specifically, but also on science itself.

THE MERRILL INVESTIGATIONS AND THE NATURE OF SCIENCE

Let us look first at the nature of science as taught and learned in the classroom described in the vignette. In fact, the classroom discussion recorded in the vignette, just prior to the commencement of the investigations, has as its subject the nature of science. "What is science?" is the first question asked by the teacher. The conversation provides an opportunity to bring out a variety of different ideas for the class to consider. The teacher has the option to reinforce all of the traditional western beliefs about science—that it is rational, objective, and impersonal, and so forth, or she can bring out other aspects of science— that it is done by groups of people, that it involves curiosity about the natural world, that the applications of science have an impact on people and on the environment, as well as on the economy. She can choose to emphasize the creativity, the precision, the adventure, the need to be methodical, or other aspects entirely. In the investigation discussion described in the vignette, the teacher's explicit goal was to uncover and begin to expand the children's notions of science, as well as their notions of who is capable of doing science.

The preinvestigation discussions and the investigations embody the process of science beginning with the articulation and choice of a question to investigate. It would be completely possible for a teacher in such a discussion to reinforce the narrowest, most exclusive notions of the process of science, but it is equally possible to use this opportunity to begin to disturb those notions, whether by introducing examples of nontraditional, non-western, or ancient science into the discussion, or by generating with the students definitions of science that are more inclusive than the ones with which they often begin.

The discussions both prior to and during the investigations are frequently students' first conversations *about* science. These conversations lay the groundwork for later conversations about who and whose interests have traditionally been served—and disserved—by science.

Beth Warren and colleagues (2001) write about the distinctions made between the scientific and the everyday in schools and elsewhere, suggesting that rigid observance of what are considered scientific qualities, "rationality, precision, formality, detachment, and objectivity" excludes that which reflects improvisation, ambiguity, informality, engagement, and subjectivity" (p. 530). These and other scholars have expressed concern that such allegiances will short-circuit the progressive possibilities of inquiry science (Eisenhart, Finkel, & Marion, 1996). The classroom discussions both before and during the investigations, as well as the investigations themselves, represent an attempt by the teachers to blur those distinctions and blend the qualities—to have the students' science questions come from "everyday" curiosity and experiences, and to approach finding answers to those questions using the students' own language and thought.

In fact, the students in this classroom are not forced (or even expected) to use the formal language of science, that is, hypothesis, control, variable, and so forth, as they plan their investigations; nor are they forced to follow steps of a strict "scientific method." The teachers help the students develop concepts of hypothesis testing and controlling for variables, but they want to be sure the students are not merely "performing" in a linguistic space that they don't fully understand. In other words, the students generate, use, and learn the concepts, and then acquire the high-status language to express those concepts.

The Merrill Investigations and Beliefs About Students

Study after study has shown that adults, both teachers and parents, underestimate the intelligence of girls. Teachers' beliefs that boys are smarter in mathematics and science begin in the earliest school years, at the very time when girls are getting better grades and equal scores on the standardized tests. Many adults think that boys possess innate mathematical and scientific ability. Girls can also achieve, they believe, but they have to try harder. (Sadker & Sadker, 1994, p. 95)

The Sadkers' (1994) research documented countless types and examples of gender bias in schools, including the subtle sexism in teachers' lowered expectations for girls' achievement, especially in the school subjects of science and mathematics. Somewhat paradoxically, higher teacher expectations for girls' classroom behavior also negatively affect teachers' attention to them, and, therefore, the quality of the education they receive:

> [W]hat teachers describe as girls' strengths in the classroom—good behavior, the desire to please the teacher, and general attention to assigned tasks—actually works against them; boys' poor behavior works in their favor. Teachers direct their attention to students who make noise and cause trouble; generally, these students are male. (American Association of University Women [AAUW], 1999, p. 62)

Teachers' beliefs about their students that have relevance for science education include beliefs about students' abilities and interests, and about what constitutes "appropriate" student behavior in the science classroom as well as in the classroom in general. All teachers construct learning environments that enact their beliefs about and knowledge of students. The extent to which those beliefs reflect biases and perceived limits of students' abilities, and the extent to which they reflect insights into students' strengths and possibilities determine the types of classroom environments they work to construct.

If a teacher believes society's message that boys are smarter than girls, the teaching she does will reinforce that. If she believes that scientists are smarter than nonscientists, or if she herself does not understand or like science, those beliefs will influence what she teaches and what she communicates to her students.

If she, however, is convinced that students and "ordinary people" can study and "do" science, by engaging their curiosity about the world around them, by being open to new ideas, conscientious, diligent, and operating with integrity and a healthy skepticism, then there is a good chance that that is what her students come to see as science. The role the students see for themselves in science will create opportunities for ongoing engagement with science. There is also the (remote but real) possibility, that if those students continue to pursue the study and practice of science, science itself could become a more inclusive endeavor.

Something as (deceptively) simple as the assignment of cooperative groups is strongly influenced by teachers' beliefs about their students. This single decision, in terms of the girls and boys in the class, may be perhaps the most crucial in the entire 6-week project. Does the teacher construct single-sex or mixed-sex groups? How does she combine and distribute "leaders" and the "followers," more aggressive children and more passive ones? And, once groups are formed, how does she prepare, monitor and guide the children so that they are respectful of each other's ideas, strengths and contributions? How does the teacher come to be aware of her students' and her own preconceptions and biases about girls' and boys' "appropriate" student roles, both individually and in groups, and how does she overcome, or at least respond, to these?

Teacher beliefs about students also come into play in how they mediate students' decisions about what to investigate. There are gender differences in the questions students have chosen for investigations. In other words, boys and girls have tended to make different choices. Girls, working with other girls, have tended to choose "consumer science" questions, often about product preference and differentiation. Boys, working with other boys, have more frequently chosen questions that involve machines or other equipment and ones that are activity-based questions, including ones about athletic performance. These choices present the teacher with powerful challenges and opportunities. Does the teacher accept or challenge the children's inclinations that largely reinforce gender stereotypes?

This is one of the times teachers have to use their knowledge and examine their beliefs about their students to assess the "teachable moment." If the teacher believes that consumer science is a "natural choice" for girls, then she is likely to accept unquestioningly the decision of a girls' group to investigate several different soaps to determine which one smells the best. If, on the other hand, the teacher believes that girls need to study something "more scientific," she is likely to encourage the girls to study the physiology of olfaction or how organic compounds smell differently depending on their functional groups. If she does not have confidence in girls' relative ability or inclination to do "hard science," she may pay less attention to this group of girls and more attention to a boys' group that is studying rockets or levers, for example.

Virginia Valian (1999) asserts that "girls spend an education lifetime in the company of adults who—often nonconsciously—underestimate the girls' math and science abilities and depress both their expectations of what they can achieve and their actual performance" (p. 64). A teacher who is aware of this will probably engage in a much more complicated decision-making process as she decides whether (or how) to encourage a group of girls in their investigation choice of fragrance preferences.

It is, perhaps, past time to explore briefly but explicitly the idea of gender and how a dichotomous key—a "scientific" sorting and explanatory system—like gender operates and ultimately misleads (Valian, 1999). First, it forces all members of a population into two groups, in this case, male and not male (female). Then, it assigns certain values and properties to each of the two groups. The grouping then assumes essential importance so that intergroup differences transcend intragroup differences. What this means, among other things, with respect to gender, is that all females in a population are considered more similar to each other than to the males in the population, so that we tend to generalize the results any studies of girls to include all girls, irrespective of race, ethnicity or socioeconomic status.

The application of an apparently simple, dichotomous key to a human and therefore, highly and multiply socialized, and complex population is both arbitrary and fraught with problems. Nevertheless, it is the system within which this chapter functions.

But, let us return to consideration of the Merrill investigations, and the example of one all-girl group's choice to investigate fragrance preference. This choice may genuinely reflect the girls' current interests, and/but it would also reinforce gender stereotypes about what girls are or should be interested in. The teacher needs to decide which is the more important teaching goal. On one hand, the teacher might choose to help the group refine their research question so that they focus on the chemistry of compounds or the physiology of smell. On the other hand, if the teacher knows that this group of girls has not shown much interest in science before, she may decide to encourage them in their choice, but/and to engage them (perhaps later) in exploring the aromaticity of chemical compounds or the targeted marketing of consumer products. In other words, the teacher's instruction and guidance of this group of girls will reflect her beliefs about girls' abilities specifically and in general, and the abilities of these female students in particular, in combination and interaction with her beliefs about what those girls can and should accomplish in science class and in life.

The Merrill Investigations and the Process of Instruction

The First Science Teaching Standard Begins

Teachers of science plan an inquiry-based science program for their students. Inquiry is often discussed in teacher preparation programs as one of the preferred methods of instruction. Yet, inquiry does not exist in equal prevalence in the classroom. Most science teachers can list reasons for the discrepancy immediately. Inquiry takes more classroom time. Inquiry is difficult to assess. Inquiry creates a heavy planning burden. It is difficult to operate in an inquiry mode and have a classroom that "looks like" what teachers and administrators often expect a classroom to "look like." (http://deepimpact.jpl.nasa.gov/educ/DesigningCraters.html)

As the curriculum designers at NASA note above, inquiry science as described in the vignette does not represent how science is taught in most elementary schools. The classroom is noisy, individual and groups of children are frequently out of their seats and sometimes out of the building, children argue, things spill, all the children seem to be doing something different, and children ask their teachers to do things (rather than the other way around). The student-initiated, student-designed small-group investigations make it difficult for the teachers to set specific content learning objectives ahead of time, and impossible to set the same objectives across the class.

In addition to being "messy" and less scripted than typical science lessons, though, another way that the investigations differ from normal elementary school science is that they teach science in a way that crosses into other traditional subjects (language arts) as well as into areas often left out altogether (project planning and presentation skills). Boys and girls tend to excel in different areas of the curriculum—boys in science and math and girls in language arts (AAUW, 2002). The investigations provide opportunities for the students to develop and expand their competence across the curriculum and skill areas. Small groups, carefully chosen by the teacher, work together with the student teachers to discuss, plan and prepare. The boys are expected to take good notes just as the girls are expected to make and use the equipment, and the teachers and student teachers pay attention to make sure that happens. The AAUW (2002) has recommended curricular changes to challenge all forms of gender inequity, including boys' underperformance in language arts.

> Areas ... where boys underenroll or underperform girls are relevant to the equity agenda.... Are there curricular changes that might encourage their engagement in these crucial areas of the curriculum? (p. 295)

For the presentations at the end of the investigations, groups prepare and then distribute sections so that everyone is responsible for speaking to the whole group. The teachers and student teachers pay attention to helping all the students develop comfort and then increasing facility in this blend of school subjects and skill areas. The *National Science Education Standards* (NRC, 1996) recognize the value of presentations like these to help develop literacy and communication skills:

> The (National Science Education) Standards also recommend that students present and share their results with other students. Presenting and sharing results with other students can have a direct connection to general literacy goals of developing effective written and oral communication skills. Students can use their skills in language arts to present and share science exploration results and conclusions with other students. (Dickinson & Young, 1998, p. 334)

The vignette illustrates a number of ways that teachers can create opportunities for all students to participate in meaningful inquiry. Specifically, the teachers in the vignette used their cultural and specific knowledge of the children to form small groups where each child was likely to have a voice and a say, and the university students allowed children to choose questions that might not be considered "strictly scientific" in other settings. The teachers also encouraged practices that would ensure that students knew their work was valued by teachers and peers. For example, students kept laboratory notebooks in which they wrote their ideas, actions taken, and investigation results. From these records, they developed posters and oral presentations to share with the class. Each oral presentation was followed by a "PQP" (Praise, Question, Polish) session, during which class members were asked, first, for "Praise," a positive statement about the presentation (what was especially interesting or well-done in the investigation), second, for a "Question" about something they did not understand or wanted to know more about, and, finally, for a "Polish," a suggestion for improving either the investigation or the presentation. The students and teachers took these presentations and PQP sessions seriously.

It is important to note another way in which the classroom teachers used their subject-area knowledge to create an inclusive classroom context. Most of the knowledge constructed by the children in the vignette was interdisciplinary and did not map directly on to the body of knowledge (science facts) that was included in their science textbooks. This increased the risks for the classroom teachers in multiple ways; it did not directly prepare students to correctly answer objective, standardized, subject-discrete tests, and it opened them up to accusations of teaching "dumb-downed" science. This interdisciplinarity, though, is much more in keeping with the tenets and goals of feminist pedagogy, which holds that the world and all real knowledge of it does not adhere to artificial disciplinary rules and boundaries.

Interactions

In the previous sections I have tried to separate discussion of the three sources of questions about inquiry science with respect to gender, but the separation belies what are, in practice, complex and dynamic interactions. The vignette illustrates how teachers' notions of science interact with their beliefs about students, the methods of instruction they employ, and the learning that results. The very selection of the investigation unit for inclusion in the curriculum suggests that the teachers believe that authentic science inquiry takes time, and that students need to—and can be trusted to—think, to ask questions, to do research, to plan, and to execute plans, with the teachers' and student teachers' guidance and participation. In other words, the children are given space and opportunity to direct their inquiry and learning.

In this unit, the teachers are acknowledging and embracing the idea that science is as much about curiosity and imagination as it is about rigor and regularity. It requires asking questions before one can set about answering them. It is as personal as it is objective. It is as much about creativity as it is about conventions. It involves conversation, collaboration and compromise, as well as individual cognition and discipline. For the girls in the class, this is especially powerful. The "scientific method" as presented in textbooks, usually downplays or leaves out entirely the creative, the conversational, the collaborative.

The teachers encourage the girls and boys to think about science and scientists, to view themselves as scientists, and to view what they are doing as similar to what scientists do. This gives the teachers the opportunity to discuss with the children such myths as "only men or white people do science," and "scientists are abnormally smart people who are very different from me," and then to work to dispel those myths, whether by finding stories about scientists who are/were women, people of color, and people with other types of nonprivileged backgrounds, or inviting visitors representing any of these groups.

You will notice, perhaps, that I am talking about the highly complex act of teaching as being on both "input" and "output"—the teacher's need to pay attention to students' comments, feelings and perceptions, and then to make sensitive and appropriate decisions about what to say and do, based on what they have heard and seen. This, too, represents an approach to teaching and learning that is more effectively modeled and developed than merely "instructed." This is a "do as I do" method rather than a "do as I say" method, designed more for effectiveness than efficiency.

This, of course, requires that the teachers are aware of their own views and how those views mesh or contrast with masculine and masculinist views of science and scientists. The teachers must be alert to their students' developing perceptions of science and of their own capabilities and then intervene through both conversation and action. For example, a teacher might ask, "Who in this class is good at science?" and then follow up with "What does it mean to be good at science?" or "What does it take to be good at science?" This provides an opportunity to explain to and show the children that all kinds of people with all kinds of talents and abilities engage in science and scientific careers and activities. In terms of action, a teacher can find and take an opportunity to reinforce behaviors in girls and boys that reflect the more "feminine" aspects of science—the collaborative, the personal, the imaginative—such as by commenting, "Kim, that is such a creative way to approach your study of paper making. It reminds me of how Barbara McClintock studied genetics in corn" (see Keller, 1983).

The Future

Earlier in this chapter, I mentioned briefly that the kind of inquiry science teaching portrayed in the vignette, and in the Merrill science investigation unit was consistent with feminist pedagogy. Teachers' beliefs about science, students and instruction, combine with self-awareness and cultural and gender sensitivity as they design and construct classroom inquiry. The model presented in the vignette and discussed in this chapter is also highly consistent with the emerging field of feminist science studies. In their publication, *Frequently Asked Questions About Feminist Science Studies*, (Association of American Colleges and Universities, 1999), the AACU authors connect their notions of scientific literacy with the nature of science, beliefs about people, and ways of inquiring about the world:

> Feminist science studies ... defines science in context, not as a disconnected, ethereal body of knowledge, but rather as something deeply rooted in the world itself, in all its messiness. It sees science as something that matters profoundly to men and women alike. Feminist science studies scholars look for ways to comprehend the sometimes mystifying connections between science and what an average citizen might call ordinary life. It also assumes that a thoughtful, observant person can ask a good question about science and, in the process of searching for or evaluating the answer, can, in fact, become scientifically literate. (p. 6)

Teachers who believe that science is not a pursuit discrete from all others, requiring special traits and skills, and teachers who believe and are committed to the idea that all their students are capable of "doing" and "learning" science, are the ones in whose classrooms inquiry science can realize its transformative potential, both in terms of the lives of their students and the future of science.

If students can identify with science as something that connects with their lives and the world they live in, as well as something they might do, they are one step closer to inclusion. Science will not be the professional goal for everyone, but if students identify positively with science, they will see a normal and accurate intersection between themselves and science. If, later, they encounter some exclusionary message, they will have reason to refute and resist the exclusion.

What power does something as relatively small as an opportunity to conduct science inquiry in school hold against sexism in science and society? Put that way, it is rather discouraging. But, if teachers can help students (girls and boys) experience science as something interesting, challenging and satisfying rather than as a set of facts collected by others scientists, then there is the potential that the students will maintain an interest in exploring the natural world. Maybe some of them will go on to have careers in science and maybe they will practice it in a way that goes beyond what has been exclusive and exclusionary.

INQUIRY FOR DIVERSE STUDENT POPULATIONS: PROMISES AND PITFALLS

Jose Rios

Scientific inquiry refers to the diverse ways in which scientists study the natural world and propose explanations based on the evidence derived from their work (National Research Council [NRC] 1996, p. 23). In translating this broad definition for classroom practice, *National Science Education Standards* (NSES) proponents also refer to inquiry as "the activities of students in which they develop knowledge and understanding of scientific ideas, as well as an understanding of how scientists study their natural world" (p. 23).

At face value, the NSES value what many multicultural educators put forth as essential qualities for good instruction. First, there is an emphasis on diverse methodologies. Allowing students to study the world in multiple ways provides a picture of science that contradicts the notion of science as narrow or static. In fact, students can begin to appreciate the interdisciplinary nature of science, where the boundaries of natural science intersect with the needs of society.

Second, this definition places added value scientific habits of mind (Irvine, 2001). Although not explicitly stated, such habits seem universal and create entrance points for students from diverse backgrounds to experience science. Given this emphasis on universality, engaging students in carefully aligned activities that promote authentic learning opportunities should result in better experiences with, and thus better knowledge of, science and scientific endeavors.

Third is the emphasis on evidence. What distinguishes scientific inquiry from other forms of study is the intricate relationship between the questions asked, the methods employed, and the conclusions drawn. According to Brown (2006),

> through formalized instruction, scientific learning communities typically seek the dual goals of creating future science professionals and scientifically literate citizens. The pedagogy supporting these goals typically involves socializing students in the conceptual content and epistemologies characteristic of the disciplines of science. (p. 100)

As seen in the vignette, the teachers strive to make science accessible for students. They assess students' understandings of science and articulate a view of science that is more than just a school subject: science involves the natural world. What one examines in the natural world, and how one studies it, depends largely on the focus of study. Given this understanding scientific inquiry, and the apparent congruence with the NSES, students should be motivated to engage what scientists do, appreciate the power of inquiry, and become more literate in doing science. So what's the problem? Using the vignette as a focal point of discussion, this section will address what is required to do science according to the NSES, the instructional implications for diverse student populations, and the potential pitfalls for inquiry-based approaches to science instruction.

Inquiry, Multicultural Education, and the Nature of Science

Since the release of *Science for All Americans* (American Association for the Advancement of Science [AAAS], 1989) and *National Science Education Standards* (NRC, 1996), scholars have written about numerous issues related to a standardized approach to science education. Some focus on issues of language differences (Lee & Fradd, 1998), gender issues (Eisenhart & Finkel, 1998), cultural conflicts (Brown, 2004), cognition and development (Aikenhead & Jegede, 1999), and curriculum reform (Shymansky, Yore, & Anderson, 2004). Other have focused on epistemology (Lehrer, Carpenter, Schauble, & Putz, 2000), power issues (Harding, 1998), and equity (Hewson, Carpenter, Schauble, & Putz, 2001). Given the complexities of meeting the needs of diverse student populations, dissonance seems to reign supreme. Yet Lee (2002) provides a direction for science education research:

> With students from diverse languages and cultures, divergent perspectives and related areas of literature need to be considered simultaneously. The current knowledge base highlights critically important and fertile areas of research that require consideration of seemingly conflicting theoretical perspectives. These perspectives and areas of literature may be merged into a theoretically coherent and sound body of knowledge. Research results will offer insights in identifying effective instructional scaffolding to enable students to conduct scientific inquiry as practiced in scientific communities while helping them recognize and value the ways of knowing and talking in their own cultures. (p. 60)

The emphasis on scaffolding provides a useful starting point for discussing instructional issues in the vignette. I will use one particular approach, Banks' approaches to multicultural curriculum reform (1994), to frame the discussion.

Approaches to Multicultural Education Reform

The Model Revisited

According to Banks (1994), there are four approaches to multicultural education reform:

Level 1:   The Contributions Approach
Level 2:   The Additive Approach
Level 3:   The Transformation Approach
Level 4:   The Social Action Approach (p. 25)

The Contributions Approach, which I refer to as the 3 Fs—food, fashion, and festivals, is a common curricular approach used in schools. Discussions of other cultures often coincide with national, regional, and local holidays. The curriculum remains the same and students are not exposed to images of people and cultures that have engaged in and promoted the field of scientific inquiry as taught in schools. Surprisingly, students learn about Rosa Parks and how her dignified act of rebellion ignited the Civil Rights Movement in social studies. Are there any similar acts of rebellion in science?

The Additive Approach is similar to the Contributions Approach in that there is no challenge to the adopted curriculum. Students receive cultural enrichment through the addition of books, lectures, units of study, and even entire courses. Although the depth and breadth of these enrichments vary greatly from one context to another, the basic premise remains the same: showcase the contributions of others in ways that do not challenge the status quo.

> Level 3, the Transformative Approach, differs radically from Levels 1 and 2. This approach ... changes the canon, paradigms, and basic assumptions of the curriculum and enables students to view concepts, issues, themes, and problems from different perspectives and points of view. Major goals of this approach include helping students to understand concepts, events, and people from diverse ethnic and cultural perspectives and to understand knowledge as knowledge construction. (Banks, 1999, p. 26)

The emphasis on knowledge construction allows students to question the voices heard in the curriculum, seek out the voices of those not heard, and explore why certain questions are pursued while others are ignored.

In science, people who are ignored often resemble the students asking the questions in the classroom.

The final level, The Social Action Approach, builds upon the experiences and knowledge gained at Level 3 by engaging students in activities that challenge the topics of study. These actions, whether civic, social, academic, or personal often result in reconstruction of knowledge at numerous levels, individual or group, and changes in the way students view the curriculum itself and their relationship to it. For example, knowing about the ecology of the school grounds is one thing: doing something to reduce pollution is another thing entirely. The former corresponds to Levels 1-3, while the latter moves students to Level 4.

According to Banks (1994), the goal of multicultural education is "to help, to care, and to act in ways that will develop and foster a democratic and just society in which all groups experience cultural democracy and cultural empowerment" (p. 27). Content knowledge and hands-on experiences are important means to democratic education. Using knowledge and experience to promote "a commitment to personal, social, and civic action, and the knowledge and skills needed to participate in effective civic action" (p. 27) should be the goal of education. With these levels in mind, let us return to the vignette.

Examining Merrill School Through a Multicultural Lens

Merrill School epitomizes what many urban educators face in this age of accountability: conflicting notions of competency, mounting pressures to teach to published standards, increasing attention to test scores, and a desire to engage students in relevant, hands-on science experiences. Merrill also enjoys a hospitable relationship with a local college. Students from the college, along with their professor and the classroom teacher, are engaged in bringing constructivist experiences to the students. Judging from the interactions and conversations, these experiences are less teacher-centered than most curricula, emphasizing student interest and participation over lecture and worksheets.

As students begin their conversations about science and conducting scientific investigations, it is evident that the curriculum is not bound by the calendar. There is a 6-week window for investigating questions of their choice and the goal is to do what scientists do. That means asking good questions, designing investigations and procedures, doing the experiment, interpreting results, and sharing what was learned with other students in the class. According to Peterson and Jungck (1988), students are engaging in the 3 Ps of science—Posing, Probing, and Persuasion. Given the importance of doing science in this classroom, students' classroom experiences are aligned with the NSES, which place inquiry at the center of instruction.

With the emphasis on inquiry, this classroom has moved beyond Level 1, the Contributions Approach. Here, all students are engaging in scientific activities. Although there is still room to use historical and current personalities to highlight who does science and how they do it, the instructors chose to focus on the students and promote their engagement in scientific activities. Inquiry is now viewed as a process that gives "occasion for deeper interaction and relationship with the phenomena-greater potential for further development of understanding" (Exploratorium, 1998). Students no longer see science as something outside their experiences. Rather, they enter the realm of authentic science.

Yet entering the realm of science can be costly for students. "Although the acculturation of the values, epistemic beliefs, and genres of discourse consistent with those of science can provide learners with educational and social opportunities, there are also potential cultural costs" says Brown (2006, p. 96). Assuming the language and processes of science neglects the notion that students come to school with their own cultural capital (Seiler, 2001). This capital is built from sociocultural experiences that shape the ways in which they see and interpret the world. As long as there is no conflict between the work of school, and the world of home, learning is easy. However, identity, experience, and worldviews can lead to radically different experiences with science curricula (Gilbert & Yerrick, 2001).

Of all of the levels, this classroom seems aligned with Level 2, the Additive Approach. Since science instruction is tied to preservice teacher education, it is safe to assume that instruction is different from the regular curriculum. Some of those differences may include more time, greater individualized attention, increased emphasis on group work, and opportunities to learn about one topic in depth. Depending on the district, this approach constitutes an enrichment to the establish curriculum. In fact, if the teacher aligns instruction with established standards, then this classroom experience is in addition to and not in place of the adopted curriculum.

Lee (2002) argues that given this approach to the curriculum, teachers are addressing issues of student identity by allowing students to pursue questions of their own design. Allowing students to draw from their cultural experiences can lead to greater participation and success in science activities (Warren, Ballenger, Ogonowski, Rosebery, & Hudicourt-Barnes, 2001). Equally important, according to Lee, is the notion that an inquiry-based approach to science reflects an epistemological understanding of science (Lehrer et al., 2000). Students engage in model-based reasoning in the same ways that scientists construct and reconstruct models of natural phenomena. Yet with the constraints of time, equipment, materials, and budget, can we truly say that students are truly free to pursue their interests?

At some point, a decision is made about the feasibility of the focal topic. This decision, whether made by the students or, more often than not, the teacher, reflects the value-laden nature of science. What is valued in school science reflects what is valued by science: one just needs to look at what's available and allowable in schools. According to Brown (2006), these curricular and instructional practices "may either inadvertently, or more directly, favor students from particular backgrounds or more privileged ways of speaking" (p. 100). Harding (1998) would take this argument one step further by pointing out the androcentric nature of science and that schools mirror this view through its curriculum. The curriculum, in this case, means more than books and worksheets: it is what questions students are encouraged to pursue or not pursue. Given that children have limited content and experiential knowledge in science, their classroom experiences are often "simplified forms [of science] that children can participate in, comprehend, and communicate" (Lee, 2002, p. 42).

Given the limitations of school science programs, what is left is a narrow view of what counts as science, how one does science, and how one communicates scientifically. The NRC (1996) point out clearly that science is "a way of knowing that distinguishes itself from other ways of knowing or other bodies of knowledge" (p. 201). Questions are focused and measurable; research designs are replicable; results are quantitative; results are shared using a common language for greater clarity and ease of interpretation. This way of knowing favors objectivity and gender, race, culture, and sexual orientation have no bearing on scientific activity. Yet this emphasis on the universality of science (Stanley & Brickhouse, 2001) often presents problems for students from diverse backgrounds. Given the limitations of school science programs, how does one move to a transformative approach? In many ways, this approach runs counter to what is proposed in the NSES standards. To begin this discussion, I want to draw from a past experience with high school students.

Transforming Instruction by Asking Different Questions

As a graduate student, I was privileged to work with high school students from underserved communities in Illinois, Puerto Rico, and Wisconsin. The program, called the Summer Science Institute, was an eight-week, summer, residential enrichment program for high school students. Students chose one area of science—animal behavior, genetics, or physiology—and participated in research projects under the guidance of other graduate students. They also received instruction in data analysis, science writing, and technology. Although we encouraged students to pursue topics of interests to them, we were limited by time, space, material, budgets, and what students already knew about the topics. Year after year, students proposed projects like:

- Is body fat an indicator of fitness?
- Do male and females do [insert a behavior here] the same way?
- Is one [insert a phenotype here] more prevalent in the population than others?

One summer, however, the genetics group asked a compelling question. The genetics group consisted of fours girls and three boys, with a core group from Chicago, Illinois. That year, the Chicago Police Department sanctioned a study looking at the relationship between finger print patterns and ethnicity. The goal was simple: find consistent patterns according to ethnic groups and you can narrow down the field of suspects at a crime scene. According to the students, preliminary results indicated that such patterns were emerging and that police were considering putting their initial findings to the test in the field.

To put it mildly, the students were upset. Citing ongoing tensions between the police and the African American communities, they did not trust the system and feared bias in the study. On the street, they knew that "brothers were bothered all the time." Was this study another way to identify African Americans more easily and make police work quick and simple?

We were amazed by their passion and candidness. This topic touched a nerve and the motivation to pursue this topic clearly was there. Not only did students want to design their own study examining the relationship between fingerprint patterns and ethnicity, they wanted to learn as much as possible about (a) current and historical arrest rates according to ethnicity, (b) other research projects linking a genotype or phenotype to ethnicity, (c) political backers of the study and (d) results of previous pilot studies. Given the approach taken by this group of students, one could say that they were transforming their experience in the genetics classroom. Although a well-designed study was still the focal point, students were concerned more about the potential victims of the study than the objectivity of their results. According to Banks (1994), these students were concerned about "the voices of the victors and the vanquished" (p. 26). More importantly, they were thinking critically and developing "the skills to formulate, document, and justify their conclusions and generalizations" (p. 26). By keeping people at the center of their study, and striving to use research to promote social change, these students made progress toward Level 4 of Bank's model—The Social Action Approach.

As the program progressed, the students spent as much time discussing historical facts and personal anecdotes as they did designing their study. What astounded me the most was that despite their disdain for the sociopolitical issues of the topic, they worked very hard at removing their subjectivities from the study. Issues like location, randomization, consistency, validity, and reliability were kept at the forefront. They conducted pilot studies to perfect their fingerprinting technique, evaluated numerous sites for ethnic diversity, tried out sample scripts for approaching prospective subjects, and designed data collection and analysis strategies for clarity and completeness. In the end, they spent two weeks planning before they collected their first real fingerprints. At the end of the data collection period, the group had amassed a sample of 500 fingerprints! Impressive for any small-scale research project.

Motivated by a desire to prove the Chicago police wrong, the students worked diligently at analysis. Day and night, they entered data, compared notes, examined patterns, and discuss emerging results. In the end, they found out that some ethnic groups in their study showed consistent fingerprint patterns. Although there were limitations to this study, the students took their findings seriously. They had designed an objective study and the results challenged their core beliefs. In many ways, this was the first time that they had experienced congruency between their personal cultural priorities and those of their science instructors (Lee, 2004). With greater congruency comes the opportunity to promote "deeper learning than would have been possible through the simple transmission of information" (p. 85).

According to Wallace and Kang (2004), there are two elements of success tied to promoting inquiry in the classroom:

> One element of success is that children have positive attitudes toward inquiry. Students like to be involved in asking their own questions and formulating ways to answers those questions. A second element of success is that students improve their ability to ask researchable questions and to coordinate questions with knowledge claims and evidence as they become more accustomed to inquiry-based learning. (p. 939)

In transforming their experience with genetics instruction, these students supported Lee's (2002) assertion that effective and congruent instruction, "enable students to conduct scientific inquiry as practiced in scientific communities while helping them recognize and value the ways of knowing and talking in their own cultures" (p. 60).

Judging from the limits placed on Merrill students (time, materials, safety), and the focus on asking "good" questions, the teachers may have constructed barriers inadvertently between teaching science as a "rhetoric of conclusions" (Schwab, 1962) and transformative experiences

(Rodriguez, 1998). Although providing opportunities for students to engage in inquiry is consistent with Schwab's vision of science instruction, it falls short of connecting science experiences to real world issues that affect students directly. According to Rodriguez (1998),

> By not directly addressing (making visible) the ethnic, socioeconomic, gender, and theoretical issues that influence the teaching and learning of science in our schools, documents such as the NRC Standards end up being a compendium of half-articulated good intentions, with little guidance on how the proposed substantive changes can be implemented at the classroom level. (p. 592)

Growing crystals is fun and students can become great investigators. However, these types of activities should serve to introduce inquiry and teach basic science skills. Transformative science teaching and teaching for social action involves a greater degree of risk-taking, one that teachers must be prepared for since science curricula rarely reflect the world views and experiences of diverse student populations. It "will take a lot more than good intentions to help teachers work with growing and ethnically diverse pupil population" (Rodriguez, 1998, p. 592).

Transforming Instruction by Taking Social Action

When students move from transformation to social action, they take "personal and social actions related to the concepts, problems, and issues they have studied" (Banks, 1994, p, 27). With the genetics group, the very act of engaging the topic of fingerprinting and suspect identification addressed the personal part of social action. The issue had great significance to them and to their communities. The motivation for examining the topic in detail, and putting the ideas to a rigorous test, came from genuine concerns about existing tensions at home. Yet in order for this activity to move past the personal, students needed additional avenues for discourse with other audiences. Fortunately, the program had built-in requirements for this level of discourse, although we learned that internal discussions are far different from external discussions.

Consistent with the idea that "all science has to be reported" (Reiss, 1993, p. 26), we required students to produce a scientific paper, a poster, and present their project in a public symposium. Parents, teachers, University of Wisconsin professors, and members of the community attended the symposium. The intent of the symposium was to introduce students to different forms of discourse. The paper and posters were intended for scientists, while the public presentation was geared for a general audience.

The latter was fairly easy for every group because we emphasized the non-scientific nature of the public presentation. "Keep it real" was the motto.

According to Fusco (2001), the presentations allowed students to "create science and science-like performances, tools, and discourses that are extensions of their lives, cultures, and communities" (p. 862). Yet Fusco did not want to "imply that no culture of science practice exists and that students should not be acquainted with it" (p. 862). Rather, she advocates for an approach to science education where "the methods of learning science are informed not just by science or what scientists do but by the many ways of understanding of the world and by the expressions of those understandings" (p. 862). Although some of these expressions are unrecognizable to those entrenched in traditional forms of scientific discourse, students provided translations of their personal discourse in ways that scientists could understand—papers and posters.

Although we were satisfied with this level of social action, opportunities to take this discourse beyond the confines of the university were missing. In hindsight, I wish that we had provided opportunities for the students to take their acts on the road. In this case, they could have sent copies of their paper to important constituents in the Chicago community. They could have requested audiences with key members of the Chicago police department to share their results and concerns about the initiative. These types of discussions are consistent with the notion that science is situated within specific contexts and that these contexts influence what is studied, how something is studied, and what is done with the results. According to Reiss (1993), "science inevitably reflects the interests, the values, the unconscious suppositions and the beliefs of the society that gives rise to it" (p. 24). As much as the students wanted to refute the basic premise of the fingerprinting study, they had the opportunity to engage in rich discussions with the greater community, both scientific and political. Taking discussions of science outside of schools challenges the "discourse of invisibility" (Rodriguez, 1997) in the NSES and promotes Barton's (1998) notion of "reflexive science" that "welcomes diverse aims, interests, and positions" (Seiler, 2001, p. 1002).

LESSONS LEARNED ABOUT INSTRUCTION AND STUDENTS

Students in the Summer Science Institute (SSI) had many advantages that they do not experience in the typical public school: small classes, integrated curricula, teachers who are researchers, evening tutorials, and increased access to materials and supplies. In some ways, we tried to create a utopia for science teaching and learning. Even with these advantages, I learned many lessons about inquiry that have informed my current practice as a science educator. These lessons include knowing thy community and thyself, focusing on basic science skills, and creating spaces for discourse.

Lesson 1—Know Thy Community and Thyself

Knowing thy community involves more than just understanding the demographics of your school. As important as it is to know whether the community is predominantly African American with a growing Eastern European immigrant population, teachers need to look beyond ethnicity. Data on social economic status, parental involvement, political tensions, and corporate contributions are also important. As we learned in SSI, knowledge of current topics in the community can served as a powerful focus for science curricula. There are some topics that lend themselves easily to scientific study: pollution, conservation, disease, and fitness are just a few. However, the local newspaper can provide a databank of recent community issues that students may find interesting and worth studying. I encourage teachers to keep back issues of magazines on hand. I also model ways of posting current scientific events in the classroom, using both print and electronic media. Given the growing use of computers in schools and classrooms, it is easier for teachers to access current information quickly.

Equally important is for teachers to look at themselves and identify the perspectives, biases, and idiosyncrasies that define them. According to Cochran-Smith (1995):

> In order to learn to teach in a society that is increasingly culturally and lin-guistically diverse, prospective teachers need opportunities to examine much of what is usually unexamined in the tightly braided relationships of language, culture, and power in schools and schooling. This kind of exami-nation inevitably begins with our own histories as human beings and as edu-cators—our own cultural, racial, and linguistic backgrounds and our own experiences as raced, classed, and gendered children, parents, and teachers in the world. It also includes a close look at the tacit assumptions we make about the motivations and behaviors of other children, other parents, and other teachers and about the pedagogies we deem most appropriate for learners who are like us and who are not like us. (p. 500)

Often teachers assume a color blind approach to science education (Howard, 1999), one that stresses perceived common values (i.e., the teacher's values) to the detriment of recognizing, and building on, stu-dent differences. Part of creating congruent instructional experiences for students involves making the classroom experience less congruent for you, the teacher, and more congruent for the learners. As suggested by Lee (2003), increasing congruence brings increased relevance and accessibility. Teaching for diversity means negotiating new territories with students, ones that strengthens the alignment between what is expected in school and what students bring from home (Lee & Fraud, 1998).

Lesson 2—Focus on the Basics

According to Barba (1998), engaging students in inquiry requires mastery of certain basic science skills: classifying, communicating, identifying variables, inferring, measuring, observing, predicting, using numbers, and using space/time relationships. When students have difficulty with inquiry-based activities, it can be traced back to problems with basic science skills. Barba argues that inquiry combines these basic skills into a new set of skills, integrated science skills: controlling variables, defining operationally, experimenting, formulating hypotheses, and investigating. As we did with students in SSI, the first part of the summer focused on revisiting and sometimes reteaching basic science skills before we engaged in designing and implementing investigations.

With classroom teachers, I spend much of my time examining current science curricula, assessing which basic skills are prerequisite to these curricula, and what skills are taught through laboratory activities. Understanding prerequisite science skills is especially important because teachers can plan and supplement their curricula with short diagnostic activities that reveal existing strengths, deficiencies, or misconceptions. Too often teachers assume that children, especially English language learners, come to the science classroom with multiple deficiencies (Sleeter & Grant, 1994). This perception of deficiency often sends a message that science is outside the experiences of these students and that they must learn to think in a whole new way. As we learned in SSI, many students get science: they only need more experiences to hone their existing skills, correct existing misconceptions, and learn new ways of studying familiar and unfamiliar problems.

Lesson Three—Create Spaces for Discourse

School-based science curricula often limit student discourse. Content is fixed, materials are listed, activities are scaffolded, and you can find answers in the back of the book. However, more science curricula are providing opportunities for students to asked relevant questions that extend their interactions with scientific content. These efforts are a step in the right direction. However, these opportunities are still bound by the curriculum and are not always relevant to students. Either the teacher is faced with making connections between students' interests and the focal curriculum or having students find those connections themselves. I would propose a third option—create separate opportunities for exploring inquiry.

As illustrated in the vignette, it is possible to engage students in inquiry outside of the required curriculum. It may mean negotiating time with other subjects and teachers, giving up another activity, or learning to integrate content in new ways. Whatever approach a teacher chooses, students should have opportunities to discuss current issues, prioritize topics for study, and negotiate time lines with the teacher. In fact, by observing student discourse, teachers can learn about students' ways of "explaining, questioning, arguing, establishing trust, and the like" (Rosebery, 2004, p. 6). In this scenario, the teacher acts as an advocate and mentor, who supports student involvement while ensuring that students have successful experiences with inquiry. More importantly, this discourse is an important part of the process of inquiry, and students should be encouraged to revisit their questions, make connections between their studies and their community, and share what they are learning with each other and the community outside their classroom.

CONCLUSION

Teaching science as inquiry can be a powerful approach for improving science education for all. Studies that focus on teachers' professional development (Huffman, Thomas, & Lawrenz, 2003), instructional practices (Kahle, Meece, & Scantlebury, 2000; Von Seeker & Lissitz, 1999), or student identity (Brown, 2004) are identifying some key variables for greater success in science. Establishing a link between certain school-based practices and achievement in science is a promising area of study. However, as Loucks-Horsley and Matsumoto (1999) point out, these studies are small in scope scale and do not generalize to other contexts. Until then, we should continue to explore the intersections between what we works for diverse populations of students and what works in science education. Specifically,

> science educators must engage in academic research and pedagogical innovation that seeks to explicitly address the notion of students' discursive identity development and its implications for science learning ... if science educators fail ... science will continue to be divided on an ethnic, linguistic, and gender basis. (Brown, 2006, p. 122)

TRANSFORMATIVE INQUIRY: IMPLICATIONS AND CONCLUSIONS

Liza Finkel

Throughout this section and elsewhere in this book, the authors have argued that inquiry-based science is a distinct improvement over traditional models of school science instruction. They have also pointed out that there are questions that need to be raised if inquiry-based science classrooms are going to provide opportunities and access for all students, and not only for those who are already successful in more conventional science classrooms. Implementing an inquiry-based science curriculum without considering the specific and differing needs of all students is not likely to address the challenges science teachers face in providing access to diverse groups of students.

Although the specifics of each chapter differ, the conclusions reached by Finkel, Greene, and Rios are similar: inquiry-based science instruction has the potential to truly reform science education, and even the lives of the students who experience it, when students' interests, imaginations, and needs are seriously considered. These authors also conclude that to be truly meaningful, inquiry-based science education must offer the potential for transformation, of curriculum, teachers, students, and even science and society itself. It is this vision of what I will call transformative inquiry-based science education that I will attempt to illustrate in this final chapter.

Analyzing the Vignette: Potential and Limitations

The vignette that accompanies this section offers one illustration of an inquiry-based science classroom that includes many of the aspects of transformative inquiry-based science advocated by these authors. Students are expected to identify their own questions; they are supported in developing investigations that are feasible and appropriate for the setting within which they work; they conduct the investigations they design; they collaborate with each other and with more knowledgeable others (teachers and university students); and they share their work in a classroom forum. In addition, students learn that this kind of science learning is important because 6 weeks of class time is devoted to this work and because their work and the conclusions of their work are taken seriously.

The vision of inquiry described in this chapter addresses many feminist critiques of science and science education with its emphasis on peer collaboration, authenticity, and support from caring adults; one that can be summarized with the following quote from Elaine Howes (2001):

They [the teachers] want science to be communal, nurturing, embodied, and connected for their students. They hope to create classrooms in which these ethics prevail. They want their students to learn scientific content, but they want it to happen in an atmosphere that realizes a kind of scientific activity that welcomes the whole self, welcomes questioning and open exploration, and denies the inaccessibility of scientific knowledge and practice to all but a few of the social and intellectual elite. (p. 154)

The classroom described in this vignette shows many of the ways that teachers can meet those goals within ordinary classrooms, operating under the constraints provided by reduced funds, increased curriculum standardization, and mandates for extensive standardized testing.

At the same time, there are limits to the ways that students in the classroom depicted in the vignette participate in scientific inquiry. In his essay, "Inquiry for Diverse Student Populations: Promises and Pitfalls," Jose Rios argues that the vignette depicts a classroom that fits James Banks' second approach to multicultural education "The Additive Approach" in which "ethnic content [is integrated into] the curriculum [through] the addition of content, concepts, themes and perspectives ... without changing its basic structure, purposes, and characteristics (Banks, 2003, p. 231-32). Greene, in her essay, "Gender and Inquiry in the Classroom: Contexts and Contests," however, argues that the work of the students in the vignette is "consistent with the emerging field of feminist science studies." She quotes the volume *Frequently Asked Questions About Feminist Science Studies*, (Association of American Colleges and Universities, 1999):

Feminist science studies ... defines science in context, not as a disconnected, ethereal body of knowledge, but rather as something deeply rooted in the world itself, in all its messiness. It sees science as something that matters profoundly to men and women alike. Feminist science studies scholars look for ways to comprehend the sometimes mystifying connections between science and what an average citizen might call ordinary life. It also assumes that a thoughtful, observant person can ask a good question about science and, in the process of searching for or evaluating the answer, can, in fact, become scientifically literate. (p. 6)

Rios would probably agree with that statement but wants to go one step further and presents a story of his own to illustrate what a multicultural inquiry-based science classroom might look like. Rios describes a summer enrichment program during which a group of students, who he refers to as "the genetics group," came to their summer school experience primed to address a social issue that had directly impacted their lives and the lives of their families and friends. Motivated by a Chicago Police Department study on the relationship between fingerprint patterns and ethnicity, these students wanted to carry out their own investigation of this topic, and at the same time "learn as much as possible about a) current and historical arrest rates according to ethnicity, (b) other research projects linking a genotype or phenotype to ethnicity, (c) political backers of the study, and (d) results of previous pilot studies." (p. 138, this volume).

Rios argues that this example comes closer to illustrating Banks' third and possibly even fourth approaches to multicultural curriculum, "The Transformation Approach" and "The Social Action Approach" (Banks, 2003, pp. 233-238) than does the vignette.

Some may argue that it is unfair to compare the events in the classroom presented in the vignette with the description presented by Rios. After all, there are a number of salient differences between the two groups of students and the settings in which they work. First, the students in Rios' story were older, and came to scientific inquiry with more reading, writing, and science skills and background knowledge than the fourth and fifth graders in the vignette. Second, Rios' students were passionate about the topic they were studying before beginning to conduct scientific inquiry about it, and also had a strong sense that a social injustice was being perpetrated through the Chicago Police Department study. And finally, Rios' students were not constrained by the regular school day, school year schedule or curriculum because they were participating in a summer enrichment program.

To some degree, I would agree that this kind of comparison does not help us. In fact, it could easily lead some to say that the kind of inquiry described by Rios is: (1) impossible to replicate in ordinary public school classrooms, (2) something that can only happen if the combination of students, teachers, and issues is "right," or (3) something that only older students can do. I disagree with all three of those claims, and think that a close look at the similarities between the vignette that begins this chapter and the situation Rios describes is a good way to begin to understand how this kind of transformative inquiry can be created in everyday classrooms, for all students, and by most teachers.

In order to proceed with such an analysis, it is important to ask what about the two stories is similar? First, in both cases students were able to choose the questions that interested them, with the help of more knowledgeable, caring, others. In the summer school story students in the "genetics group" chose to investigate the possibility of a relationship between fingerprints and ethnicity, a topic that emerged from their concerns about a current issue facing their community. Other summer school students chose to investigate questions like: "Is body fat an indicator of fitness? Do male and females do [insert a behavior here] the same way? [and] Is one [insert a phenotype here] more prevalent in the population than others?" (Rios, p. 137, this volume). In the fourth or fifth grade classroom, students chose to investigate questions about their bodies, familiar foods and objects, and physical or natural features of the world around them. These two sets of questions are not all that different from one another. In both cases, students chose to investigate topics they knew and wondered about and in most cases, even the older summer school students described by Rios chose questions more like those created by the younger students. The biggest difference between the question asked by the genetics groups and those asked by the other students was that most of the high school students and the fourth and fifth graders did not connect their questions to larger social issues. I believe that with help, they could have made those connections.

With assistance and guidance from their teachers and the university students working in their classrooms it would be possible for students to expand a question like: "If paper is made from the pulp of wood, can it also be made from the pulp of oranges?" to include an investigation into the economic and environmental costs of paper use and production. Or to expand a question like: "What brand of soap smells the best?" to include an investigation into how companies market products to kids and how marketing influences students' decisions about what products to choose. Similarly, a question like "Is body fat an indicator of fitness?" raised by high school students in the summer school setting, could be expanded to include an investigation into gender and race-related conceptions of body image. Of course, these are only a few possible ways to expand student inquiry, and there is no guarantee that these larger questions will be ones that will inspire students. They would, however, give students a chance to see their questions from more than one perspective, an essential feature of Banks' transformation approach, and could lead them to "make decisions and take actions related to the concept, issue, or problem studied (Banks & Banks, with Clegg, 1999)," a key feature of Banks' Social Action Approach (Banks, 2003, p. 236).

Second is the potentially interdisciplinary nature of the investigations that students in both settings pursue. None of the questions fit easily into one discipline, one chapter of a science textbook, or require only one set of skills. Students cross disciplinary boundaries with the science they investigate, with the broader questions they address, and with the skills and habits needed to carry out, analyze and present the results of their work. Both feminist and multicultural critiques of science education as described by Rios and Greene in this section draw attention to the interdisciplinary nature of science as it is practiced in the "real" world, and to the need for teachers to help students see that science is not a subject that exists in a vacuum isolated from others. By providing students with the opportunity to investigate real problems, teachers can also help them see how those problems intersect with other typical school disciplines as well as other aspects of culture and society.

Finally, in both cases, students were required to present their work to an audience of interested others. Parents, teachers, university students and faculty and peers were all invited to attend a formal presentation of the students' work. In neither case however, did students have the chance to present their work to a larger audience, one whose decisions might be influenced by the work the students had completed. Genetics group students would have benefited, as might the Chicago Police Department, from the chance to present their work to Police Department Task Force members, or to community groups concerned about the results of the police department study. Elementary school students studying economic and environmental issues related to paper production and use might benefit from making a presentation to their school board about paper purchasing choices in the school district. These meaningful presentations are another step on the road to social action, providing opportunities for students to see their work put to use in an authentic and personally important context.

Responding to feminist and multicultural critiques of inquiry-based science requires an expanded view of what counts as inquiry. It is not sufficient for students to ask questions about scientific phenomena without also beginning to explore the ethical, cultural, and social implications of those questions. If inquiry-based science is to become transformative, teachers must take an active role in helping students develop questions that are connected to concepts and issues beyond those included in the more traditional science curriculum, or to see the ways that the questions they develop are connected to those broader concepts and issues. They must also help students see the interdisciplinary nature of the questions they choose to answer, as well as find opportunities for students to share the results of their work with a broader audience whose decisions and actions might be influenced by the work the students have done.

CONCLUSION

The authors of the chapters in this section take seriously feminist and multicultural calls for changes in our vision of what constitutes inquiry-based science instruction. They argue that, while inquiry-based science instruction addresses some of the concerns raised by critics of more traditional science pedagogy and curriculum, we must do more if we are to truly find ways to engage all students in science. If our goal is to transform science education so that all students have the opportunity to participate in school-based science, and in science beyond school, we must go beyond simple models of inquiry in the classroom. We must also find ways to create transformative inquiry-based science instruction, in which students not only learn science concepts, but also begin to explore the social implications, ethical complications, and personal meanings of the science learned in school.

Teachers play an essential role in this process. It is not easy or risk-free to help students to explore ethics, culture, or socially relevant issues in schools. Nor is it something that most teachers are prepared to do. This kind of teaching requires a broad knowledge of both science content and other disciplines. It requires time for both planning and teaching. It requires access to resources like internet connections and telephones to allow students to contact relevant others. It requires flexibility and a degree of independence from constraints of testing and standardized curriculum, though I am confident, and others have shown, that this kind of instruction prepares students to do as well or better on standardized tests than other, more traditional, forms of instruction (see Newmann, Marks, & Gamoran, 1995; and Newmann & Wehlage, 1995.) And it requires trust on the part of parents and administrators that teachers know what is best for their students.

None of these conditions is easy to come by, but if teachers, administrators and teacher-educators do not work to make them the norm rather than the exception in schools, we are not likely to find ways to help all students actively participate in and learn science. If we do not recognize that scientific knowledge is used by many people in their everyday lives at home and at work, and if we do not help students understand that the kind of knowledge and ways of knowing that science represent are useful to them, we will not have changed anything.

REFERENCES

Aikenhead, G., & Jegede, O. (1999). Cross-cultural science education: A cognitive explanation of a cultural phenomenon. *Journal of Research in Science Teaching*, *36*, 269-287.

American Association of University Women. (1999). *Gender gaps: Where schools still fail our children.* New York: Marlowe.

American Association for the Advancement of Science. (1989). *Project 2061: Science for all Americans.* New York: Oxford Press.

American Association for the Advancement of Science. (1993). *Benchmarks in scientific literacy.* New York: Oxford Press.

American Association of University Women. (2002). *Course-taking patterns. The Jossey-Bass Reader on gender in education.* San Francisco: Jossey-Bass.

Arellano, E. L., Barcenal, T., Bilbao, P. P., Castellano, M. A., Nichols, S., & Tippins, D. J. (2001). Case-based pedagogy as a context for collaborative inquiry in the Philippines. *Journal of Research in Science Teaching, 38*(5), 502-528.

Association of American Colleges and Universities. (1999). *Frequently asked questions about feminist science studies.* Washington, DC: Author.

Banks, J. A. (1994). *An introduction to multicultural education.* Boston: Allyn & Bacon.

Banks, J. A. (2003). Approaches to multicultural education reform. In J. A. Banks & C. A. McGee Banks (Eds.), *Multicultural education: Issues and perspectives* (4th ed., pp. 225-246). New York: Wiley.

Banks, J. A., & Banks, C. A. M., with Clegg, A. A., Jr. (1999). *Teaching strategies for the social studies* (5th ed.). New York: Longman.

Barba, R. (1998). *Science in the multicultural classroom* (2nd ed.). Needham Heights, MA: Allyn & Bacon.

Barton, A. C. (1998). Reframing science for all through the politics of poverty. *Educational Policy, 12,* 525-541.

Barton, A. C. (2003). *Teaching science for social justice.* New York: Teachers College Press.

Berry, A., Mulhall, P., Loughran, J. J., & Gunstone, R. F. (1999). Helping students learn from laboratory work. *Australian Science Teachers' Journal, 45*(1), 27-31.

Bleier, R. (Ed.). (1988). *Feminist approaches to science.* New York: Pergamon Press.

Brown, B. (2004). Discursive identity: Assimilation into the culture of science and its implications for minority students. *Journal of Research in Science Teaching, 41,* 810-834.

Brown, B. (2006). "It isn't no slang than can be said about this stuff": Language, identity, and appropriating science discourse. *Journal of Research in Science Teaching, 43,* 96-126.

Chinn, C., & Malhotra, B. (2002). Epistemologically authentic inquiry in schools: A theoretical framework for evaluating inquiry tasks. *Science Education, 86,* 175–218.

Cochran-Smith, M. (1995). Color-blindness and basket making are not the answers: Confronting the dilemmas of race, culture, and language diversity in teacher education. *American Education Research Journal, 32,* 493-522.

Crawford, B. A. (2000). Embracing the essence of inquiry: New roles for science teachers. *Journal of Research in Science Teaching, 37*(9), 916-937.

Dickinson, V. L., & Young, T. (1998). Elementary science and language arts: Should we blur the boundaries? *School Science & Mathematics, 98*(6), 334-339.

Edmondson, K. M., & Novak, J. D. (1993). The interplay of scientific epistemological views, learning strategies, and attitudes of college students. *Journal of Research in Science Teaching, 30*(6), 547-559.

Eisenhart, M., & Finkel, E., with Behm, L., Lawrence, N., & Tonso, K. (1998). *Women's science: Learning and succeeding from the margins.* Chicago: University of Chicago Press.

Eisenhart, M., Finkel, E., & Marion, S. F. (1996). Creating the conditions for scientific literacy: A re-examination. *American Educational Research Journal, 33,* 261-295.

Exploratorium. (1998). *Inquiry descriptions*. Retrieved January 1, 2006, from http://www.exploratorium.com/IFI/resources/inquirydesc.html

Fusco, D. (2001). Creating relevant science through urban planning and gardening. *Journal of Research in Science Teaching, 38*, 860-877.

Gilbert, A., & Yerrick, R. (2001). Same school, separate worlds: A sociocultural study of identity, resistance, and negotiation in a rural, lower track science classroom. *Journal of Research in Science Teaching, 38*, 574-598.

Hart, C., Mulhall, P., Berry, A., Loughran, J., & Gunstone, R. (2000). What is the purpose of this experiment? Or can students learn something from doing experiments? *Journal of Research in Science Teaching, 37*(7), 655-675.

Harding, S. (1998). *Is science multicultural? Postcolonialisms, feminisms, and epistemologies*. Bloomington: Indiana University Press.

Hewson, P. W., Kahle, J. B., Scantlebury, K., & Davis, D. (2001). Equitable science education in urban middle schools: Do reform efforts make a difference? *Journal of Research in Science Teaching, 38*, 1130-1144.

Howard, G. R. (1999). *We can't teach what we don't know*. New York: Teachers College.

Howes, E. (2001). Visions of "science for all" in the elementary classroom. In A. C. Barton & M. D. Osborne (Eds.), *Teaching science in diverse settings: Marginalized discourses and classroom practice* (pp. 129-159). New York: Peter Lang.

Huffman, D., Thomas, K., & Lawrenz, F. (2003). Relationship between professional development, teachers' instructional practices, and the achievement of students in science and mathematics. *School Science and Mathematics, 103*, 378-387.

Irvine, A. D. (2001). Russell on indoctrination. *Inquiry: Critical Thinking Across the Disciplines, 20*, 20-26.

Jegede, O. J., & Okebukola, P. A. (1992). Differences in socio-cultural environment perceptions associated with gender in science classrooms. *Journal of Research in Science Teaching, 29*, 637-647.

Kahle, J. B., Meece, J., & Scantlebury, K. (2000). Urban African-American middle school science students: Does standards-based teaching make a difference? *Journal of Research in Science Teaching, 37*, 1019-1041.

Keller, E. F. (1983). *A feeling for the organism: The life and work of Barbara McClintock*. New York: Freeman.

Keller, E. F. (1985). *Reflections on gender and science*. New Haven, CT: Yale University Press.

Lee, O. (1997). Scientific literacy for all: What is it, and how can we achieve it? *Journal of Research in Science Teaching, 34*, 219-222.

Lee, O. (2002). Promoting scientific literacy with elementary students from diverse cultures and languages. In W. Secada (Ed.), *Review of Research Education* (pp. 23-69). Washington, DC: American Educational Research Association.

Lee, O. (2003). Equity for linguistically and culturally diverse students in science education: A research agenda. *Teachers College Record, 105*, 465-489.

Lee, O. (2004). Teacher change in beliefs and practices in science and literacy instruction with English language learners. *Journal of Research in Science Teaching, 41*, 65-93.

Lee, O., & Fradd, S. H. (1998). Science for all, including students from non-English-language backgrounds. *Researcher, 27*, 12-21.

Lee, O., Fradd, S. H., & Sutman, F. X. (1995). Science knowledge and cognitive strategy use among culturally and linguistically diverse students. *Journal of Research in Science Teaching, 32*, 797-816.

Lehrer, R., Carpenter, S., Schauble, L., & Putz, A. (2000). Designing classrooms that support inquiry. In J. Minstrell & E. van Zee (Eds.), *Teaching science in the inquiry-based classroom* (pp. 80-99). Washington, DC: American Association for the Advancement of Science.

Lemke, J. L. (2001). Articulating communities: Sociocultural perspectives on science education. *Journal of Research in Science Teaching, 38*(3), 296-316.

Loucks-Horsley, C., & Matsumoto, C. (1999). Research on professional development for teachers of mathematics and science: The state of the scene. *School Science and Mathematics, 99*, 258-271.

Martin, B., & Brouwer, W. (1993). Exploring personal science. *Science Education, 77*(4), 441-459.

McKinley, E., Waiti, P. M., & Bell, B. (1992). Language, culture and science education. *International Journal of Science Education, 14*(5), 579-595.

Minstrell, J., & van Zee, E. (Eds.). (2000). *Teaching science in the inquiry-based classroom*. Washington, DC: American Association for the Advancement of Science.

Moss, D. M. Abrams, E. D., & Robb, J. (2001). Describing student conceptions of the nature of science over an entire school year. *International Journal of Science Education, 23*(8), 771-790.

Moss, D. M., Abrams, E. D., & Robb-Kull, J. (1998). Can we be scientists too? Secondary students' perceptions of scientific research from a project-based classroom. *Journal of Science Education and Technology, 7*(2), 149-161.

Namenwirth, M. (1988). Science seen through a feminist prism. In R. Bleier (Ed.), *Feminist approaches to science* (pp. 18-41). New York: Pergamon Press.

National Research Council. (1996). *National Science Education Standards*. Washington, DC: National Academy Press.

National Science Teachers Association. (1988). *Scope, sequence and coordination of secondary school science* (Vol. 1). Washington DC: Author.

Newmann, F. M., Marks, H. M., & Gamoran, A. (1995). *Authentic pedagogy and student performance. Research report from the Center on Organization and Restructuring of Schools*. Madison: University of Wisconsin.

Newmann, F. M., & Wehlage, G. G. (1995). *Successful school restructuring: A report to the public and educators by the Center on Organization and Restructuring of Schools*. Madison, WI: University of Wisconsin, Madison, Center on Organization and Restructuring of Schools.

Peterson, N., & Jungck, J. R., (1988, March/April,). Problem-posing, Problem-solving and Persuasion in Biology Education. *Academic Computing*, 14-17 & 48-50.

Rodriguez, A. (1997). The dangerous discourse of invisibility. *Journal of Research in Science Teaching, 34*, 19-38.

Rodriguez, A. (1998). Strategies for counterresistance: Toward sociotransformative constructivism and learning to teach science for diversity and understanding. *Journal of Research in Science Teaching, 35*, 589-622.

Roth, W.-M., & Barton, A. C. (2004). *Rethinking scientific literacy*. New York: Routledge Falmer.

Reiss, M. J. (1993). *Science education for a pluralist society*. Buckingham, England: Open University Press.

Rosebery, A. (2004, May). *Some thoughts about culture and the preparation of science teachers for urban classrooms*. Wingspread conference on Urban Science Education. Racine, Wisconsin.

Sadker, M., & Sadker, D. (1994). *Failing at fairness: How our schools cheat girls*. New York: Touchstone.

Schwab, J. J. (1962). *The teaching of science as enquiry*. Cambridge, MA: Harvard University Press.

Seiler, G. (2001). Reversing the "Standard" direction: Science emerging from the lives of African American students. *Journal of Research in Science Teaching, 38*, 1000-1014.

Shymansky, J. A., Yore, L. D., & Anderson, J. O. (2004). Impact of a school district's science reform effort on the achievement and attitudes of third- and fourth-grade students. *Journal of Research in Science Teaching, 41*, 771-790.

Stanley, W. B., & Brickhouse, N. W. (2001). Teaching sciences: The multicultural question revisited. *Science Education, 85*, 35-49.

Sleeter, G., & Grant, C. (1994). *Making choices for multicultural education: Five approaches to race, class, and gender*. Englewood Cliffs, NJ: Merrill.

Solano-Flores, G., & Nelson-Barber, S. (2001). On the cultural validity of science assessments. Journal of Research in Science Teaching, *38*(5), 553-573.

Stanley, W. B., & Brickhouse, N. W. (2001). Teaching Sciences: The Multicultural Question Revisited. *Science Education, 85*, 35-49.

Valian, V. (1999). *Why so slow? The advancement of women*. Cambridge, MA: The MIT Press.

Von Secker, C. E., & Lissitz, R. W. (1999). Estimating the impact of instructional practices on student achievement in science. *Journal of Research in Science Teaching, 36*, 1110-1126.

Warren, B., Ballenger, C., Ogonowski, M., Rosebery, A. S., & Hudicourt-Barnes, J. (2001). Rethinking diversity in learning science: The logic of everyday sense-making. *Journal of Research in Science Teaching 38*(5), 529-552.

Wallace, C. & Kang N.-H. (2004). An investigation of experienced secondary science teachers' beliefs about inquiry: An esamination of competing beliefs sets. *Journal of Research in Science Teaching, 41*(9), 936-960.

SECTION IV

STANDARDIZED TESTS AND INQUIRY: HOW THE ACCOUNTABILITY MOVEMENT ACTS TO PREVENT CHANGES IN SCIENCE CLASSROOMS

Sherry A. Southerland, Eleanor Abrams, and Todd Hutner

EDITORS' NOTE

Describing Section IV's Use of
Inquiry in the Classroom

Section IV, with its analysis of the interaction of the accountability movement and adoption of classroom inquiry, is largely focused on the educational goals of classroom inquiry. We see a close analysis of instructional goals, while Section IV is largely mute as to the manner in which classroom inquiry is to be enacted.

The essays in Section IV suggest that the assessments overwhelmingly emphasize scientific content knowledge, although we must recognize to a lesser extent more current standardized test are beginning to measure knowledge derived from learning about inquiry as well. To the minimal extent that these assessments require students to analyze data or make assertions of data, then they can measure knowledge and skills constructed from learning to inquire. Thus, Eleanor argues, if teachers understand their role to be the preparation of their students for standardized testing, then the goals of their classroom inquiry should support such preparation.

The essay by Sherry Southerland and Todd Hutner suggests that science educators have been so ineffective in influencing policy, particularly as it relates to assessment because we have been muddled in our own

Inquiry in the Classroom: Realities and Opportunities, pp. 143–168
Copyright © 2008 by Information Age Publishing

goals, as they examine the many ways "scientific literacy" has been defined and discussed. While they urge us to adopt a more uniform and explicit emphasis on the democratic equality goal of science education—on that would emphasize scientific content knowledge, knowledge of inquiry, and knowledge about inquiry—as students use these knowledge to make sense of their world and to make informed personal decisions. It follows, therefore, classroom inquiry as a part of a broader teaching repertoire would have a similar range of goals.

VIGNETTE

Three teachers look at each other politely as they pour their coffee. Each of these teachers comes from a different middle school in the district, and each is the "lead" science teacher at their school. Two of the women know each other from a district science teachers' organization, but the third, a man, is less well known to these women. These three middle school teachers have been "invited" by their district science coordinator to review a set of science kits for possible adoption by the district the following year. Each of these three teachers viewed the invitation with a mixture of interest and disdain. The interest stemmed from each of them had used similar kits in their university methods courses and two of them even in their early years of teaching; each remembered these experiences fondly. Part of the disdain came from the timing of the "request," the last full planning day of school. The other part of the disdain came from the different teachers' view of inquiry in their curriculum, as will be evidenced during their day working together.

As is the case with most new groups, at first the talk is somewhat formal and stilted as they group begins their assignment. It is only as the coffee and doughnuts kick in and they gain some comfort with one another that the three teachers begin to "speak their minds." At first they decide to each look over a separate module in the series, but a soon a flurry of comments such as "come over here and look at this" changes the three separate teachers into a trio pouring over a single module.

The one they somehow settle on for a joint analysis is a module on devoted to teaching students how models are developed in science, what the role of models are in science, and what the characteristics of models are. At first glance, it is an unassuming assortment of materials (i.e., black boxes taped shut filled with some sort of material that makes a sound as the box is moved, worksheets, overheads). After a while the talk over this module becomes so loud it can be heard from the hallway:

Margaret: *Oh, I remember doing this one or somethin' like it, years ago. You give these boxes to the kids, and get them to design what the interior of the box looks like based on the "data" they collect by listening. Oh, that was really...*

Karen: (jumps in) fun, yeah, I remember doing this in my methods class, it was fun to argue about what you thought the inside of the box looked like.

Margaret: Yes, fun, that's part of it. But I remember it was this really cool activity to get the notion of models. To help them understand what a model is and what it isn't—that a scientific model isn't some sort of exact replica of the thing its modeling. Oh yeah.... (she drifts off).

Mathew: Yes, I've done something much like this. But I've used a demonstration with a tube going into a box filled with water, and it is up to the students to figure out, based on patterns of water movement when they blow into the tube, what the inside of the box is like. Both these activities work on the same principle, but my version is better. Because I do it as a whole class, with the students telling me what to do, and we put our interpretations on the board, so I know what they are finding out. This module does have a neat idea, but I think there are better ways to teach the same concept. Ways that are much easier to pull off in a room with too many kids already. I mean, who wants to pass out 15 of the boxes and pair of their kids, or worse, pass out 30 boxes, and listen to all those marbles slamming around inside? I mean, that's just mayhem. That's just a recipe for disaster, at least in my classroom, in my school.

By this point in the discussion, Matthew has raised his voice, and Margaret sizes him up with one eyebrow raised. Karen senses the tenseness and works quickly to try to "smooth" over the turbulence.

Karen: Yeah, Matt, I see what you mean. If you could somehow do the same activity, but as a whole class, yeah, that would be as good, and sure it would be easier. Oh, I'd love to get a description of that water-tube contraption, maybe I'll use that next year with my honors class.

Margaret: (Shaking her head yes slowly, but looking directly at Mathew) Yes, I see how your way would be easier, in terms of management and materials and such. But too many of my students "tune out" when we do a whole group discussion of something, so that 4 or 6 of them really get into what we are trying to figure out, but who knows about the rest?

Matthew: Isn't that always the case though? A teacher really only has the attention of a few of their students, at least in a general science class. The rest really don't care.

Karen: (jumping in) I know, that's why I try to do fun things so I can grab the attention of more of them. But afterwards we get to real work, *the definitions, the formulas. But unless those activities are really wild and fun, yes you're right, I have the attention of just a handful of my students.*

Margaret: *(looking puzzled) I think I'm lost, or missing something. (pause) This module is designed to help students learn about models, and it is trying to do it through maybe a low level of inquiry—maybe low level 2. I mean the teacher or the kit has pretty much laid out the question, but it is up to the students to determine how they will answer it, and it is up to the students to come up with the answer. So, a low level two inquiry (she says pursing her lips), 'cause the box itself pretty much limits how the students can do the investigation.*

As Margaret is talking, Matthew has gone back to looking at the materials in the box, leaving only Karen closely attending to Margaret's comments. The room is quiet for a long two minutes, then Matthew speaks still with is eyes focused on the materials in the box.

Matthew: *Well that's just fine and good Margaret, and maybe in your school you have time and energy to think about "levels of inquiry." But my kids are not the "high performers" yours are, and everyone knows it. What I need are things to teach my kids enough science to pass that test at the end of the year. And while these kits are cute and "fun", and your ideas come straight out of the Science Teacher, I work in the real world. Where I've got too much science content to cover to spend a period passing out materials and letting my kids get lost THEN trying to bring them back together. I mean in that same period where you would have my kids spread from here to kingdom come, shaking a box with marbles, I could define models, show them examples of different scientific models, give them something to read, 'cause God knows we've got to teach reading in science class now, and THEN give them a writing assignment. I mean, come on. This is the real world and my principle is constantly breathing down my departments' neck to get the scores up, reading scores, math scores and NOW science scores. I don't even know why the district is wasting our time here. What teacher in this district has time for this fluff?*

Matthew is clearly upset and moves quickly and deliberately away from the table and the kits to look out the window. Again the room is silent for what feels like a long period of time. Karen, ever the hostess, jumps in quietly.

Karen: *Well, I do feel like this kind of teaching has a place. Inquiry I mean. Doing things. Letting kids see the fun of science. There still*

has to be room for that, or what are we? Just people who assign
things out of the book? Who just read off the test questions for the
day? No, I want to teach science. So, in those windows of time after
we've covered what we need to cover or when the kids aren't ready
to do more reading or more worksheets, then I think these kits will
be great. Really, they will help up remember that science can be fun.

Margaret: *(Sounding as frustrated as Matthew did earlier) Isn't it more than*
that? (Shaking her head.) I know I have a pretty cushy situation,
and I know that my kids tend to score well on the state tests so I
don't have the same pressures you do Matthew. But part of the rea-
son, and I know it is just part, is that we teach them well. We use
inquiry in my school because I think that is the best way for them to
learn and remember science content. Because through inquiry they
will begin to understand how science is done and how to make
judgments based on evidence. Yes, you could define a model for
them and show them some models, but will they understand what
models are? Will they understand what a model is supposed to do
and not supposed to do? Will they be able to apply that knowledge
next time you get to a model in your teaching? Yes, inquiry can be
fun and yes it takes time, but most importantly this approach of
having the kids come to the answer with our support, that helps
them understand and remember the science we're supposed to be
teaching.

Matthew: *(sharply) And who has time for that?*

Margaret: *Those who make time. (pause). Look, I'm not saying to throw out*
the book and yes we have to help the students pass those darn tests.
But isn't our job also about teaching them science, teaching them
ideas, skills, ways of thinking they can use everyday? So, for me the
big ideas, the hard ideas, the things we need to use over and over in
my discipline, those are the ideas I teach through inquiry. That way
I don't have to teach them over and over and maybe, just maybe,
the kids will remember them even after they walk out of my class-
room.

Again there is a long pause in the conversation. The two women continue to
look through the kits but in a lackluster way. Matthew continues to stare out the
window.

Matthew: *Well, we just won't come to an agreement on this now. Let's just*
get through these things so I can get back to packing up my
classroom.

INTRODUCTION

Sherry Southerland

In some ways the now-common requirements of standardized assessment represents some of the most contentious issues in the discussion of inquiry, and in this chapter we will explore some of the areas of controversy, contradiction, and contention as we consider the role standardized assessments play as barriers to classroom-based inquiry. But before we begin this analysis, we must recognize that assessments can and do shape the nature of student learning. Not only can assessments be summative—serving as a description of what a student has learned, they are also formative—serving to shape (whether deliberately or not) the nature of the learning students engage in (Black & William, 1998). Most of the attention of parents, administrators and policymakers is on summative assessments ("How well are 12th grade students scoring on science assessments? Or "What is my child's grade in science"), and we know that what a teacher focuses on in assessment tells students, implicitly or explicitly, what is valued in that classroom. Students think "If my teacher says that "big ideas" are important but she only tests on the glossary terms in the back of my book, then I'm going to learn the glossary terms in the back of my book." So, assessments serve both a summative and formative role, and that dual role MUST be recognized as we consider them. It is important to recognize that assessment can and should be an important part of inquiry in the classroom. As discussed in the introduction, science education has move past traditional Piagetian notions in which learners were thought to come to a science understanding through the manipulation of materials ("learning by doing"). Instead, as mentioned throughout this volume, particularly in Section 1 and Section II, more current ideas about learning suggest that science understandings are largely constructed during the "talk" about what student have done, a Vygotskian emphasis on the role of social negotiation in the construction of meaning. Thus, it is through composing an explanation of a science activity and arguing about that explanation that students come to an understanding of the activity. Likewise, assessments shape what is learned and many argue that assessment is a fundamentally important aspect of teaching and learning (Gallagher, 2006).

So, what accounts for the uneasy relationship between classroom based inquiry and standardized assessments? It is not as though the inquiry movement has ignored the role of assessments. Indeed, the National Science Education Standards (National Research Council [NRC], 1996) lays out the content of science they understand to be central to scientific literacy, the pedagogy which should be central to teaching this content (classroom-inquiry), and the central role of assessment in this process of teaching and learning. The Standards suggest that reform based science teaching requires attention to each of these three facets—content, pedagogy, and assessment, and the authors describe that the use of only the content of the standards while ignoring the pedagogical and assessment aspects of the standards serves to defeat the entire purpose of reform. To support teachers in their adoption of classroom-based inquiries, the NRC developed a book focusing on the role of assessment in shaping student learning, Classroom assessments and the National Science Education Standards (NRC, 2001). The focus of this text is to describe the optimal use of formative assessments, ways in which teachers can better understand what a learner knows so that they can better craft instruction—optimally allowing for increased student growth and understanding of science.

That notion of the role of assessment in shaping student learning is very distinct from the idea of summative, standardized assessments. As the NRC (2001) describes and every teacher and child in the U.S. educational system knows all too well, as a direct result of No Child Left Behind legislation that had its origins in the Nation at Risk report (National Commission on Excellence in Education [NCEE], 1983), the United States is engaged in the use of standardized, statewide, summative assessments. The goal of these assessments is to rank schools, make decisions about funding patterns for those schools, and often influence teacher salaries, and students' scores on the science version of these assessments have recently begun to be factored into these decisions. In many states in the United States, those same statewide assessments are used as a deciding factor in student promotion.

The primary goal of these summative, statewide, standardized assessments is not intended to directly shape student learning, but as a means of accountability for school districts and administrators and teachers that work within those districts. Through the system of rewards and incentives, schools whose children score well and show continued growth on these measures are rewarded, so presumably the nature of the teaching in those schools will continue to improve. Schools whose children fail to do well or to show adequate progress in their learning will lose funding, and this presumably serves as a strong message to change or improve the quality of teaching and learning, so that children in those schools will show improvement on those measures.

If one steps away from the context of schools and children and examinations, the accountability movement does seem to present an opportunity to shape instruction, for the assessments serve not only a summative function but also a formative function for teaching. Although the literature is scant in this regard, there is more and more anecdotal and research based evidence to suggest that teachers are indeed shaping their instruction in response to their students' achievement on these standardized measures, that is teaching to the test—and the test in question is their state's standardized assessment (Hamilton, Stecher, & Klein, 2002; Settlage & Meadows, 2002; Whitford & Jones, 2000). A common assumption is that teaching involving high stakes leads teachers to abandon practices that address students' varying learning needs in favor of those practices that ensure high scores (Delandshere, 2002; Herman, 1992; Gordon & Reese, 1997; Sacks, 1999; Stiggins, 2004). Because of the of nature of the accountability measures, teachers hesitate to adopt teaching practices that focus on student understanding—instead they tend toward practices that they perceive as being the most successful in covering the wide range of material students will be assessed upon (Shaver, Cuevas, Lee, & Avalos, 2007). So, statewide assessment and classroom based science-inquiries are often seen as having contradictory, mutually exclusive goals, as reflected in our dueling teachers in the vignette that opened this section and as experienced by the many reform-minded teachers who spend time trying to convince their administrators of the efficacy of inquiry approaches.

How we do find ourselves in this position? And more importantly, how can we resolve this dilemma in ways that will allow for better student understanding of science? That is the focus of this section. For this discussion, we recognize that any reform of teaching, and particularly science teaching, is a very difficult, long-term process that requires both structural changes in the system and personal changes in the knowledge and beliefs of teachers, administrators, and policymakers that work within and influence that system (Brooks, 2005; Gess-Newsome, Southerland, Johnston, & Woodbury, 2003; Tyack & Cuban, 1997). The first essay in this section will focus primarily on some of the structural changes required, and the second will focus primarily on the personal changes required.

ASSESSING STUDENT UNDERSTANDING IN
AN INQUIRY-BASED LEARNING ENVIRONMENT

Eleanor Abrams

The reason many teachers become teachers is the desire to help their students to become successful learners excited by their content. As little children, these future teachers can be found playing school with other friends, siblings, or if there are no willing humans, stuffed animals sufficed. As these children are pretending to be the teacher, they are lecturing to their class, reading a book to their students, or even sternly reprimanding their stuffed animal students to pay attention. In my years of observing children pretending to run a classroom, I have never once seen these budding teachers pretend to administer a state-mandated test. Of course, that may change in a few years as our conception of what a teacher is supposed to do changes and these students become the kind of teacher they observe. As teachers of science in this age of testing and accountability, sadly we have moved far away from our dream of helping students become excited about learning science.

The pressures on grown up science teachers are at all time high. Education is being used as a political issue to win campaign elections. And why not? What parents do not want the best education possible for their children? It is also not surprising that education is a major issue on most of the political campaign trails. Education has been swept up in the accountability movement that started in the 1990s with the citizens finding out the Army was paying $100 for a toilet seat. As people became disenchanted with how the government was spending their tax dollars, they demanded an accounting of how the money was spent. This idea quickly spread to education. Parents wanted to see that their children were receiving a quality education for their tax dollars and they had their doubts. The widely publicized Trends in Mathematics and Science Study (TIMSS) (National Center for Education Statistics, 1999) showed U.S. students lacking in science and mathematics when compared to other developed countries in the world.

Blue ribbon panels studied the countries that were succeeding in teaching their students mathematics and science and found that many of those countries had a national curriculum or national standards to guide the teachers in deciding which concepts and skill to teach. Many of those countries also had a high stakes national test for the students.

In response two national science organizations developed a set of national standards. *Benchmarks for Science Literacy: Project 2061* (American Association for the Advancement of Science, 1993) and the *National Science Education Standards* (National Research Council [NRC], 1996), both espoused similar guidelines about what should be taught to students. Many states followed suit and developed their own state guidelines for what science needed to be taught to their students in their state. However, there was a need to guarantee that teachers were held accountable for teaching to the standards.

States vary greatly in how they assess students understanding of the science standards. The No Child Left Behind Act mandates testing for science beginning in the year this text is published, 2007. However, even before this requirements, many states did test students' comprehension in science through tests, mostly in multiple choice formats. And, many states are beginning to tie student performance to funding for the school. If sufficient progress is not made in student performance on these tests, then the control of the school could be relinquished to the state. It is not uncommon for states to tie minimal scores to being able to graduate to the next grade or to high school graduation.

Within this climate of strict accountability through high stake testing, how does a teacher try to meet the teach science through inquiry? Let us look at the positive aspects of this climate from veteran science teachers. Research has found that teachers think that the science standards to be useful guides in helping them prioritize what to teach during the year (Clark, Shore, Rhoades, Abrams, Miao, & Li, 2003; Shaver, Cuevas, Lee, & Avalos, in press). In addition, the national standards and most of the state standards emphasize the need to teach about inquiry through inquiry-based methods. However, teachers overwhelmingly express concerns about the negative impact of test preparation has on science instruction (Saka, 2007; Shaver et al., 2006). They feel that the tests do not adequately show what a student has learned about science over the entire year. State assessments are expensive to administer and multiple choice test items tend to be the least expensive formats to grade. However, inquiry skills and knowledge about inquiry are often difficult to assess through multiple-choice formats, so inquiry is de-emphasized in most state assessments. In addition, one yearly assessment does not take into account the teachers' more thorough assessments of the students' understanding of science. So how does a teacher remain committed to teaching inquiry-based science and not become constrained to teaching to the test?

There are no easy answers for that very important question except to refer back to the vignette that started this section on assessment. Margaret was trying to make the point if we teach our students well then they will do well on the state assessments. She feels that inquiry is the best way from her students to learn and remember science content. Her philosophy is a sound one, from a science teacher educator's point of view. Margaret does not worry about the test; she worries about teaching her students science. However, she does have the support of the school. Matthew comes from a school were test scores are the measure of success but he feels unsure, like many teachers, how to guarantee his students will be successful based on that one measure (Kauffman, Johnson, Kardos, Liu, & Peske, 2002).

Margaret's school philosophy is echoed in the Coalition of Essential Schools, a model of schooling in which students engage in in-depth and rigorous learning. They expect all students to learn a small number of core skills and areas of knowledge. The Coalition of Essential Schools has found that setting high standards while personalizing instruction results in increased student achievement on a variety of measures including state assessments (CESNationalweb). If teachers can focus on teaching their students well rather fearing their students will not succeed on one assessment, teachers still have quite a bit of freedom to teach the way they want to teach and to create assessments they know will help students monitor their learning and assist science teachers in preparing science lessons designed to meet the changing needs of their learners.

I will outline four driving principles when thinking about creating effective assessments for students immersed in inquiry-based learning. When constructing assessments, it is important to keep in mind the following consideration: having a clear idea of what you hope your students will learn or be able to do; knowing your reasons for assessing your students; designing the assessment to reflect the way the students learned; and determine who is doing the assessing. Since assessments determine how effective the lessons are in supporting student learning and are a measure of how well the students are progressing, the need for effective assessments are paramount to determining if you are teaching your students well.

ASSESS WHAT YOU WANT YOUR STUDENTS TO LEARN

The first driving principle for assessment construction is no matter how you assess, you need to assess what you want your students to learn. This is a simple premise but it is difficult to put into practice. As you remember from the introductory chapter of this book, inquiry has many acceptable definitions. Some of the authors' definitions described inquiry as a way to teach and some researchers defined it as something to learn. A teacher needs to know if it is important to assess the students' content knowledge, process skills, or knowledge of the process.

However, research shows that assessments often do not match the teacher's goals or the main emphasis of the lesson (Yinger, 1980). Often assessing content is easier than assessing how students are doing inquiry. It is difficult for teachers to develop common criteria for achievement on open-ended inquiry tasks across students, unless the criteria becomes so generalized and disconnected from the content and the context of the activity as to fit all students (University of Illinois, Inquiry Group). However if you are clear with your students on what you want them to learn, there are multiple opportunities to gather information on student learning. You can observe, your students can create and reflect, and everyone can discuss. Inquiry leads learners in different directions and learning can seem fragmented but that doesn't mean learning has not occurred.

Hein and Lee (2000) in their book about science inquiry offer two criteria by which to judge whether an assessment would be useful to evaluate student learning in an inquiry learning context. First, does it address how well students are able to carry out physical processes, such as measurement, observation, experimental design, problem solving to name a few. This measures how well students "do" science. Second, the level does it address the level of students' thinking and reasoning skills? A teacher could look at students' ability to draw evidence-based conclusions or evaluate the students' knowledge of science concepts. NRC (2000) has similar criteria called learning outcomes and adds a third learning outcome that states that teachers need to assess students' understandings about inquiry (the process of science knowledge construction). Depending upon your objectives for that lesson, you could assess one of those learning outcomes or a combination of them.

Another consideration in your planning is how deep you want your students to learn the learning outcomes. NRC (1996) asks educators to consider the three learning outcomes of inquiry-based education in the light of knowledge and understanding. They define these two terms in their book as:

> Scientific knowledge refers to facts, concepts, principles, laws, theories, and models.... Understanding science requires that an individual integrate a complex structure of many types of knowledge, including the ideas of science, relationships between ideas, reasons for these relationships, ways to use the ideas to explain and predict other natural phenomena, and ways to apply them to many events. Understanding encompasses the ability to use knowledge, and it entails the ability to distinguish between what is and what is not a scientific idea. (p. 23)

On a more superficial level, students will be able to show their knowledge of: the process of doing science; science facts, principles, laws, theories, and models; and the process of how knowledge is constructed through inquiry. However, students with a more sophisticated understanding will be able to use and apply that knowledge.

Teachers have to consider realistically the breadth of the knowledge to be learned and the depth the knowledge that would be understood in the scope of their lesson. This goal seems to be beyond the time that most teachers have in their school day while paying attention to preparing the students for the standardized testing they will experience. However, without the proper planning, many teachers, like Matthew in the vignette, rely on more traditional forms of lessons and assessments.

Assess the Reason You Are Assessing Your Students

The second driving principle in the construction of assessment is to consider the reason you are assessing the students. There is increasing emphasis on assessment by administrators and politicians as a way to determine what students have learned and to ultimately determine the quality of education received by those students. This reason has overshadowed teachers' other reasons for assessment.

Here is a case in point. My fourth grade son was subjected to two national and two state assessments this year. These assessments spanned over 6 weeks of the school year, greatly diminishing the teacher's ability to teach her students. I asked several of the fourth grade teachers what they expected to learn from the assessments and heard a common reply. The teachers stated that the information garnered from the assessments will not benefit their classes because they will not receive the results of these assessments until this school year is almost over. I asked if they thought the information would be helpful in modifying their instruction for the next year. They replied, only moderately, because the classes of students varied so greatly in their abilities and knowledge, that they found application of patterns from one year only marginally helpful in modifying their instruction the following year. They did recognize that the assessments captured content that was consistently omitted by all teachers in that school.

Summative assessments or tests designed for the purpose of making final judgments about student achievement and instructional effectiveness is an admirable goal, if done with restraint and moderation. By the time summative assessment occurs, students have typically exited the learning context. While large scale summative assessments such as state or national testing can make a difference in instructional practice, it does not influence the teachers as much as the summative assessments administer to their students, because they see the outcome of these assessments immediately.

Summative assessment has overshadowed two other reason teachers want to assess their students. Two other kinds of assessments are diagnostic assessments and formative assessments. Diagnostic assessments are used to gather information about what students already know about a particular science concept and are able to do prior to instruction. They are often overlooked in a busy school day but can provide a method for teachers to plan their lessons based upon existing student knowledge. Examples of diagnostic assessments include graphic organizers, journal entries, and pretests. These can be very effective in determining how ready students are to engage in inquiry-based instruction.

Formative assessments occur throughout the learning task. Teachers use them to determine what their students are learning so they can tailor their instruction to better meet the needs of their students. These assessments can inform the students how well they are learning so hopefully the students can make needed corrections in their learning strategies and become more successful in science. Popular examples of formative assessments are conferences, observations, quizzes, and journals.

Create Assessments That Reflect the Way the Students Have Learned

There is a third driving principal to keep in mind when creating assessments is to design assessments that reflect the way a student has learned. Because inquiry learning is contextualized, much of the assessment method should be authentic. The task of the student should related and relevant to their learning experiences and ideally embedded with in the curriculum.

There are a variety of types of constructed response tasks that have the benefit of allowing the learning the opportunity to show what they students know while learning about a topic of interest to learners. Some examples include portfolios, presentations, performance tasks, demonstrations, and interviews. One of the limitations of such assessments is that they are not necessarily reliable when analyzed using traditional psychometric approaches (reliability and validity). In contrast, tests of intelligence, aptitude and achievement, which typically employ standardized multiple-choice test, can fare well with these approaches, while more non-traditional, contextualized assessments often fare more poorly, Because of their misfit with traditional pyschometrics such assessments are often seen as less useful for gauging student understanding on a large scale.

Contextualized assessments are designed to reveal what students have actually learned through their learning experiences. They allow the students to demonstrate and reflect on their complex knowledge and skills. A personalized approach to assessing student achievement better aligns with constructivist learning principles. It assumes that everyone can understand the same things in different ways; respond to assessments in different ways, and think at their own rate. Therefore useful contextualized assessments should have personalized content and to allow students to perform in ways that will allow them the best change to show what they know.

Keep in Mind Who is Doing the Assessing

The fourth principle to keep in mind is who is doing the assessment. Students feel that teachers determine what is assessed and how it is assessed. Teachers feel that administrators determine those factors. Administrators feel politicians are the arbiter of those decisions. I am sure the politicians would say they are simply responding to taxpayers' demands for high quality education for the children. Everyone wants the same goal—our students to be successful in learning science (although the authors of the second essay in this section may argue with this statement). Research has shown that training students in self-assessment so that they understand the purposes of learning and what they need to achieve is an effective way of raising of the academic performance of low performing students as well as benefiting those students who are already performing well (Black & Wiliam, 1998). This research suggests that it is less about how students are assessed but with what criteria students' work is assessed by that determines student learning. It is my argument that this finding opens the door for student generated or teacher-student co-constructed assessments.

SUMMARY

The piece that is missing in this conversation is how the four driving principles inform the way teachers assess inquiry. There are many inquiry-based assessments available in books, professional journals, and online. NRC (2001) offers a rubric that approaches those principles based upon seven dimensions as seen in Table 1.

NRC (2001) highlights the importance of who decides the quality of the students' work—the student, the teacher, the school, or the science community. The importance of the content(s) or skill(s) to be learned will determine the demand placed on the assessment to uncover the depth of student learning.

State-wide assessments will not be going away any time soon. Teachers need to focus on the tools that will enhance their science curriculum and to help their students learn science well. Assessing student understanding as they are immersed in an inquiry-based learning environment in ways congruent with their goals for the inquiry experience is one essential tool that can help students succeed.

THE "PROBLEM" OF INQUIRY: THE DIVIDE BETWEEN EDUCATING FOR CREDENTIALING AND EDUCATING FOR A DEMOCRACY

Sherry A. Southerland and Todd Hutner

As has been widely discussed in this volume, the current emphasis on inquiry in the classroom comes to us via the reform movements (American Association for Advancement of Science [AAAS], 1989, 1993, 2000; National Research Council [NRC], 1996, 2000), and it is important to note that these reforms have a threefold nature; content, pedagogy used to teach that content, and assessment to be employed to measure student learning. Yet, only the content portion of these reform messages seem to be filtered to states and districts, and so onto classrooms. The

Table 1.   National Resource Council Rubric

	On Demand	-->		Over Time
Formats	Multiple Choice, True/false, Matching	Constructed Response, Essays	Investigations, Research Reports, Projects	Portfolios, Journals, Lab Notebooks
Amount of time	typically ~1 min 2-3 min with justifications	1-2 min short answers 5-15 min open-ended responses	days, weeks, or months	months or even years
Whose questions? (audience for the answer)	anonymous or the teacher's	anonymous or the teacher's	the teacher's or the student's	the teacher's or the student's
What kind of questions?	posed narrowly	posed narrowly	posed more openly	varies
Source of answer	anonymous or the teacher's	The student's	the student's	the student's
What kind of answers?	right/wrong	extent of correctness	standards or criteria for quality	standards or criteria for quality
Resources available during assessment	usually none	none or some equipment	equipment, references	equipment, references
Opportunity for feedback, revision	none	usually none	usually some from teachers and peers	usually some from teachers and peers

pedagogy and assessment nature of the reforms have been largely sidestepped, and in many instances have had remarkably little influence on classroom teachers, district coordinators, or state administrators.

What accounts for the assimilation of the reforms' science content, but the widespread sidestepping of the accompanying pedagogy and assessment? What situation creates the "problem of inquiry" exemplified by the dueling teachers in the opening vignette? It is our argument that traditional science teaching (and that which is most in concordance with current accountability movements at the national and state level) has a very different goal that that of the science reform movement. Traditional science teaching and that supported by current accountability systems is largely based on a drive for educational credentials; in contrast, the goal for science education as portrayed in the national reforms is that of the preparation of knowledgeable citizens. We argue that it is the contradiction of these drives—education for credentials and education for democracy—(not length of period or lack of supplies or even the content knowledge of the teacher) that is at the heart the "problem with inquiry."

To best understand this argument, we look to the work of Labaree (1997, 2000) who describes that current the American educational system is based on a mixture of three rival educational goals:

(a) Social efficiency (in which schools are used to prepare student to "carry out useful economic roles with competence"; looks to produce a competent workforce, and sort students into jobs that match their abilities).
(b) Democratic equality (in which schools are prepare students to "take on the full responsibilities of citizenship in a competent manner"; to create a citizenry well versed in the American political community and able to lead productive lives as members of society).
(c) Social mobility (in which schools are to provide "individual students with the competitive advantage in the struggle for desirable social position"; the role of schools with this goal is to search for the most capable students and select them for the important roles in society).

Each of these goals has enjoyed different periods of predominance: When one goal is favored, the other two are to some extent ignored. Rarely do two of the goals exert any real influence at a given point. Clearly these goals suggest very different answers to many important questions; is schooling to serve the needs of political or economic forces? Should students be nurtured toward similar or different endpoints? But as Labaree (2000) points out the social efficiency and social democracy goals share one thing: they view education as a public good, something that touches everyone in a community.

The emphasis on community good stands in stark contrast to the third goal, that of social mobility. As Labaree (2000) points out, social mobility conceives of schooling as an individual good, something that benefits the consumer of education. As he describes, "From this angle, education exists because of what it can do for me or my children, not because of its benefits for democracy or the economy" (p. 30). This educational goal results in a push for the grading, sorting and selection of students. A quick look at the accountability movement suggests that the goal of this movement is much in line with social mobility—which manifests itself as a drive for credentials. This social efficiency goal is attractive to many in that it "puts a democratic face on the inequalities of capitalism" (Labaree, 1997, p. 72), meaning that the achievement of academic credentials for an individual allows a wide range of possibilities for the achievement of higher social status. This goal of achieving a higher social status, of the possibility of social mobility is dear to many, in that it presents schooling as the conduit of the "American dream."

If the purpose of education is understood to be the acquisition of credentials for the individual for the eventual goal of social mobility, then the goal of an individual engaged in schooling becomes the completion of activities that allow for those credentials. Labaree (1997) describes this as the problem of "seat time" as an exchange rate for credential, but one can understand minimum attainment on most statewide science assessments in the same manner. If the credentials of science credits in high school, middle school, even elementary school begin to rely on, or, in some cases revolve around, satisfactory performance on standardized science assessments, then the goal of science learning is not the USE of knowledge of science, but adequate performance on assessments.

We argue that the education for credentialing approach to schooling seen in the accountability movement (which can be understood to have its grounding both in social mobility the social efficiency) stands in stark contrast to the goal of education via the science education reform movement, which can best be typified by the *democratic equality* goal of schooling. Since the work of Dewey (1916), a strong thread in discussions of science and science teaching has been the need for all citizens to have a grasp of science so that they can make reasonable judgments about it and interact knowledgeably with it (Brickhouse, 2006; Rudolph, 2005). Clearly, the need for an educated citizenry knowledgeable about the fundamentals of science is central to the current calls for science education reform. As described so eloquently in *Project 2061* (AAAS, 1989):

> Education has no higher purpose than preparing people to lead personally fulfilling and responsible lives. For its part, science education—meaning education in science, mathematics, and technology—should help students to develop the understandings and habits of mind they need to become compassionate human beings able to think for themselves and to face life head on. It should equip them also to participate thoughtfully with fellow citizens in building and protecting a society that is open, decent, and vital. America's future—its ability to create a truly just society, to sustain its economic vitality, and to remain secure in a world torn by hostilities—depends more than ever on the character and quality of the education that the nation provides for all of its children. (Introduction, para 2)

This notion, that scientific knowledge should be useful for everyone, not to become scientists, but to allow them to "participate thoughtfully with fellow citizens", to "build and protect a society" is a powerful one. It forces science educators to consider the utility of the knowledge they are teaching, past the notion that "We always teach this in biology" or "They'll need this when they go onto college chemistry." Science teachers must begin to ask question such as: Will these concepts help students make sense of their worlds? Are students learning science in a meaningful way? Can they apply what they are learning in real life situations? With scientific literacy as a goal we can no longer to teach to the five percent of our students who may be targeted for a science career, instead, this goal forces teachers to go about their work in a way that science be made available to everyone, as again was describe in that moving preface to *Project 2061*:

> The set of recommendations constitutes a common core of learning in science, mathematics, and technology for all young people, regardless of their social circumstances and career aspirations. In particular, the recommendations pertain to those who in the past have largely been bypassed in science and mathematics education: ethnic and language minorities and girls. (para. 12)

This version of scientific literacy, one that emphasizes a fundamental knowledge that is useful to all learners for their "walking around lives" (Brickhouse, 2006, p. 6), can be easily understood within the goal of education for democracy. It is this goal of science learning that places a premium on classroom-based inquiry, in that this approach to science teaching and learning is one that allows for students to construct a meaningful knowledge of scientific content as well as learn to form explanations from evidence. Thus, if one has the goal of scientific literacy, then classroom inquiry is well positioned to be a tool to help reach that goal. To complement this pedagogy and educational goals, assessments that measure students' knowledge and their abilities to apply that knowledge would be a visceral part of such inquiries, both on a formative and summative level.

Although the goal of scientific literacy has been a visceral aspect of reforms begun in the 1980s, and the notion of science education for a democracy has been with us since the early portions of the 1900s, few teachers, administrators, or policymakers beyond the community of science educators share this goal. Most members of the American public still think of science as something only a limited number of students will be interested in and only a fewer number of students will excel in. Science is thought by many as an educational luxury that should be made available to a few only when more pressing matters are attended to. Many preservice teachers enter the profession with this mindset, as they hope to teach that reified group of students that are able to grasp the complexities of science.

What is the problem with the social mobility view of science education? The view of science as so difficult for most learners and so dispensable for many excuses a wealth of ineffective teaching practices. It allows teachers, districts, and states to assess students on a largely superficial level, as deep, meaningful, applicable knowledge of that material is not expected. It allows for the assessment of students on a vast range of material, as a wide range of "coverage" becomes the substance of the credential; if a deep, applicable knowledge is not a goal of learning, then the rigor of the classroom becomes the sheer volume of material covered. It allows teachers to dwell on the arcane in their teaching, because science is not seen as something that is applicable to one's life. In short, when scientific literacy fails to replace the goal of teaching science for credentials, we produce another generation of citizens who, although they may have science "credentials" such as passing high school chemistry or physics, do not have the fundamentals of science needed to make informed personal and societal decisions.

As was reflected in the vignette that opened this section, and a look at most science classrooms, a review of many textbooks or analysis of statewide assessments clearly demonstrates that the clarion call of scientific literacy heard within the science education community is often muted or distorted as we move outside the boundaries of the science education research community and go into schools. We must admit that outside of our small community and teachers that work within this community, the norm is to teach science so that students can receive the needed science credential to allow them passage in later educational endeavors or graduation requirements. We must acknowledge that in the credentialing classroom that is assessed via statewide-standardized assessments that emphasize large volumes of science content, inquiry has little place.

If classroom-based inquiry is a useful approach to supporting students' understanding of science and abilities to think scientifically, how can we better support its use? How can we help educational systems construct their practices inform not only for the content standards, but also for the standards for pedagogy and assessment? It is overly simplistic to say, "We have to change statewide assessments!" although this must be done, as inquiry was not a prominent pedagogy in schools even before the widespread implementation of standardized assessments. Instead, we suggest we can no longer afford to bemoan the absence of literacy in the thinking of most classroom teachers, administrators and policymakers, as we depend on the graces of a handful of teachers such as Margaret in the opening vignette to enact inquiry. Instead, we must make active steps to bridge the divide between education for credentialing and education for democracy, taking a page from the playbook of the curriculum developers of the 60s and 70s. But, instead of focusing all our resources on curriculum development, we must follow the guidelines established by the NRC (1996) and others (Southerland, Smith, Sowell, & Kittleson, 2007) and begin to work actively not only with curriculum developers, but also teachers, policymakers, and assessment companies to design prototypes supporting the kinds of teaching, learning and knowledge necessary we understand to be necessary for scientific literacy. Certainly, taking a close look at states in which inquiry is more common, such as Delaware

(Kittleson, 2006) might shed some light on how systemic change might be approached. Then we must be able to show the efficacy of these experiences, approaches and materials, efficacy that can be demonstrated in standardized ways.

But we argue that our first step in this process is to better define what is meant by scientific literacy. Indeed, this term has been so widely employed that it has begun to mean almost everything, and so nothing. A quick review of national policy statements over the last 10 years reveals a number of usages of the term "scientific literacy": "Students need to be scientifically literate for job preparation." "A higher degree of scientific literacy needed by our citizens to succeed in global competition." "More students must become scientifically literate if the United States is to regain the forefront of scientific advancements." None of these usages of this term seems particularly aligned with the way in which this goal is outlined in the national reforms. Instead in the vernacular of educational policy, scientific literacy seems to be more akin to social efficiency notions of education--that is the notion of education for the preparation of workers—not the preparation for citizenship in a democracy. Unfortunately, the envelope of this term has been stretched even within our own community, with Bybee and Fuchs' (2006) recent call for a social efficiency goal for science education—that of producing a new wave of workers prepared for the demands of the increasingly technologically demanding workforce.

We argue that such co-opting of this term has been made possible by our weak definitions of scientific literacy. Beyond outlining the goal of literacy, actually describing what such literacy would look like for teachers and learners has been absent in the national reforms. And without clarity on the part of science education reformers, the goal is easy subsumed and adopted for other purposes—just as the national standards have been subsumed and adopted for the goal of social efficiency approach to science learning. In Piagetian terms, scientific literacy has been assimilated into the prior schema for science teaching and learning, a process that required virtually no changes pedagogy or assessment. This vague and ambiguous notion has had such little impact outside of our community for the same reasons that it has had little real, meaningful impact within our community. By meaning so many different things to so many educators, *scientific literacy* has come to mean very little at all.

Science educators must have frank discussions about what we understand our predominant goal to be—that of democratic equality (as suggested by the original reform documents), that of social efficiency (as suggested by Bybee and Fusch and many other attempts to shape policy) or that of social mobility (as currently emphasized in the accountability movements). What are our goals and how are they different from those suggested and employed by others? Then we must describe what scientific literacy should and should not include (i.e., although recognition of the states of mitosis and meiosis are recognized as a standard of biology classes, is such information needed for a student to be scientifically literate?). We, ourselves, need to set the boundaries of this construct, solidifying the notion into a firm construct, one that can be shared in a more informative, useful manner outside of our community, one that can be insightful in shaping the work of others involved in science education. To begin this discussion, we offer the work of DeBoer (2002) and his nine goals for science teaching:

1. Teaching and learning about science as a *cultural force* in the modern world.
2. Preparation for the *world of work*.
3. Teaching and learning about science that has direct *application to everyday living*.
4. Teaching students to be *informed citizens*.
5. Learning about science as a particular *way of examining* the natural world.
6. Understanding reports and discussions of science that *appear in the popular media*.
7. Learning about science for its *aesthetic* appeal.
8. Preparing citizens who are *sympathetic to science*.
9. Understanding the nature and importance of technology and the *relationship between technology and science*.

- DeBoer, himself, seriously questions if all these goals can be achieved in science education. We agree, and suggest that as we consider K-12 science instruction with its attendant increasingly diverse student demographics combined with the ever magnifying effects human activity has on our natural world, we should focus our efforts primarily on:

1. Teaching and learning about science that has direct *application to everyday living*.
2. Teaching students to be *informed citizens*.
3. Learning about science as a particular *way of examining* the natural world.

Clearly, these goals are debatable. Indeed, they need to be debated. Once we agree as a community on the central goals of science education, then we must present a firm, operational vision of what a scientifically literate student knows and should be able to do. Following this, we must actively work outside of the boundaries of our community and become viscerally involved in shaping state policy documents, in crafting text-book, curriculum, and the preparation of current and future teachers for this new portrait of science learning. But, as teachers continually remind us, the revision of assessment is a fundamentally important aspect of this system, and if classroom-based inquiry is to be a common approach to developing students' literacy, then fundamental changes are needed in the science assessments employed in many states. What would assessment of scientific literacy look like if we are to measure students' "walking around" knowledge? What is a reasonable scope of content to allow for meaningful learning of science? It is time to formalize our goals and fully enter such discussions.

IS THERE ROOM FOR INQUIRY IN A WORLD OF ACCOUNTABILITY?

Sherry Southerland and Eleanor Abrams

In Section IV, we have had two responses to the role of inquiry in a world of accountability. The first essay points to the possibilities of craft-ing assessments to take advantage of the strengths of classroom-based inquiry for engendering student learning—and through that demonstra-tion securing a role of inquiry in more science classrooms. The second essay suggests that the problem is not just that of assessment, but that the issue is a much deeper one. Southerland and Hutner suggest that the organizing framework for science instruction must be changed for inquiry to have a real role in science instruction, a change that can only be engen-dered by science educators' work in every step of the educational pro-cess—without forgetting that assessment is a visceral part of this process.

It is important to point out that reformers readily acknowledge of the role of assessment in learning—and we understand and accept both the formative and summative function of assessments. However, as Brickhouse (2006) reminds us, we must acknowledge that the measurement of true components of scientific literacy is difficult. Despite this difficulty we must be mindful of the role assessments do place on learning--and we must remain critical of our measures. Whatever the assessments we employ, we must be careful to keep the assessment true to the scientific competencies that should be our goals.

Given the high stakes nature of current accountability efforts, teachers often teach to the test. But if the assessments they were to use adequately measured students' progress toward scientific literacy, and if they were constructed according to standards with a reasonable scope of content given the depth of knowledge sought (DeBoer, 2002), *then* teaching to the test may not prohibit the use of classroom-based inquiry, but *require* such inquiry.

REFERENCES

American Association for Advancement of Science. (1989). *Science for all Americans.* Retrieved from http://www.project2061.org/publications/sfaa/online/intro.htm. Washington. DC: Author.

American Association for the Advancement of Science. (1993). *Benchmarks for science literacy: A Project 2061 report.* New York: Oxford University Press.

American Association for the Advancement of Science. (2000). *Designs for science literacy.* New York: Oxford University Press.

Black, P., & William, D. (1998). Assessment and classroom learning. *Assessment in Education, 5*(1), 7-74.

Brickhouse, N. W. (2006). Editorial: Celebrating 90 years of Science Education: Reflections on the gold standard and ways of promoting good research. *Science Education, 90*(1), 1-7.

Brooks, J. (2005). *The dark side of school reform: Teaching in the space between reality and Utopia.* Lanham, MD: Rowman & Littlefield.

Bybee, R. W., & Fuchs, B. (2006). Preparing the 21st century workforce: A new reform in science education. *Journal of Research in Science Teaching, 43*(4), 349-352.

Clark, M., Shore, A., Rhoades, K., Abrams, L. Miao, J., & Li, J. (2003). *Perceived effects of state-mandated testing program on teaching and learning: Findings from interviews with educators in low-, medium- and high stakes test states.* Boston: National Board on Educational Testing and Public Policy.

Coalition of Essential Schools: Essential resources for schools change. (1998-2002). Retrieved from http://www.essentialschools.org/

DeBoer, G. (2002). Student centered teaching in a standards based world: Finding a sensible balance. *Science & Education, 11*(4), 405-417.

Delandshere, G. (2002) Assessment as inquiry. *Teachers College Record, 104*(7), 1461-1484.

Dewey, J. (1916) *Democracy and education. An introduction to the philosophy of education.* New York: Free Press.

Gallagher, J. (2006). *Teaching science for understanding: A practical guide for middle and high school teachers.* Upper Saddle River, NJ: Prentice Hall.

Gess-Newsome, J., Southerland, S. A., Johnston, A., & Woodbury, S. (2003). Educational reform, personal practical theories, and dissatisfaction: The Anatomy of change in college science teaching. *American Educational Research Journal, 40*(3), 731-767.

Gordon, S. P., & M. Reese. 1997. High-stakes testing: Worth the price? *Journal of School Leadership, 7*(4), 345-68.

Hamilton, L. S., Stecher, B. M., & Klein, S. P. (2002). *Making sense of test-based accountability in education.* Retrieved May, 29, 2004 from http://www.netLibrary.com/urlapi.asp?action=summary&v=1&bookid=81653

Hein. G. E., & Lee. S. (2000). Assessment of science inquiry in *Inquiry: Thoughts, views, and strategies for the K-5 classroom*. Washington, DC: National Science Foundation, Inquiry Group at the University of Illinois, http://www.inquiry.uiuc.edu/index.php

Herman, J. L. (1992). *Accountability and alternative assessment: Research and development issues* (CSE Technical Report 348). Los Angeles: University of California, Center for Research on Evaluation, Standards, and Student Testing.

Kauffman, D., Johnson, S. M. Kardos, S. M., Liu, E., & Peske, H. G. (2002). "Lost at Sea": New teachers' experiences with curriculum and assessment. *Teachers College Record, 104*(2), 273-300.

Kittleson, J. M. (2006). *Epistemological beliefs and epistemological practices in elementary science education.* Unpublished doctoral dissertation, University of Delaware, Newark, DE.

Labaree, D. F. (1997). Public goods, private goods: The American struggle over educational goals. *American Educational Research Journal, 34*, 39-81.

Labaree, D. F. (2000). Resisting educational standards. *Phi Delta Kappan, 82*(1), 28-33.

National Center for Education Statistics. (1999). *Trends in International Mathematics and Science Study 1999 Results.* Retrieved from http://nces.ed.gov/timss/results.asp

National Commission on Excellence in Education. (1983). *A nation at risk: The imperative for educational reform. A report to the nation and the Secretary of Education United States Department of Education by the National Commission on Excellence in Education.* Retrieved June 30, 2006, from http://www.goalline.org/Goal%20Line/NatAtRisk.html

National Research Council. (1996). *National Science Education Standards.* Washington, DC: National Academy Press.

National Research Council. (2000). *Inquiry and the national science education standards.* Washington, DC: National Academy Press.

National Research Coucil. (2001). *Classroom assessment and the National Science Education Standards.* Washington, DC: National Academy Press.

Rudolph, J. L. (2005). Inquiry, instrumentalism, and the public understanding of science. *Science Education, 89*(5), 803-821.

Sacks, P. (1999). *Standardized minds.* Reading MA: Perseus Books.

Saka, Y. (2007). *What happens to our reform minded beginning science teachers?* Unpublished doctoral dissertation, Florida State University, Tallahassee.

Settlage, J., & Meadows, L. (2002) Standards-based reform and its unintended consequences: Implications for science education within America's urban schools. *Journal of Research in Science Teaching, 39*(2), 114-127.

Shaver, A. Cuevas, P., Lee, O., & Avalos, M. (2007). Teachers' perceptions of policy influences on science instruction with culturally and linguistically diverse elementary students. *Journal of Research in Science Teaching, 44*(5) 725-746.

Southerland, S. A., Smith, L., Sowell, S., & Kittleson, K. (2007). Resisting unlearning: Understanding science education's response to the U.S.'s national accountability movement. *Review of Research in Education, 31*(1), 45-77.

Stiggins, R. J. (2004). New assessment beliefs for a new school mission. Phi Delta Kappan, *86*(1), 22-27.

Tyack, D., & Cuban, L. (1997). *Tinkering toward utopia: A century of public school reform.* Cambridge, MA: Harvard University Press.

Whitford, B. L., & Jones, K. (2000). Kentucky lesson: How high stakes school accountability undermines a performance-based curriculum vision. In B. L. Whitford & K. Jones (Eds.), *Accountability, assessment, and teacher commitment: Lessons from Kentucky's reform efforts* (pp. 9-24). Albany: State University of New York Press.

Yinger, R. J. (1980). A study of teacher planning. *Elementary School Journal, 80*(3), 107-127.

SECTION V

TEACHER KNOWLEDGE AND ENACTING INQUIRY

John Settlage, Lee Meadows,
Mark Olson, and Margaret Blanchard

EDITORS' NOTE

Describing Section V's Use of
Inquiry in the Classroom

Section V keenly reflects many of the conceptual complexities inherent in classroom inquiries, even as these conceptual complexities are situated in the practical difficulties teachers face daily. Thus, once the use of inquiry is described in systematic ways, the chapters in Section V reveal a wide variation—and that wide variation is aptly portrayed in the rivaling views by the intern, cooperating teacher, and university supervisor at play in the opening vignette.

GOALS OF INQUIRY

In Lee Meadow description of his own experiences in "pulling off" the reforms, his primary and overriding goal was largely that of using inquiry **for construction of scientific knowledge** as is the goal of the Mark Olson in the second essay in Section V—although in this regard, Olson's use of this goal is much more tacit than the very explicit goal of Meadow's—perhaps due to Meadow's context as a classroom teacher for this essay. John Settlage's essay is more difficult to categories, a hybrid in our description.

Inquiry in the Classroom: Realities and Opportunities, pp. 171–229

His call to change our approach to inquiry from a pedagogical technique to a skill set hits upon **learning to inquire**, as students are expected to develop their inquiry skills.

MEANS OF ENACTMENT OF INQUIRY

On the second point in our descriptive frame, there is more agreement. Two of the essays in Section V (Meadows and Settlage) take particular care to further critique the common conception of Level 3/open inquiry as the hallmark of reform-based science teaching (a pedagogical misconception critiqued throughout this volume). Indeed, Meadow's essay charts his pathway away from Level 3/open inquiry toward more **guided and structured approaches (Levels 1 and 2)**—a pathway that makes particular sense given his central goal of the use of inquiry for the construction of scientific knowledge. Categorizing Settlage's take on this issue is more difficult, as he critiques open inquiry as well as critiquing the use of inquiry as an overly vague notion that has hampered much of our attempts at science education reform. If one to were to equate Settlage's "inquiry skills set "with process skills, then the means of his enactment could be quite simplistic, residing around Levels 0/1 (structured) inquiries. However, if his skill set is mindful of authenticity of tasks and critiques of overly simplistic approaches to inquiry, then perhaps this skills set approach could leave room for carefully selected Level 3/open inquiries.

Olson's narrative and paradigmatic accounts of science does not necessarily suggest a particular form of enactment of inquiry—indeed, one can see a role for both narrative and paradigmatic approaches in each of the levels of inquiry.

PHYSICAL SCIENCE VIGNETTE: HEAT AND TEMPERATURE

Standing behind a long demonstration table, the intern begins presenting her physical science lesson to the ninth graders. "Before we move forward with our studies of heat and temperature, I would like to review some of the equipment and ideas we've used over the past few classes." Moving to the far end of the table, she holds up an object for the students to see. "We began this unit by exploring this pulse  *glass.[1] As you remember, when we hold it, the red liquid moves inside the tube. Can someone describe the two competing ways to explain what is happening?"*

A student volunteers that heat from one's hand flows into the pulse glass and pushes the red liquid (methylene chloride dyed to make it visible) so it moves from one bulb to the other. Another student proposes that the heat from the intern's hand increased the motion of the particles that make up the liquid and that increased activity caused the liquid to expand.

Without commenting, the teacher steps over to the next collection of objects on the demonstration table—a small coffee maker and three insulated cups. She asks, "Who can remember the investigation we did with these materials?" The students recount how they measured the temperature of tap water in one cup, the temperature of an equal volume of hot water in the second cup, and then predicted the temperature of the water when mixed in a third cup. Again the teacher does not comment but simply moves to the next set of objects on display: an insulated cup adjacent to several metal blocks (brass, aluminum, and copper) each of which has a small hook projecting from its top. "What about this activity?" Several students are jointly able to explain how they had heated the metal blocks and then measured the increase in water temperature upon immersing each one into the cup.

The intern positions herself in front of the last display of objects. "Today we will be working with these objects which I believe will be familiar to all of you. Here I have an assortment of metal knives, forks and spoons along with a dishtowel. In fact, I have enough of these for each table to examine. Before you send a representative from each group up here to retrieve your equipment, I have two questions I would like for you to consider: How do you think these objects will feel like when you touch them? How do you predict the silverware will feel compared to the towel?

"I also have two thermometers that will remain here at the front. One is bundled with a rubber band inside several pieces of silverware and the other is wrapped inside a dishtowel. As you are writing observations in your science notebooks about the silverware and towels at your desk, I will call groups up to examine these thermometers."

At their desks students notice that the silverware is cooler to the touch than the dishtowels. They are surprised to find that when they read the thermometers, the silverware and dishtowel at the intern's table have the same reading. The students are perplexed by the incongruity. The silverware feels cooler, yet they are reluctant to distrust what they detect with their senses. They doubt the accuracy of the thermometers, they question whether the intern's materials were identical to their own, and they repeatedly touch the towels and silverware to confirm their initial impressions. Some students become frustrated when the metal does not feel cool any more, even though they realize it is because of their repeated touching. One student asks, "How can they be the same temperature when the metal feels colder than the cloth?" *This question becomes the starting point for the intern's lecture about heat and temperature.*

"What you've been running into are the ideas of heat and temperature. In everyday conversation, we tend to think of these as being very similar. But for scientists, heat and temperature are very different concepts," explains the intern. The intern defines temperature as a measure of molecular motion while heat is a measure of energy transfer. As a class, they create a two-column chart with everyday heat and science heat as the headers. They identify ordinary experiences they have

had with hot and cold objects. Under the two columns they describe how those would be interpreted with the contrasting explanations. For example, putting ice into a drink is described as "adding cold" in everyday heat language, but using science heat language, the drink cooled because heat was transferred to the ice and contributed to its melting. The intern guides the students to use the two perspectives to explain various phenomena without positioning science heat as superior to everyday heat explanations.

Returning to the materials she used to introduce the day's lesson, the intern encourages students to recognize that in everyday language, cold and hot are often thought of as substances that are opposite each other. In contrast, the science perspective is that a cold object contains less heat compared to a warmer object. Heat can be added to or removed from an object but there is no such thing as cold. This last idea raises a lot of controversy among the students: "What do you mean there's no such thing as cold?" "It's cold in the winter." "I'm cold right now!" "Food in my refrigerator is cold."

Returning to the silverware and dishtowel activity, the intern guides the students to resolve the discrepancies between their sense of touch and the thermometers' readings. The everyday heat explanation is that the silverware holds more cold than does the towel. In contrast, the science heat explanation is that heat from the students' fingers moves more rapidly to the silverware than to the towel and what felt like cold is actually the transferring of heat energy out of their fingers registering in their sense of touch as a perception of cold. The Science heat perspective is reinforced by a section from the textbook the teacher has the class read. There they find that "coldness" depends upon how quickly an object conducts heat. A tile floor conducts heat more quickly from bare feet than does a rug. While everyday heat would suggest that bathroom tile is colder than a bath mat, they are actually the same temperature. The science heat perspective explains the difference in the perceived coldness as due to variations in the rate of energy transfer.

To encourage students to apply the difference between everyday heat and science heat explanations, the intern provides a written description of a scenario to each group and asks them to use two perspectives of heat to explain what is happening. For example, one group is asked to explain why on a cold winter day it is dangerous to put one's tongue on a metal pole but it's not a problem to lick a nearby tree trunk. In the closing portion of the class, each group shares their scenarios and explanations with the rest of the class. Moments before the dismissal bell rings, the intern distributes a homework activity designed to have the students find additional everyday heat and science heat examples over the weekend.

Analyzing the Lesson

After the students have exited, the intern walks the back of the room to join the two other adults who have been observing her lesson. One person is the mentor *teacher whose classroom has become the intern's final training ground; the other is the university supervisor who was also the intern's instructor for science methods. The intern sees that the copies of her lesson plan she had provided are covered with handwritten remarks.*

"Nicely done," says the supervisor. "We were just commenting about how much better you've become at making effective use of time. You didn't rush to finish the lesson because time was running out but you also didn't run out of activities before the bell rang."

"Thanks," says the intern knowing compliments typically precede criticisms. "Even though the lesson was not especially open-ended, it seemed to me that most of the students were beginning to grasp the distinctions between heat and temperature."

"I also thought it was a very well organized lesson," says the mentor. "However, I felt you could have done more in the way of hands-on activities without so much lecturing. Even though there was a little bit of time in which the students were feeling the silverware and towels, I don't think that's really enough to qualify as being truly a hands-on activity."

The intern responds saying, "It seemed to me that the students had participated in enough investigations in the last several days that it seemed necessary to help them pull their ideas along a little further. Even though the students weren't working with equipment in groups, I felt as if it was appropriate to run this lesson as a guided inquiry. I was hoping I could receive feedback on how well I addressed the Five Essential Features of Inquiry," referring to the supplement to the original National Science Education Standards.

"Technically I guess you were addressing all the elements. But this really wasn't inquiry: you were providing way too much structure," suggests the mentor. "For example, even though there was a question posed before they worked with the silverware and dishtowels and, I admit you did have them attempt to form explanations based upon what they noticed, it was awfully teacher centered. And as we all know, the students aren't going to learn and retain the material unless they have lots of hands-on experiences."

"I would have to agree," said the supervisor. "This isn't really a criticism of the lesson because it did proceed very smoothly. Well, let me think about that: there was a lot of chaos when the students were shouting over each other and not waiting for you to call upon them. But let's set that aside. Even though this was a nicely organized lesson, I don't think it is appropriate to suggest that it was an inquiry lesson. While I recognize these are young teenagers and appreciate that they come from backgrounds where questioning authority may not be culturally acceptable and all that stuff, they still deserve to experience authentic inquiry and not such a cookbook approach where the teacher is pretty much running the show."

The mentor addresses the supervisor. "From my perspective, it's not all that necessary for the students to do the same sorts of science as the professionals do. The Standards are fairly clear that school-based inquiry is not identical to what hap-

pens in research labs. My concern was based more in the fact that the students weren't having enough direct experience with the materials. It seemed too much of the lesson involved talking and not enough with doing.

The intern interrupts: "I completely agree with the need for the students to have hands-on experiences. But given what we had accomplished during labs up until today, my impression was that this lesson was an opportunity to try to pull together all of those activities and ideas into something that made sense to them. At some point it seems the students expect the teacher to provide information to them. As much as they enjoy activities, I'm not so certain they really understand the ideas unless I help to guide them. Another thing I was hoping you would give feedback about were my explanations for heat and temperature. Ideas like molecular motion and energy transfer are so abstract that I'm not sure whether I am clear enough in my definitions and examples. Any thoughts?

"I thought you did an exemplary job with explaining. You used examples all of the students could appreciate. Also, I was pleased that you help to scaffold your explanations by writing terms on the board to reinforce what you were saying," says the mentor. "As a suggestion for improvement, I would urge you to pay attention to the state curriculum framework. You didn't include that within your written lesson plan."

"Yes, I must confess that I neglected the state standards in my planning. I suppose I'm so focused upon gathering materials and writing the lesson that I continue to forget to reinforce what's in the framework," the intern admits.

"But I think this is something you could have included in the lesson. Ideally, you would introduce the targeted standard at the start of the lesson, return to it partway through, and then make sure the students are using the correct terms on the homework," the mentor suggests. "It's just that in this day and age, we have to make sure that not only do the students learn the science but they learn it in ways that will allow them to show their understandings on the achievement tests."

"I guess I'm somewhat less concerned about the state frameworks," says the supervisor. "But I believe in the goal of scientifically literacy. Since you asked about your explanations, I would agree that they were clear enough for these students. And yet it seems you fell short of really driving the ideas home. One technical drawback is that you didn't stress the difference in the units of measure for heat versus temperature. Hopefully you can introduce Joules and the Kelvin scale in a later lesson."

"I'm not so sure that fits into ninth grade scientific literacy," says the mentor—to the intern's relief.

"I suppose there are different levels of scientific literacy and I saw this as an opportunity to advance these students beyond a basic level," the supervisor says. "Related to this is the absence of any discussion about the historical development of heat and temperature concepts. I'm always amazed about how students' misunderstandings parallel the history of science. I cannot help but believe that relating stories about the caloric view would be interesting to students. I'd

recommend you find ways to infuse the history of science in your lessons, if for no other reason than to make your lectures more lively."

"My recommendation is that you avoid having to rely quite so much on lecture and invest more time in having the students do hands-on activities. In addition, if the activities are going to be legitimately identified as 'inquiry' then you must allow the students a great deal more free choice in how they perform the activity. In addition, make sure you are finding ways to connect good lessons to the state science frameworks," advises the mentor.

"My recommendation would be not to neglect history of science in your lessons. I know that Benchmarks includes such material within science curriculum. It seems that sharing this information will contribute to your students' science literacy and help them better recognize the intellectual pathways of professional scientists. And I would concur with the need to use activities that more closely align with the unstructured approaches that are consistent with the work of real scientists," proposes the supervisor.

TEACHER KNOWLEDGE ABOUT INQUIRY: INCORPORATING CONCEPTUAL CHANGE THEORY

Lee Meadows

The intern, the mentor, and the supervisor in the vignette all appear to be dedicated educators. None of them sounds lazy, burned out, or resistant to change. But they each have different beliefs about what should happen in the classroom. These differences are not minor, however, and they personify the larger issues of science teaching today. Most public school teachers in America face a crushing load of conflicting demands. The classroom is more diverse: Teachers must serve an increasingly broader audience of culture, language, and economic status. Accountability has increased significantly over the last decade: States have implemented high-stakes tests and No Child Left Behind is raising the stakes even higher. Today's students are the millennial generation (Oblinger & Oblinger, 2005). Their steady diet of cell phones, instant messages, and Web browsing leaves them bored and restless in the traditional classroom. Any one of the issues might be dealt with in isolation, but teachers must do it all. None of the demands being forced on teachers are presented as simply an option. The key question then becomes how to make sense of the conflicting voices.

The answer to those conflicting voices is not simple, however. The realities teachers face in American classrooms are much too difficult for a simple checklist of strategies. Implementing inquiry amidst these classroom realities requires deep teacher knowledge, a combination of special strategies and perspectives that are internally related to each other and that that can be translated into effective instruction. The model proposed in this chapter provides insight on the professional knowledge teachers need to move inquiry activities from simple engagement to development of accurate and enduring scientific understandings. The model addresses the twin goals of content mastery and inquiry skills, not by forcing those to be competing choices, but by charting a middle ground where efforts in one do not necessitate sacrifices in the other.

I also do not think the answer to these conflicting voices is open-ended inquiry (Bell, Smetans, & Binns, 2005). From my experience, open-ended inquiry is an unreasonable vision for teaching given the complexities of the American science classroom. I work at a university as a science methods instructor, but I recently spent a year back in the classroom teaching ninth grade physical science by inquiry. I wanted experience teaching high school students via inquiry, so I became a regular teacher again: I graded papers, I met IEP requirements (individual education plans for special needs students), I filled out discipline referrals, and I cleaned up labs. I savored a year in the life of my ninth graders, and I experienced the conflicting voice we hear in the vignette. I also failed with open-ended inquiry (Meadows, in press). I led the teachers on my team to try a form of inquiry where students pursued their own questions and determined their own methods, but our students achieved little more than frustration (Bell et al., 2005). As the year progressed, we shifted to guided inquiry, and we began to see success. The model I propose in this chapter grows directly out of these classroom experiences.

The model calls on two large pieces of teacher knowledge necessary for inquiry-based science teaching. These are the knowledge and skills necessary for guiding and facilitating student inquiry and the knowledge and skills necessary for guiding and facilitating students' conceptual change. Each can be thought of as a cycle of evidence and explanation, as shown in Figure 1. The top cycle in Figure 1 shows the cycle of evidence and explanation that students must move through in inquiry and how teacher knowledge about guiding inquiry is at the center of the cycle. The goal of this cycle is student understanding of the scientific evidence they encounter. The bottom cycle in Figure 1 shows the cycle of evidence and explanation that students must move through, under the teacher's watchful supervision, during conceptual change and how teacher knowledge for orchestrating discourse is at the center of the cycle. The goal of this cycle is student understanding of the scientific ideas that develop from the evidence they have collected. To play out the model, I will begin with the intern's lesson to consider how she supported students' understanding using teacher knowledge about guiding and facilitating both inquiry and conceptual change. We will then look deeper at the model with an example from my teaching with ninth graders.

EVIDENCE AND EXPLANATION IN INQUIRY

The proposed model for use in high school classroom has teachers guiding and facilitating students' work to create a constant interplay between evidence and explanation. Evidence is scientific data, and it is typically, though not always, generated from hands-on investigations done by the students. Inquiry is the process students go through to encounter the evidence that serves as the source of scientific ideas. Explanations are created by the students in an effort to make sense of evidence. Orchestrating discourse refers to the kinds of small- and large-group talk that teachers facilitate to guide students through the process of moving around the cycle of evidence and explanation until the students have constructed in their minds strong understandings of the science content as it grows out of the science process.

This model is a classroom application of the *National Science Education Standards* (NSES). Standard B of the NSES teaching standards calls for teachers to orchestrate discourse, an aspect of science teaching described by other contributors to this volume within the introductory section and in the assessment section. This approach to science teaching stands in contrast with teacher lecture, which has consistently been shown by research to fail in getting students to internalize the scientific ideas (Bransford, Brown, & Cocking, 1999). The model draws the ideas of evidence and explanation from the five Essential Features of inquiry presented in *Inquiry and the National Science Education Standards* (National Research Council, 2000), a key resource teachers can tap to better understand the how's and why's of inquiry.

The intern exemplifies teaching according to the model throughout her lesson. She consistently referred students to scientific evidence that they had either seen or collected themselves. The lesson was built around students' interaction with kitchen utensils serving as the direct evidence that they would consider while formulating understandings about heat and temperature. But beyond hands-on instruction, the intern encouraged conversations with her students so that they could make sense of the evidence they had collected. If you look through the vignette, you will see how much of her talk was with students, not at them. She was engaging them in conversations about the evidence. She was orchestrating discourse.

A key difference between this model and traditional science teaching is the shift in who creates the explanations. Traditionally, science teachers give students the explanation. They will perform a demonstration and

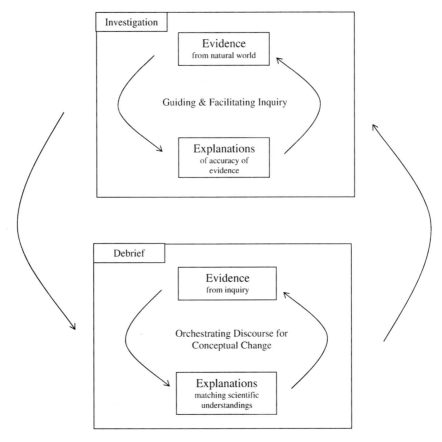

Figure 1.   Teacher knowledge for inquiry.

then explain to the students what happened. They will overview a key science concept (i.e., a scientific explanation) and then have students work
through a lab showing this concept in action. They will also create lectures
explaining key ideas of science in clear and interesting ways. Research
findings from cognitive science (Bransford, Brown, & Cocking, 1999) and
science education (Driver, Squires, Rushworth, & Wood-Robinson, 1994)
have consistently raised questions about how much students really learn
in teacher-centered instruction. The model, therefore, shifts the role of
developing explanations from the teacher to the student. The teacher
guides the process to make sure the students' explanations jibe with
accepted scientific theory, but students have to shoulder the thinking
responsibility required for explaining the evidence they have seen.

Consider how the vignette presents the intern's lecture following the students' initial interaction with the kitchen utensils. It is really not a lecture at all. She does begin with a burst of teacher talk, setting the stage and giving a definition, but she then moves smoothly into orchestrating discourse with a two-column graphic organizer. Through talk with her students, she guides them to make sense of evidence that they saw that day, in previous lessons, and in real life in terms of the concepts of everyday heat and science heat. In the rest of the lesson she continues to craft dialogue with her students, guiding them to confront the discrepancies between their thinking and the scientific evidence they are examining. In terms of Figure 1, the lesson moves smoothly back and forth between the top and the bottom cycle so that students understand the evidence they have encountered and how the evidence leads them to scientific explanations of heat.

Figure 2 adds specificity to the model in Figure 1 by integrating inquiry with teaching for conceptual change. Figure 2 shows four phases of instruction and how in each phase the teacher links facets of inquiry instruction and conceptual change instruction. The Inquiry column in Figure 2 gives the five essential features of inquiry, as they appear in *Inquiry and the National Science Education Standards*. The Teaching for Conceptual Change column in Figure 1 gives typical steps of a conceptual change lesson. You may not be very familiar with teaching for conceptual change, however. Conceptual change teaching (Suping, 2003) is the approach to science teaching that targets students' misconceptions so that they abandon those non-scientific ideas and latch on to more scientific understandings of how the world works.

Linking inquiry and conceptual change teaching in one model, as shown in the details of Figure 2, gives teachers the powerful knowledge they need to guide students to learn deep ideas of science, how science works, and thinking skills at the same time. Rather than teaching in fragmented ways to achieve these goals, teachers can use a unified method to address many of the competing voices staking claims to their classrooms.

As shown in Phase 1 of Figure 2, teachers begin teaching according to the model by engaging learners in science and assessing their prior understandings. For the model to work, the science content to be studied has to be engaging for students. If today's students cannot see the relevance of the science they are studying, they typically will not engage in the intellectual work the model requires. Content selected by the standard of science (American Association for the Advancement of Science [AAAS], 2001; Rutherford & Ahlgren, 1990) fits this criteria, though. When the content helps students understand their world, then teachers can guide students to identify questions they have that engage them in the science

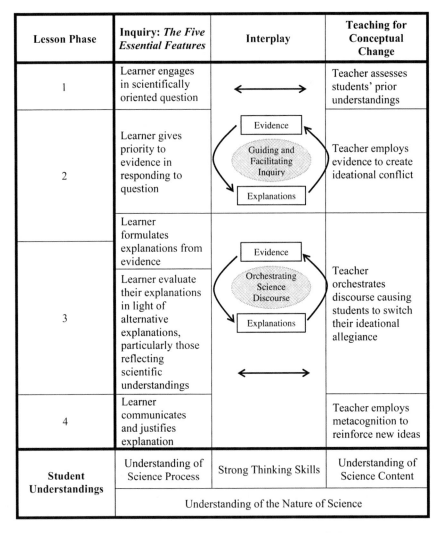

Lesson Phase	Inquiry: *The Five Essential Features*	Interplay	Teaching for Conceptual Change
1	Learner engages in scientifically oriented question	←→	Teacher assesses students' prior understandings
2	Learner gives priority to evidence in responding to question	Evidence / Guiding and Facilitating Inquiry / Explanations	Teacher employs evidence to create ideational conflict
3	Learner formulates explanations from evidence Learner evaluate their explanations in light of alternative explanations, particularly those reflecting scientific understandings	Evidence / Orchestrating Science Discourse / Explanations ←→	Teacher orchestrates discourse causing students to switch their ideational allegiance
4	Learner communicates and justifies explanation		Teacher employs metacognition to reinforce new ideas
Student Understandings	Understanding of Science Process	Strong Thinking Skills	Understanding of Science Content
	Understanding of the Nature of Science		

Figure 2.   Overlaying the lesson with inquiry and conceptual change descriptors.

they are about to study. The intern did this in the vignette lesson by focusing on a topic with rich practical applications for students to make sense of their world. Heat is powerful concept for student understanding because an "enormous variety of biological, chemical, and physical phenomena can be explained by changes in the arrangement and motion of atoms and molecules" (AAAS, 1993, p. 17).

In Phase 1 of the model, teachers also assess students for prior knowledge about the science they are about to study. The typical technique here is uncomplicated—it is mainly asking open-ended questions and accepting all student responses (Harvard-Smithsonian Center for Astrophysics, 1997). Open-ended questions cause students to respond in depth about their understanding. Accepting all answers keeps students talking about their ideas without signaling them that their ideas are wrong. You can see the intern doing this during the review at the beginning of the lesson. Students respond to her questioning about past experiments, but the intern accepts their answers "without commenting." The purpose of this is not to leave students in confusion or misunderstanding, but rather to get students to express their own understanding so that the teachers can collect evidence about what their students are thinking. If teachers attempt to correct wrong ideas at this early point in the lesson, students typically shut their thinking down and move into a mode of just waiting for the right answer from the teacher rather than thinking things through for themselves.

The intern's lesson shows students engaging with evidence in many different forms. Her lesson mixes hands-on activity with a demonstration. Maximizing student engagement, the intern gave each group of students a set of material so that they could get as close to the phenomena as possible. But, she also needed a special set up—the bundled thermometers at the front of the room. She did this to ensure that students were not corrupting the data by transferring body heat to the utensils bundled around the thermometer by picking them up with their hands. So, she used more of a demonstration format where the students came forward to collect evidence by observing one piece of equipment. This is the evidence the intern used to confront student misconceptions, as shown by the student who said, "How can they be the same temperature when the metal feels colder than the cloth?"

As the students collect evidence, Phase 2 of Figure 2 shows that teachers guide the students to begin the process of explaining the data. Teachers have to execute a balance here, however. They need to let students struggle with the data to make sense of it, but not let them struggle so much that they become overwhelmed and frustrated. The vignette shows this balance with students at times expressing frustration, challenging their teachers' explanation, or engaging in controversy with each other. Sometimes, making sense of evidence is just hard intellectual work, and American students typically resist it. Traditional teaching does not require this type of intellectual work from students because they can be passive and still succeed. With support and training, however, students can learn to make sense of data, and the key benefit of this portion of instruction is the development of students' thinking skills.

Phase 2 of instruction is also when teachers begin to point out the conflict between the evidence and students' misconceptions. The intern could have done this when she introduced the idea that, according to science, there is no such thing as cold. Her students pushed back on this idea, probably because they think of cold as a real substance that moves into objects to drop their temperature. The intern skillfully prepares students to make sense of this conflict by introducing earlier in the lesson the distinction between scientific ideas and everyday understanding. Teachers are not trying to dispel students' misconceptions yet during Phase 2, though. They are mainly helping students recognize that the data conflicts with the ideas they had coming into the investigation. This can occur informally as teachers move around the room during the lab or after the lab when students are working in small groups to develop their initial explanations.

At this point in the lesson, the inquiry cycle of Figure 1, students are engaged in science. They see how the topic relates to questions important to them, and they have interacted with actual evidence useful in answering their questions. They have also begun the process of trying to explain their data in such a way that they see answers to their questions. They are getting their minds, as well their hands, on the science. Often they also recognize conflicts between the data and their original ideas.

At this point teachers move to the bottom cycle of Figure 1 and Phase 3 of Figure 2. From an inquiry perspective, they guide the students to evaluate their explanations in light of the evidence. From a conceptual change perspective, they orchestrate discourse to encourage students to switch their intellectual allegiance to a more scientific understanding. Typically, this happens in large group dialogue. The teacher develops the kind of respectful dialogue where, while one student talks about their explanation of the science, the other students are listening for how well the explanation fits the data. If students or the teacher see flaws in the thinking, they challenge it based on the data. Throughout, the teacher monitors the dialogue to make sure that student misconceptions are challenged using the evidence from the lab.

The intern could have done this in her lesson to help students make sense of the conflict they were sensing between the temperature of the thermometers bundled in the utensils and the towel. At this point in the lesson, students have talked about the phenomena in their small groups and some students are beginning to be able to explain the data. The intern could simply say, "Who would like to tell me your understanding of why the thermometers read the same temperature?" She then waits until Lupe, one of her students, volunteers and talks out her explanation. Rather than immediately confirming Lupe's idea, though, by saying, "Right, Lupe...." or "Well, not really...," the intern would then continue to orchestrate discourse by saying to the class, "You've heard Lupe's explanation. Who can build on Lupe's ideas and help us understand better what's going on?" Again, she waits until Natasha, another student, volunteers her understanding. The intern continues to guide the dialogue, drawing out students' explanations of the evidence they have encountered. She uses her expert knowledge of science content and process to guide students toward explanations that rely upon evidence and in line with correct scientific knowledge.

Phase 4 of the model helps students solidify their new understandings. From an inquiry perspective, the learners communicate and justify their findings. From a conceptual change perspective, the teacher deploys metacognition to reinforce new understandings of science. This portion does not necessarily require a traditional lab report. Teachers would better consider the communication forms relevant to answering the question that began the investigation. Students can create posters or brochures, they can explain their findings to parents or siblings, or they could take a position on a scientific issue. They can also accomplish Phase 5 informally, such as through a journal entry. The intern used an informal activity for Phase 5 by requiring the students to react to a funny scenario, the licking of a metal pole on a cold day. The example is sure to start a lot of snickers around the room, but it forces students to solidify their understanding by applying their thinking to a new context. As students communicate their new understanding, they solidify their understanding of the scientific explanation and how the evidence justifies what they encountered.

Student Understanding From Inquiry

We have taken an overall look at how the model plays out in the intern's lesson. Now, let us dig in deeper regarding the specific knowledge teachers need to have to teach via inquiry by considering the pulse glass lesson, one of the lessons the intern mentioned in her review and a lesson that I taught my ninth graders.

The pulse glass lesson lasted one class period, 50 minutes at my school. I implemented Phase 1 at the beginning of the period by having the students respond in their journals to the following question, "How does heat affect the molecular motion of a substance?" I had trained my students in a classroom routine of entering the class and looking for a posted opening task. Most of the time it was a question for them to respond to, as in the case of this lesson. They would come in, get settled, and start writing. By the time the bell rang, they were required to all be on task while I checked roll and did any other administrative tasks I needed to at the beginning of the period. I would then walk around the room and monitor their work. I would also read a few responses over their shoulders to get a sense of the range of their ideas.

By now, about 5 minutes had passed, and I then began a large group discussion. I simply asked, "Who can tell me what you wrote?" As the intern did, I would then take their answers without comment. Following the dictates of conceptual change theory, I made sure at this point of the lesson to make no evaluative comments of their responses. I did not say, "Good answer," or "Right." My only comments were something along the line of "Uh-huh" or "Okay" so that they would know I was listening.

I was also trying to develop a general sense of the different ideas in the room. For example, if the first student to volunteer said, "I think heat makes the molecules go faster," I would then ask students to raise their hands if they wrote something similar to this, allowing me to determine the proportion of the class that shared the same idea before instruction. I would then ask them to let me know if anyone had a different idea. If in response, one student offered that nothing would happen because heat cannot change molecules, I would ask students to raise their hands if they had written something similar to this response. Again, I could see how many students shared this preinstruction idea. I would continue this discussion for a total of 3-5 minutes until I had a sense of the major ideational allegiances the students had before instruction. I would often jot down notes on note cards about what my students were saying, which really surprised them: "You're taking notes on what we say?" I would use these notes in Phases 2 and 3 to focus students on evidence that either supported or contradicted their ideas going into the lesson.

The students were now ready for evidence, Phase 2 of the model. In the pulse glass lesson their collection of evidence required only 5-10 minutes because the phenomenon is simple. The pulse glass consists of a sealed glass tube with a bulb on either end; the tube joining the bulbs contains CH_2Cl_2 which is a Freon-like substance that "boils" when warmed by body heat. My students sat in groups all the time because very little of the work done in Phases 2, 3, and 4 is individualized. I had placed a pulse glass in the center of each group's lab table, and after hearing from me clear directions on how to handle this fragile piece of glassware, the groups passed the pulse glass around and explored its function. They found that the warmth from their hands would "push" the liquid. By this point in the year, my students all knew that they had to engage in the activities or lose class participation points. They did not have to understand everything that went on, but they were required to give attention to the investigation. As they explored, I walked around and monitored to see that they stayed on-task and that they handled the glassware responsibly. I also listened to their spoken observations.

After they explored, I directed them back to the focus question and instructed the groups to develop an answer (an explanation) based on the evidence they had seen from the pulse glass. Students knew to engage in this small-group discussion because I was recording class participation points and also because I might call on them during the next lesson portion, the large-group discussion, to report what they had heard from their group members. Again, they did not have to understand everything that was being said in the discussion, but they had to at least pay attention. I walked around again and monitored these discussions to make sure students were on-task and to create a sense of the explanations they were developing. Listening at this point was key evaluation for me to see if the evidence I had given the students was actually helping them to develop the target explanation, as I had planned.

At about 25 minutes into the lesson we are ready for Phase 3, almost always a large-group discussion. The students have activated their prior knowledge in Phase 1, and in Phase 2, encountered evidence and worked with peers to develop initial explanations. They now needed expert input of information to help refine their explanations.

I structured this discussion much like the beginning large group discussion of their journal responses, but at this point I would typically call on students by name rather than allowing volunteers. This technique ensures that everyone is involved and thinking. I would ask a student what he was thinking, listen to his response, but not comment on whether I thought he was right or wrong. I would then turn to another student and ask her to respond to the first student's idea. This question requires a lot of thought and engagement. This student has to have looked at the evidence, generated an explanation, considered her small group's explanation, listened to another student's response, and think about what he said in light of the evidence she saw and her thoughts about the explanation. I continued in this fashion, asking several other students for their contributions to the discussion, again expecting that my students were listening to each other's responses so that they could build on what is already been said. The only wrong answer at this stage was, "I don't know," because that response told me that a student had not been paying attention. They should all be able to comment because they have had a lot of training in these types of discussion. This was true even of many of the special needs students. They almost always could participate in the discussion.

This phase of the lesson is where I get really excited about teaching by inquiry because I hear my students thinking! By the second half of the school year, almost all of my students could participate well in a lesson taught according to this instructional model. Group after group and class after class could make initial sense of their data again and again. They needed my guidance to refine their explanations and see the details, but they were making sense of scientific questions in light of evidence. My students were not gifted or academically motivated. Most ninth grade students elect to take honors biology, but not this physical science course. I had the leftovers.

To help the students focus on the key phenomena, I began at that point in the lesson to build a graphic of the phenomena on the white board, using their explanations. My graphic showed the molecules making up the liquid in the pulse glass and the increase in their motion as the heat from the students' hands flowed into the pulse glass. I would use arrows and color to try to create a diagram that would best help them build a correct understanding of the kinetic molecular theory at work in this investigation. Here, the lesson took a subtle shift as I orchestrated discourse. Rather than accepting all ideas, even wrong ones, I began challenging students who offered explanations contrary to the evidence. Rather than telling the students the right answers, I guided the discourse so that the explanation arose from their observations of the evidence, their initial explanations, and the refinements that I gave based on my expert knowledge. A by-product of the model was that students saw that science knowledge must come from evidence, not from my authority as the teacher or even from the text. Also, they learned to trust science as something valuable, meaningful, and practical.

I finished the model with a countersuggestion, a technique suggested by conceptual change theory, to encourage them to communicate and justify their explanation and to employ metacognition. This is Phase 5 of the model. In the last 10 minutes of the lesson, I posed the following question, "One student in another class said that heat is a molecule." This was a misconception that some of my students held, and I wanted to use the pulse glass lesson to confront it directly. After letting the students ponder the question quietly for a moment, I called on a couple of students to talk out their thinking. I let the conversation go until I heard one student's response that if heat were a molecule, it could not go through the glass. "Glass is solid," she said, "and heat molecules, if there were such things, couldn't go through the glass. Since we saw heat go through the glass and make the liquid expand, we know that it's not made up of molecules." I asked the class whether this student's idea made sense, neither affirming nor rejecting her response. Instead, I gauged the expressions on the other students' faces and their initial responses to see how they were internalizing her argument.

A powerful event then happened in my classes, one I did not expect. Throughout my classes at that point, a few students asked what heat was if it was not made up of molecules. We talked that through until one student realized that heat had to be energy since it was not matter. For many of my students, the lesson appeared to be their first meaningful encounter with the concept of energy. They had learned in years past that the universe was made of matter and energy, but the reality of the concept seemed to sink in for the first time during this lesson.

The purpose of the pulse glass lesson was to help students think about heat as energy and how it affects molecular motion. Via instruction following the two cycles of Figure 1, they encountered evidence from the natural world and they used that evidence to develop stronger and more scientific ideas about how the world works. I used my knowledge of inquiry and conceptual change instruction to guide and facilitate their learning.

CONCLUSION

We have taken a detailed look at how teacher knowledge can be employed in the two-cycle model of Figure 1 to generate student understanding in the science classroom. In the investigation cycle, teachers use their knowledge of guiding and facilitating inquiry to help students gather evidence from the natural world in a way that students regard the data as believable and trustworthy. Teachers need knowledge about selecting labs that match their curriculum goals and resources on-hand. They have to be able to set up the materials students need. They have to be able to introduce the lab to students and guide the students as they work through the lab. They must monitor safety and keep students on-task. To apply these techniques to inquiry, however, teachers must possess the professional knowledge described here to help students make sense of the process of laboratory investigations so that they understand and trust the data they have collected.

In the debrief cycle, teachers use their knowledge of orchestrating discourse to guide students to make sense of the data they just collected. Again, many familiar teaching skills and techniques come into play in this cycle. Teachers must manage student behavior in small-group learning. They have to ask good questions. They have to listen attentively to student ideas, but also skillfully redirect students when their thinking is incorrect. Inquiry teachers raise these skills to a higher level, however, when they can guide small- and large-group discussions so that students internalize the scientific explanations that emerge from laboratory evidence.

Take a look at the bottom lines of Figure 1 for the results of the model. You may not have noticed these before. The bottom of Figure 1 shows how the model results in student understanding. As teachers use their knowledge to guide students again and again through the investigation cycle of the model, students develop an understanding of the process of science. They do not learn about inquiry by memorizing the five steps of some scientific method: they understand it by direct experience. As teachers use their knowledge to guide students successfully through the debrief cycle of the model, students develop understanding of science content. They do not learn by memorizing facts. Instead they see for themselves how scientific understandings are the best explanations of evidence they collected. Furthermore, as students move between both cycles, they learn to think. Their teachers constantly engage them in thinking about data and what it means. Finally, the combination of the two cycles helps students to understand the nature of science from direct experience. They realize, as my students told me, that science knowledge comes from the lab and "from talking about what happens in the lab." The model shows how rich teacher knowledge can be aptly deployed to create rich student knowledge.

Some readers will probably take issue with my focus away from open-ended inquiry. I have purposely focused on structured- and guided-inquiry (Bell et al., 2005) because of the failure of open inquiry in my classroom. I question whether open-ended inquiry is a realistic goal for real classrooms, classroom without appropriate time, materials, and mixed motivation among students. Without positive conditions for teaching and learning, I question whether open-ended inquiry can thrive. The model proposed in this chapter helps teachers implement inquiry without inappropriately directing them toward the chaos and frustration that I experienced.

By way of wrapping up this consideration of teacher professional knowledge, let us return to the dialogue among the intern, the mentor, and the supervisor. I indicated at the outset that the model would help make sense of all those voices that science teachers have pounding in their ears. In the vignette, the supervisor was concerned that the intern had structured the inquiry too much and had omitted the history of science. The model helps us get a handle on those concerns. Open-ended inquiry experiences are good for understanding how to create investigations, but the model shows that for students to understand science content, they need their teacher's expert guidance to make sense of the data they're collecting. The history of science is valuable for understanding the nature of science, one of the results of the model, and the supervisor was correct to advise the Intern to include it, something teachers using the model can easily work into debriefs when opportunities arise in the dialogue.

The mentor also had two main concerns, both addressed by the model. The first was a lack of hands-on activities and direct experiences. I am sure that you can see now that the model clearly advocates for these experiences in the investigation cycle, but the model also criticizes a hands-on-only approach. If students are only experiencing hands-on science, without the debrief component, they will not make sense of their data nor develop essential science content knowledge. The mentor's second concern was the intern's lack of focus on standards. The model allows this focus if teachers thoughtfully align student experiences so that they are investigating and debriefing the science called for in the standards.

The model will not solve all of the broad issues plaguing American science teaching, such as lack of funding for science materials or administrative support for discipline. But it can provide teachers with a way to bring order to their own teaching by making sense of the conflicting instructional voices they are hearing. More importantly, the model helps science teachers move toward the meaningful teaching and learning that drew most into the profession. They will see their students doing science meaningfully in the investigation phase. In lab, my ninth graders went from following instructions by rote to working well in teams and understanding the data they were collecting. Teachers will see their students understanding the big ideas of science and thinking in the debrief stage. My physical science students went from passively waiting for me to give them a list of facts to memorize for the test to being able to take a first attempt at explaining the meaning of the data they collected in the lab. And what will excite many teachers the most, use of the model will allow them to see their students truly engaged in science. It is like one of my students said at the end of the year: "Dr. Meadows, I don't like science, I've never liked science, and I won't ever like science. But, you know what? I like this science." She, and many of my other students, had found the value in science. They understood it.

A FRAMEWORK FOR EXAMINING PROFESSIONAL KNOWLEDGE FOR TEACHING SCIENCE VIA INQUIRY

Mark Olson

As indicated in previous chapters, there is broad enthusiasm for inquiry teaching and learning in science. As a pedagogy, inquiry has been promoted as an alternative to dry and didactic science instruction. Inquiry aims to produce learning outcomes that are more ambitious, more meaningful, more interesting, while simultaneously better at conveying the scientific enterprise and the nature of knowledge. Further, inquiry is seen as a way of enlivening classroom science and incorporating the excitement of scientific discovery. Even within the discussions about the potential benefits of inquiry teaching and learning, however, it is not entirely clear just what knowledge a teacher must have in order to success-ful enact inquiry-based lessons.

This situation is apparent within the vignette of the intern and her conversation with mentor and supervisor. There we have three actors who represent broad process-based stances taken about inquiry: an intern using inquiry as a process for connecting "everyday" experiences with sci-entific ideas; a mentor-teacher who advocates inquiry as a teaching approach that is grounded in student experience; and a university super-visor who favors including the history of science within his view of effec-tive inquiry teaching. In addition to the discord about what constitutes inquiry, there is an accompanying uncertainty about the knowledge needed by teachers. The central question of the current chapter addresses the issue of the professional knowledge required of teacher to be effective with inquiry.

I hope to make some progress on questions of what constitutes teacher professional knowledge about inquiry, and to what extent this knowledge is evidenced in the vignette. To do so, I must first acknowledge the breadth of knowledge needed to teach science, and then to focus on what is a central, yet oft-times overlooked, requisite body of knowledge about inquiry science—subject matter knowledge. To do so I introduce a frame-work that articulates what teachers need to know about subject matter in order to teach via inquiry. In doing so, I strongly suggest that efforts—whether in teacher education or teacher profession development—to improve inquiry-based instruction that do not attend to subject matter understandings (Roehrig, 2004) are also not likely to be successful.

Of course, subject matter knowledge is not the only kind of knowledge a science teacher needs. Teachers need to know many things and describ-ing the broad set of knowledge needed to teach inquiry-base science is a tall task. Such a knowledge base includes pedagogical content knowledge (Gess-Newsome & Lederman, 1999), knowledge of student learning (Bransford & Donovan, 2005), of science curriculum (Bybee, 1997, 2002) as well as the history and nature of science (Gould, 1983). In this chapter I focus on the core subject matter knowledge needed by a teacher to teach inquiry science. In doing so, I am not suggesting that subject matter knowledge is the most important element of a teacher's knowledge, but I do argue that it is essential for good teaching. While it may appear silly to even make such a statement, it turns out that despite common-sense notions of subject matter expertise—there is little consensus about the role subject matter does indeed play in teachers' knowledge. A recent review of the literature (Wilson, Floden, & Ferrini-Mundy, 2001) shows that not only is there little consensus about how much or what kinds of subject matter might be important for teaching but also how would one measure, or even recognize, such knowledge in the first place. But before we throw up our hands and walk away, I would like to offer a framework that has been productive in my thinking about science teaching.

This chapter is an attempt to make some progress in this challenge. Specifically, my goal is to provide a fresh perspective about the professional knowledge of science teachers. To do so, I show that a particularly promising place to look for the subject matter for inquiry teaching is in the instructional representations used by a teacher to teach subject matter to students. But before getting to the interesting and generative issues engaged in the vignette, I first would like to consider a framework for looking at the subject matter knowledge engaged in science classrooms

I. WAYS OF KNOWING SCIENTIFIC KNOWLEDGE

Jerome Bruner (1985, 1986) asserts that broadly there are two fundamental and independent ways of making sense of experience that he calls: narrative and paradigmatic. That is the world can be interpreted from a narrative "story-like" point of view, or from a paradigmatic "scientifically principled" point of view. Now it might seem clear that narrative is the province of poetry, drama and the humanities while the paradigmatic is what most concerns the "hard" sciences such as biology, chemistry, and the like. Not only is this not so clear-cut, it is not true. In fact, deep understanding in science makes use of *both* narrative and paradigmatic ways of knowing (Olson, 2005). That is, there are two different, and independent, ways in which to understand science—and both are needed in order to have an understanding sufficient to teach science by inquiry.

To explain, let me first make clear what I mean by narrative and paradigmatic ways of knowing, and then show why they are complementary and both necessary for teaching inquiry. Narrative ways of knowing consider the objects of science as characters in a story. There is a methods of teaching science textbook called "Science Stories" (Koch, 2004), which promotes the use of stories as a way to build students' science understanding. Such stories are not explicitly constructed around underlying principles or categories. Instead, good narratives must ultimately be compelling or believable. Though there may be somewhat "universal" storylines, these universals act more like templates—as in genre—than the principled and generative statements of paradigmatic understandings.

Paradigmatic thinking is concerned with the construction of conceptual categories, such as temperature or energy, and the ways in which these categories are used and maintained to depict a system. Paradigmatic accounts of science are about the processes and relationships of a conceptual system where scientific activities such as hypothesis testing and interpreting data are the driving components of the account. Narrative accounts of science are different. Whereas paradigmatic accounts place scientific activity at the center, narrative accounts are centrally about objects (such as plants, animals, or silverware) that take the role of main subject or lead character of a story. Both produce "explanations" or accounts of why something happens. It is in the nature of the "why" that they differ. In paradigmatic accounts action occurs due to the state of the conceptual system. In narrative accounts action occurs because an object in the system caused something to happen. Both types of accounts are important for teaching and learning science for understanding.

This framework sets the stage for considering a different way of thinking about science teachers' professional knowledge for teaching inquiry. Rather than flattening subject matter knowledge to be a storehouse of inert knowledge, or reducing inquiry teaching to be about pedagogy alone, this framework allows for a richer characterization of the knowledge and skills needed to teach inquiry. Fundamentally, I argue that deep knowledge of science involves both narrative and paradigmatic accounts and that successful inquiry teaching requires the coordination of the two. I will describe how the formulation of this coordinated knowledge for a teacher remains a dynamic process throughout a teacher's career.

II. Ways of Knowing and Teaching Science

While it is not surprising that paradigmatic accounts of science are valued, the claim that narrative accounts are vital may be a surprise. Good narrative representations of science are compelling stories about nature. They are interesting and motivating as contexts in which students can see that science is worth doing. Narrative representations play an important role in good science teaching (Egan, 1988; McEwan, 1995). When done well, teaching has a similar structure to a well-told story. In his book, *The Culture of Education*, Bruner (1996) makes an elegant argument for greater inclusion of "narratives of science" in the curriculum of science. He focuses on the potential for stories about science to combat the tediousness of what constitutes much of present science instruction in schools. By championing the role that stories of scientific discoveries might play in the classroom, he raises important issues about what is motivating and interesting about science for students. Bruner argues that a better understanding of what makes a good narrative can likely be translated into instructional practices that would make the subject matter of science come alive.

In a complementary vein, Kiernan Egan (1997) argues that developmental stages in youth learning resonate with various narrative approaches. Such narratives should be used to tap into the powerful resources of students' interests and motivation leading to the better design of curriculum. Geologists spend a great deal of their professional lives trying to figure out the details to be included in their "stories." Then they tell them. Telling these stories helps develop the paradigm for uncovering other stories and, importantly, for making predictions.

The narrative stories of science can serve important motivational and cognitive purposes. But the narrative accounts of science I am interested in examining are different from what Egan, McEwan, and Bruner describe. I am interested not in an examination of compelling stories about scientists and of discovery, but in the narratives used as explanations of phenomena. I contend that the failure to account for the ways in which narratives show up in explanations and representations of subject matter knowledge in science actually hampers learning by inquiry.

Let us examine an instructional representation of subject matter from the vignette where students touch silverware and towels at room temperature. In congruence with inquiry approaches, the intern had her students make predictions and record observations and students were surprised by what they observed—as she anticipated. However, if we examine the types of explanations that were available for students to use to make sense of their experiences, we can see important distinctions.

Although the intern explains for the students the distinctions between everyday and scientific meanings of words such as heat and temperature, and that their experiences can be described in terms of energy transfer, what she failed to provide was a connection to the conceptual framework of basic kinetic-molecular theory. With the materials at hand she could have identified the parts of the systems that had energy and indicate how energy would need to transfer in order for the systems to function. The crucial aspects of model-based reasoning, an accounting for the flow of matter and energy in a system, were not made available to the students. Therefore, the experiences that the teacher provided for the students did not serve as opportunities to practice with paradigmatic explanations. Instead, based on the experiences in the classroom, students engage relatively detailed narratives that recount important features of energy transfer, without attention to causal conceptual states. I will return to a more detailed examination of these representations of subject matter knowledge after presenting the general roles that common elements of instruction such as examples, definitions and discrepant events can play both narrative and paradigmatic roles. A comparison of the narrative and paradigmatic instructional components is summarized below:

III. Coordinating Two Dimensions of Knowing Science

Because narrative and paradigmatic ways of knowing are fundamentally independent from each other it might be puzzling to appreciate how someone might view science from both perspectives if each perspective is independent. What becomes necessary is avoiding an inappropriate use of dualistic thinking. Rather than struggling with a question about which is better and trying to determine whether narrative or paradigmatic ways of knowing are preferable, my suggestion is to consider how to coordinate these two. Instead of placing paradigmatic and narrative ways of thinking at opposite ends of a continuum, suppose understanding can be represented in two-dimensional space, as seen in Figure 3. Using a Cartesian coordinate system as an analogy, the narrative way of thinking runs along the horizontal and the paradigmatic along vertical. In this representation, narrative and paradigmatic are not in opposition to each other but rather can combine to pull into a new direction, a direction I refer to as rich understanding.

Consider how narrative and paradigmatic understandings contribute toward rich understandings in science. The relationship between narrative and paradigmatic understanding which results in rich understanding can be illustrated in a vector diagram that treats understanding as a vector "quantity" composed of a narrative understanding component and a paradigmatic understanding component. Because narrative and paradigmatic are independent, they are represented as perpendicular vectors in "understanding space" as depicted in the accompanying diagram.

If one considers understanding (U) to be a representation of the "net" understanding a person demonstrates about a science topic, we can decompose that understanding into narrative (N) and paradigmatic (P) contribution factors. Therefore, a characterization of a person's overall understanding is the vector sum of these two components. I consider these understandings of knowledge representations to be heuristic and even as they provide a novel way to consider how knowledge is represented in science classrooms.

By deconstructing instructional representations from the science classroom into these components a number of interpretations can be made. First of all, to represent understanding as a two-dimensional construct is richer than the more common single dimensional construct wherein knowledge is described as ranging from shallow to deep. This alternative representation is helpful because it affords a more descriptive and analytic characterization of the ways teachers use examples, demonstrations, labs and so on, in science. There is much to learn in learning to teach science, and teachers learn much about their subject

Table 1.   Comparisons of Instructional Representations

Instructional Representation	Purpose	Rationale
Role of **examples** in narrative accounts	To serve as illustrations of phenomena.	Multiple experiences with phenomena (examples) promote ability to associate ideas with instances
Role of **examples** in paradigmatic accounts	To serve as opportunities to explain phenomena in terms of a model.	Multiple experiences with phenomena (examples) promote ability to establish patterns in explanations.
Role of **definitions** in narrative accounts	To provide essential "facts" of the story	Facts are the elements that are connected together by phenomena/events that serve like actors in a play. Chronology plays an important role.
Role of **definitions** in paradigmatic accounts	To provide the essential "facts" and/or as principles that apply across the phenomena.	Facts are the elements that are connected together by principles and processes. These processes depend on the state of the system.
Discrepant events in narrative accounts	To increase the sense of drama and interest. The unexpected is motivating because the story is more interesting	Accounts are memorable and interesting when they include the element of surprise.
Discrepant events in paradigmatic accounts	To provide the opportunity to use an explanatory model in a new context or to establish the need for model adjustment or limitation.	Models are powerful and satisfying when they can explain a broad range of phenomena.

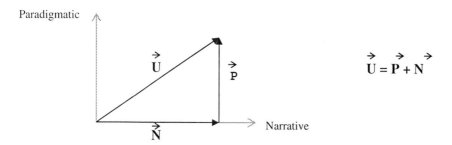

Figure 3.   Two-dimensional representation of understanding space.

matter in the course of teaching it. The best way to learn something is to teach it. But what it is that one learns in the course of teaching science is uncertain (McDiarmid, Ball & Anderson, 1989). For the case of learning to teach inquiry-based science, both the way in which teachers understand their subject matter has important consequences for what students can learn in classrooms.

IV. Learning to Teach Science Using Inquiry

In the vignette, it appears the Intern has worked hard to engage her students with a rich set of heat and temperature phenomena. The examples she uses, such as the heat capacity of metals, the pulse glass, thermometers and various opportunities to make observations and measurements, are standard and typical within physical science instruction. To be sure, her efforts to communicate for her students the differentiations between everyday and scientific conceptions of heat indicates rather sophisticated views about students' science learning. It is only through careful consideration of the knowledge representations that we notice opportunities for improvement.

If we consider that a primary goal of science is to generate explanations of natural phenomena, we can also consider a very simple version of how such knowledge is produced and tested. At its most basic level, science makes use of data in order to establish patterns that are then accounted for by conceptual explanations or theories as espoused by Lee Meadown in his chapter, "Teacher Knowledge About Inquiry: Incorporating Conceptual Change Theory." While there is certainly flexibility and recursive relationship between these categories (Anderson, Lohma, & Sharma, 2005; Duschl, 1990) relying upon scientific activity to move between data, patterns and explanations is useful for our look at the teaching practices of this intern and her teaching about thermal phenomena.

During the debriefing with her mentor and university supervisor, the intern expresses that she felt that most of her students were beginning to grasp the distinctions between heat and temperature and that they had participated in sufficient investigations to do so. While the vignette is not detailed enough for strong claims about the sufficiency of the investigations and for students' abilities to distinguish concepts, there are reasons to ask questions. Windschitl (2004) compellingly demonstrates that new teachers often have "folk" notions of inquiry that are largely shaped by their own experiences as science learners in traditional classrooms. Such a background does not often provide the foundation upon which to develop productive notions of scientific inquiry and in fact, tends to produce understandings that merely mimic the practices of inquiry.

The intern asks "how well" she did in this lesson. To answer requires more than what the mentor and university supervisor offered (which was to recommend devoting additional time to hands-on activities and to also utilize the history of science as a context in which to organize lessons). I think this intern deserves a different, and more substantive, kind of response. First, we will examine the kinds of learning opportunities that students were provided in the lesson. Second, we will classify the learning opportunites as to their role in the lesson: in what ways did they serve as data, patterns or explanations? Finally, we will examine the relationships among data, patterns and explanations to judge whether they constituted narrative or paradigmatic or coordinated accounts of the phenomena.

Let us begin with the questions that the Intern first poses to her class:

"Can someone describe the two competing ways to explain what is happening?"
"Who can remember the investigation we did with these materials?"

Each question invites students to remember information from previous activities. While this is no doubt important and necessary, the Intern does not ask her students to use this knowledge in any way beyond recall. She is treating the earlier activities as experiences to be remembered in much the same way they may be asked to recall a story. Missing within this teacher question is any signal to the students that they are to draw upon a more generalized understanding of heat. The students are being encouraged to recall an episode but they are not invited to coordinate these episodes with broader conceptualizations. In terms of the framework, the narrative way of thinking is occurring but without the paradigmatic component. In effect, the story is being recalled, with equipment and phenomena playing the role of characters and plot, but without simultaneously drawing attention to the underlying concept, the literary equivalent of its theme, moral or message. The questions posed by the teacher promote student thinking along the narrative dimension but not the paradigmatic.

For the most substantive aspect of instruction, the intern asks her students to make predictions about how the silverware and towel will feel when touched. This strategy can be important for at least two reasons. First, it provides the teacher with a sense of what ideas the students have about the phenomena and second, it serves as a motivating context for students because they are likely puzzled and want to learn why. What is less obvious about this particular instance is that the subject matter also changes. Earlier in the vignette, the questions were about distinctions between the variables temperature and thermal energy. But the silverware example adds an additional conceptual element related to the concept of thermal conductivity, which is about how fast energy is transferred in a material. The earlier conceptual framework provided by the intern, does not provide the necessary basis for incorporating the new observations into a coherent systemic understanding. The remaining option is for students to remember this experience as another narrative experience.

What is centrally important in the effort to learn by inquiry is to examine enough data, experiences often in narrative form, to uncover or develop patterns in those experiences. It is in the effort to explain these patterns that paradigmatic accounts are necessary. Looking at the vignette from this "data, patterns, explanations" standpoint we can assess the likelihood that sufficient cases have been engaged by students in order to see patterns in the data, and what type of explanations were engaged to account for the patterns. From the details provided in this vignette, I think it is clear that sufficiency has not been met. The pulse glass, the heat capacity lab, and the silverware activities do not provide a compelling set of experiences from which to extract robust patterns that can be explained by students in a conceptual way. That is, they do not serve as a foundation for a model-based, paradigmatic understanding of these phenomena.

What seems more likely is that students will remember each of the activities as a discrete episode or event in a larger story about heat and temperature. Granted this story has "real characters" and that phenomena will likely be accurately named and associated with the right examples (as in "can someone describe the two competing ways to explain what is happening," and "what happens when you stick your tongue to a frigid pole"). This is all of the evidence in the vignette that students are building the capacity to "know the story" of heat and temperature. They are given new vocabulary such as "science heat" and "everyday heat" with which to describe phenomena. But they are not provided with the conceptual hallmarks of paradigmatic reasoning: a conceptual model that identifies the physical elements of the system and how energy flows in that system.

It is interesting to note that the mentor's and supervisor's feedback are also along the narrative dimension alone. The mentor wanted students to have more hands-on experiences, and to reduce the amount of time the teacher was merely talking. This apparently presumes that the students would be able to inductively generate and make use of the distinctions between temperature, heat, science heat, everyday heat, thermal conductivity and so on. While it seems likely that students would improve their abilities to associate concepts with phenomena if they have a rich and illustrative experiential base, such learning would be in the form of narrative accounts of the phenomena. This is because the conceptual model required for paradigmatic reasoning is not available from observation and experience alone. The model is instead a mental construct used to interpret experience (Driver, Asoko, Leach, Mortimer, & Scott, 1994). Likewise, we can construe the supervisor's feedback to include more examples from the history of science as advice that such examples will be more vivid and memorable to students. While this is also likely to be true, it fortifies the students' experiential base along the narrative dimension alone.

What is missing in this lesson and from this feedback is a conceptual model that links all of these terms and ideas in a functional way, that is, along the paradigmatic dimension. Such an account makes clear that temperature is an intensive variable, thermal energy is an extensive variable, that heat is a function of both temperature difference and thermal conductivity, and how energy flows in the system. For students to learn to use such a model to make productive and useful explanations of phenomena is still a major challenge. Further, it is not simply a matter of learning how to use this mode but for students to also articulate how this model compares and contrasts with their notions of everyday heat (Wiser & Amin, 2001) that focuses on more implicit and commonly-held notions of hotness. This is what I mean by needing both narrative and paradigmatic accounts and to be able to coordinate between the two.

It is important to note that I am not arguing for the supremacy of paradigmatic accounts over narrative accounts. I am arguing that teachers require subject matter knowledge from each perspective in order to effectively teach inquiry-based science. Although the Intern indicates a rich set of narrative understandings through her selection of examples and demonstrations, conspicuously absent is the lack of explicit attention to model-based, conceptual explanations. I will next explain the importance of coordinating such a rich narrative terrain with opportunities for paradigmatic explanations for students to successfully learn via inquiry.

Central to notions of scientific inquiry is the generation and pursuit of scientific questions. But what knowledge is needed in order to ask and answer scientific questions? My answer, unsurprisingly, is both narrative and paradigmatic knowledge of phenomena. The intern in the vignette did a good job of engaging students in interesting examples of phenomena such as with the pulse glass and the silverware/towel investigation. While general model-based accounts for the matter and energy flow in a system may be paradigmatic in structure, when left disconnected from actual phenomena they are also meaningless. It is in the ability to coordinate between the conceptual model and its application in a narrative context that powerful understanding is demonstrated. Obviously, if an intern is going to create such opportunities for her students, she must understand science in that way herself. This is the import of the earlier discussion about looking for patterns in their experiences. To see the patterns nominated as important from a model-based perspective is neither trivial nor simple. To conceptualize the feeling of cold tiles as the result of an abstract entity called energy transfer is to coordinate between narrative experience and paradigmatic explanation. Where are the teacher's questions that would encourage these forms of knowing? I claim that questions that are fruitfully explored via inquiry are ultimately in the service of exploring, testing or constructing a conceptual model of phenomena,[2] where such exploration is in the generation and examination of patterns in data.

Conclusions and Further Considerations

This examination of teacher knowledge required for inquiry science focused on the role of the teacher's knowledge about science as it related to teaching students to engage in inquiry. I frame the subject matter knowledge for teaching inquiry as having two components. One component, the narrative dimension, provides concrete illustrations of a phenomenon in the form of a story. Narrative has a powerful role in how we come to understand something and science abounds tales of individual's ideas. One that comes to mind is Watson and Crick's story about developing the now iconic double helix representation of DNA's structure (Watson, 1968). The *Double Helix* recounts the ways in which evidence from a variety of sources was used in a concerted effort to piece to together a conceptual model. But just as the chemical bonds are only pieces of a larger whole, the stories of science, including stories of inquiry processes, do not automatically lead to a rich representation of science. To this mix is the need for coordinating these experiences with a larger and more inclusive type of conceptual explanation. Paradigmatic accounts allow for the coordination of these conceptual explanations with narrative accounts of experiences with phenomena.

When describing the professional knowledge teachers need about inquiry in order to create opportunities to learn science for understanding with their students, this requires combining narrative stories of inquiry with paradigmatic principles. Beyond tales about how a fresh perspective led to new discoveries, a paradigmatic way of thinking recognizes the commonalities across these stories including the value of creativity and the need to strive for objectivity. The obverse is equally true: giving students only the paradigmatic explanations (e.g., "scientists don't let their personal perspectives influence the data they gather") for inquiry lacks the vitality of real-life examples. The DNA model was such an intellectual accomplishment because of the coordination between the bits and the whole. The individual paper pieces representing the component molecules had to be organized in a way that aligned with other data Watson and Crick had obtained. The architecture of the DNA molecule reflects a successful joining and alignment of parts. In much the same way, the professional knowledge of teachers requires the coordination of narrative and paradigmatic thought processes. In particular, facility in describing both components when teaching students about inquiry plots a trajectory that differs from the all-or-none dispositions of the intern's mentor and supervisor.

In important ways, this chapter parallels the vignette. I have provided limited data to support the patterns that I assert. I claim that the narrative and paradigmatic ways of knowing help to understand what occurs within the vignette. I have, in fact, not conclusively demonstrated that. But I can use the framework to reflexively interpret my account: I have hypothesized a conceptual model for the knowledge structure of subject matter understanding for teaching inquiry science. I have used this model to account for elements of the vignette germane to inquiry instruction and student learning. I have explained the relationships between these elements and how they both promote and inhibit learning in science.

In the effort to inform the discussion about prerequisite teacher knowledge for teaching inquiry science, I hope this account raises doubts about the adequacy of its own explanation. In so doing, I assert that this is what scientific inquiry is: generating questions based upon the interrogation of conceptualizations of experience. To do so is to take part in a broader aspect of knowing in science and education through the testing of assertions, data and patterns, and the attempted coordination with other knowledge claims. An articulation of the differences in explanations can deepen our understanding of the system. What begins as a perhaps vague and suggestive explanation becomes refined and more powerful or not! This is just how science scoots along: by conducting inquiries into accounts of phenomena to produce explanations, and also importantly, by making earnest efforts to explore how some conceptual roads are more or less productive.

This framework may be helpful by promoting conversations about science teacher knowledge. It does not dismiss the narrative understandings that many teachers hold. Instead, this framework unequivocally values narrative understandings as an essential dimension of understanding. The agenda that I have begun to lay out hints at what it might mean for a teacher to continue to expand their professional knowledge about science. It also sheds light on the resources that are important for teachers in order to develop the subject matter understandings necessary for teaching science by inquiry. Being able to discuss, teach and learn with more explicit attention to coordinating the narrative and paradigmatic accounts is likely to improve communication about what types of subject matter understandings are being engaged by both teacher and student. It is in this spirit that I have offered the coordination of narrative with paradigmatic ways of thinking and teaching as a vantage point for observing and discussing teacher knowledge about inquiry.

MOVING PAST A BELIEF IN INQUIRY AS A PEDAGOGY: IMPLICATIONS FOR TEACHER KNOWLEDGE

John Settlage

The ultimate purpose of the bee is not exhausted by ... any of the processes the human mind can discern. The higher the human intellect rises in the discovery of these purposes, the more obvious it becomes, that the ultimate purpose [of the bee] is beyond our comprehension.

—Tolstoy (1898)

When it comes to questions about teacher professional knowledge about inquiry, I have arrived at my current way of thinking during two decades in the profession. As an intermittent science teacher (e.g., Southerland, Kittleson, & Settlage, 2005) and perpetual teacher educator, I have struggled with the implications of inquiry. This has happened because I have had to consider the role of inquiry within my own teaching and I often field questions from practitioners about inquiry. Something I sensed early in my career and repeatedly reinforced over time has been my skepticism about inquiry for all its allegedly hallowed power. Especially when it comes to open inquiry, I find claims of its sanctity to be unconvincing. However, as a teacher educator, I shouldn't simply discard some claim unless it can be replaced with something that is better. As a consequence, I will address the issue of teacher professional knowledge even as I call into question the status of open inquiry as the only way to teach science.

The professional knowledge required of teachers involves the blend of content knowledge and pedagogical knowledge that supports their students' engagement in inquiry. The departure from other views about teacher knowledge for inquiry is that I do not view inquiry as a teaching approach. Instead, inquiry describes desired learning outcomes for students. More specifically, the essential features of inquiry as portrayed by the National Research Council (2000) represent inquiry—as a skill-set to be developed in students. In this author's view, a shift is long overdue: we should abandon efforts to teach *by* inquiry in favor of teaching *for* inquiry. The implications for teacher professional knowledge created by this transformation are significant. But before entering into a consideration of that issue, we must distance ourselves from open inquiry.

PERSISTENCE OF SUPPORT FOR OPEN INQUIRY

Within the vignette, the mentor contrasted between "closed vs. open" in a way suggesting that undirected investigation represents the purest form of inquiry, a view we can trace to the post-Sputnik era (Schwab, 1960; Shulman & Tamir, 1973). The standard mentor applied to evaluating the presence of inquiry was the degree to which the students were in control of their investigations of scientific materials. The more influence and control exerted by the teacher, the further the lesson departs from inquiry. It is this author's view that this represents an erroneous interpretation of inquiry. Furthermore, this misrepresentation is not confined to this fictionalized situation or a quaint relic from a previous generation of science education reform. Instead, this view is widespread throughout contemporary discussions about effective science teaching. In brief, the belief in a hierarchy where open, unstructured inquiry is viewed as the pinnacle of science teaching excellence is not only inaccurate, but the perpetuation of this conviction has the potential to undermine the goal of scientific literacy for all learners.

Throughout this book, and with increased frequency within science education literature, individuals are describing the limitations of open inquiry. [See Section II on student knowledge, Section III on instructional context, and Section IV on student diversity]. The reader could question whether promoting open inquiry is an actual problem or something we only imagine. Where, one might ask, would a teacher develop the idea that open inquiry is the best way to teach science? What is there within the written material about science teaching practices that would inform teachers about the appropriateness of inquiry teaching? Two sources this author consulted were materials about inquiry published and promoted by the National Science Teachers Association (NSTA) as well as a convenience sampling of science methods textbooks commonly used at the preservice level. The purpose for examining these materials was to uncover evidence that would suggest that the 1960s predilection for open inquiry persists until today.

The National Science Teachers Association offers several texts through its NSTA store that reinforce the preeminence of open-ended inquiry. For example the advertisement for *Inquiry and Learning: Realizing Science Standards in the Classroom* (Layman, Ochoa, & Heikkinen, 1996) reads: "Keep it real: Sure the theory of inquiry-based learning sounds great—less lecturing, more exploring. But how does inquiry-driven learning look and feel in a real classroom? Read this to find out." Here inquiry is represented as an alternative to lecturing. Another example from the NSTA store is: "Inquiring minds want to know plenty of hands-on ways to transform younger students from passive listeners (maybe) into an active, engaged community of budding scientists. Which is just what this book is designed to help you do." What a great idea! Students will not have to be attentive spectators because they can be proto-scientists. Inquiry is proffered as a path out of the mind-numbing classrooms of old. Inquiry is promoted as an alternative to traditional teaching. Such rhetoric reinforces the one-dimensional continuum where teacher-centered instruction is located at one end and student-centered activity is situated at the opposite extreme (Martin, 2003).

For preservice science teachers, a similar message is transmitted via their college textbooks. For example, one secondary text describes the need for teachers to "make the transition from a traditional mode of instruction to an inquiry-based mode" (Chiappetta & Koballa, 2006, p. 157). In the next section of the same text, the authors listed 11 concerns expressed about using inquiry: time, materials, coverage, discipline, administrators, and so on. Nowhere in this list is there any refinement of the various levels of inquiry. Instead the movement toward open inquiry is cast as emancipatory. On occasions, science methods texts are less ambiguous. One such example in a book for future elementary teachers asserts that: "The essence of an inquiry unit involves turning students loose as investigators of an intriguing system of variables" (Etheredge & Rudnitsky, 2003, p. 20). Consulting science methods textbooks (e.g., Krajcik, Czerniak, & Berger, 2003; Lederman, Lederman, & Bell, 2004) reveals an absence of any distinctions among varied forms of inquiry. In short, these textbooks contain only passing references to inquiry as an instructional goal, as substantiated by the *National Science Education Standards* (NSES), with no information about the variations of this approach, let alone information cautioning teachers about the shortcomings of open inquiry.

It is this author's opinion that this message about the problems of open inquiry is not being satisfactorily transmitted from university campuses into K-12 classrooms. The reality is that open inquiry is being actively promoted within science in my state as an idealized instructional approach. Many of my fellow contributors to this book might question whether open inquiry is all that insidious. Unless those who have thought hard about the challenges of open inquiry take this situation seriously, then we may well find ourselves in a political tussle over extremes. In this regard, it seems we should learn from our reading education colleagues who have had to sustain battles between whole language and scripted instruction. It is not hard to imagine a legislative debate about science curriculum instruction in which open-inquiry and discovery are pitted against direction instruction and textbook-based teaching. The very real possibility, again summoning the reading education situation, is that the latter option would be prescribed within legislated mandates.

INQUIRY AS A STUDENT SKILL-SET

Is inquiry what we expect students to do? Or is inquiry what we do to students? Perhaps it's a little of both? How might we decide? In consulting the NSES we can uncover how inquiry is described within the chapter devoted to science teaching standards to see whether inquiry was depicted as a pedagogy. At the very least, the word "inquiry" appears within the chapter on science teaching standards 35 times but appears 115 times within the science content chapter. While the NSES is not a definitive source, the stance its developers provide is informative:

> *Inquiry* into authentic questions generated from student experiences is the central strategy for teaching science. Teachers focus *inquiry* predominantly on real phenomena, in classrooms, outdoors, or in laboratory settings, where students are given investigations or guided toward fashioning investigations that are demanding but within their capabilities.... Nevertheless, teachers can take an *inquiry* approach as they guide students in acquiring and interpreting information from sources such as libraries, government documents, and computer databases. (italics added, NRC, 1996, p. 31)

By and large, the NSES associates "inquiry" with student activity (sometimes conjuring a "spirit of inquiry"). However, as this excerpt illustrates, inquiry can also be referred to as an approach to instruction as one of multiple models from which teachers can select. Notably, the notion of an "inquiry approach" or "inquiry-based teaching" are mentioned only rarely within the standards and with very little specificity. Time and again, inquiry is described as the skills, physical and mental, in which students are to engage as a necessary component of their science learning.

This leads us to a bold assertion: inquiry is not pedagogy but rather a student skill-set. In other words, developing students' abilities to perform and participate in inquiry is a goal for science education, at the classroom level as well as more systemically, as seen in Table 2. The instructional approaches used to develop this collection of inquiry skills within students is varied and could include very open-ended activities. But it would be equally appropriate to employ highly-structured activities, even without direct experience or actual objects, as a mechanism for developing inquiry skills. Put another way, the goal of developing an inquiry skill-set within science learners does not dictate a singular teaching approach.

Table 2.   Five Essential Features of Inquiry (NRC, 2000)

1. Learner engages in scientifically oriented **questions**
2. Learner gives priority to **evidence** in responding to questions
3. Learner formulates **explanations** from evidence
4. Learner **connects** explanations to scientific knowledge
5. Learner communicates and **justifies** explanations to others

The inquiry skill-set is more sophisticated than a list of discrete process skills. As valuable as it is for students to become more skilled with objectively collecting information (observing), generating explanations for what they notice (inferring), and so on, there is legitimate concern about teaching process skills out of context or divorced from a larger goal such as developing accurate scientific conceptions. The inquiry skill-set is defined by the five essential features of inquiry. The issue about whether a teacher elects to provide more or less structure as the students develop their skill-set is immaterial—at least in terms of whether or not an activity qualifies as being inquiry. Whether the teacher leaves the source of the question for an investigation open to the students or decides that the class would be better off if the question they investigated came directly from another source such as a textbook is really not the issue. What is crucial in determining the quality of inquiry within an activity is the extent to which students are actively involved with all five essential features.

The Vignette and an Inquiry Skill-Set

Within the vignette, there was conflict among the three actors' views about the presence and quality of inquiry within the lesson. The intern relied upon the essential features of inquiry (NRC, 2000) as her guide for judging the extent to which inquiry found its way into the lesson. From her perspective, the presence of inquiry is evaluated by considering whether each of the five elements was present. In contrast, the mentor equated inquiry with an open-ended and experiential approach to a lesson. While acknowledging the existence of the essential features framework, his interpretation of the lesson was that it fell short of being an inquiry lesson because it was too structured and teacher-directed.

The desired learning outcome of this lesson would seem to be for the students to differentiate between everyday and scientific notions of heat. While the distinctions between heat and temperature are canonical within physical science, the misconceptions about these topics are exceedingly resistant to change (Laburú & Niaz, 2002; Lubben, Netshisaulu, &

Campbell, 1999; Wiser & Amin, 2001). In an apparent effort to discern whether students understand the distinctions between heat as a common sense versus a scientific perspective, the Intern assigned the students to describe scenarios involving hot and cold by drawing upon the alternative explanations. Finally, the intern provided a collection of small group and whole class interactions, involving a combination of direct experience and conversation, in an effort to address the targeted understanding.

Where might we attempt to locate the inquiry within this scenario? Inappropriately, given the desire to distance inquiry from a particular teaching approach, would be the effort to judge how the teaching itself was inquiry. This unhelpfully pushes us to negotiate between the opposing traditional, direct instruction and open-ended scientific inquiry (cf. Furtak, 2006) when we should attend to opportunities for students to develop their science inquiry skill-set. Using the NRC (2000) essential features, we could first determine whether a scientifically-oriented question was used to engage the students. Although on the surface it might seem to be a purely sensory experience, the discrepancy between the coolness felt when touching silverware and the dish towel compared to the thermometer readings would seem to provoke a question: why are the temperatures the same when the objects feel like they are not equally warm? Second, we can assess whether evidence is given priority to discussing the question and, thirdly, whether explanations are derived from the evidence. Although introduced with considerable teacher guidance, the students are expected to discuss evidence (e.g., perceptions vs. thermometer readings) as they struggled to resolve the disparity. Fourth, learners connected their activities to the understandings of the larger scientific community because the intern had the students read a textbook passage explaining how a tile floor and a rug exhibit similar properties to those of the silverware and towel. Finally, by having the students transfer this knowledge, especially in contrasting everyday and scientific heat through their writing, the Intern assisted the students with communicating and justifying explanations to others.

Given the continua for the five essential features of inquiry (NRC, 2000) it is feasible to impose greater or lesser amounts of teacher directedness across each of the features. Even though some educators might object to imposing structure upon the students during this lesson, by using the essential features as a checklist, to claim that this lesson supplied opportunities for the students to refine their use of the entire inquiry skill-set is warranted. Asserting that this cannot be an inquiry lesson because there was too much teacher involvement represents an inaccurate conflating of student actions with instructional practices. When inquiry is defined as a skill-set that students are to develop then the methods used to accomplish these, while not entirely incidental, have less pertinence relative to the question about whether this was an inquiry lesson. In other words, if the desire is to develop inquiry within students then the instructional techniques should be used in the service of that goal. Otherwise, if the goal is to teach in a certain way (e.g., inquiry-based lesson) then we will be elevating the attributes of the container over the contents it is expected to deliver.

The professional knowledge needed by a teacher is specific to supporting the development of the inquiry skill-set in students. This contrasts with a more typical view of inquiry teaching as being noninterfering. Fortunately, this shift provides substantive guidance that fills the void of only relying upon student-centeredness as the guiding principle. In its place, we in fact have a schematic that diagrams two dimensions simultaneously: the essential features of the science inquiry skill-set and the degree by which the teacher supplies structure for any given activity. In place of the more detailed descriptions provided by the NRC (2000) the cells, in Table 3, are filled for the time being with roman numerals to signify the range from considerable teacher control (i.e., I) versus very little teacher control (i.e., IV). We should envision these as levels without falling into the trap of viewing the labels as hierarchical. What is important in assessing whether an activity is legitimately "inquiry" is not represented by a score or tabulation of the number of Level IVs but instead whether all five essential features are addressed—at any Level from I to IV.

Within the vignette, the intern provided the question to the class, directed the students to make certain observations, and then encouraged them to propose how to explain the evidence. Then, the students were directed toward their textbooks to develop connections with scientists' explanations and finally they were told to compare scientific and everyday explanations about heat by writing about the same scenario from the two perspectives. Were the students using the inquiry skill-set? Yes, because all the essential feature elements were practiced by students at different levels as indicated by the shaded cells within Table 3. If we treat inquiry as a suite of student learning goals (i.e., the skill-set) then our criteria for inquiry shifts to consider whether the students had the opportunity to develop their skills. The degree of teacher structure fades to insignificance because the teaching is serving student learning.

Having situated inquiry within the realm of learning, one might wonder what limits exist for developing the inquiry skill-set. While the supervisor and mentor may have pushed for Level IV across all essential features as being a suitable goal, this is not necessary. Admittedly, there are circumstances where such methods would be appropriate such as when middle school students are expected to create an original science fair project on a topic of their own choosing. Conversely, because of the students' backgrounds and the nature of a topic, the teacher might be

Table 3. Schematic for Supporting the Inquiry Skill-Set Development (Vignette Levels are Shaded Gray)

	Learner Controlled	←	→	Teacher Structured
A. Question source	IV	III	II	I
B. Using evidence	IV	III	II	I
C. Explaining	IV	III	II	I
D. Connecting	IV	III	II	I
E. Justifying	IV	III	II	I

very directive in how a lesson is implemented—and be justifiably supporting inquiry despite the directedness of the lesson. One instance where this seems necessary would be as students attempt to explain the retrograde motion of Mars since the students would be supplied with the question as well as the data sources. Again, what constitutes an inquiry lesson is not the pedagogy but the opportunities for students to participate in all five essential features. By reconsidering the criteria for inquiry we have an avenue for advancing our discussions about students' science learning and appropriate teaching strategies.

TEACHER KNOWLEDGE REQUIRED FOR INQUIRY

The advocacy for teaching by inquiry has generated more confusion than clarity, including an absence of information regarding the requisite knowledge for teachers. Especially from those who view open inquiry as the goal, the message is a radical version of "less is more" in which student-centeredness reigns supreme and structure provided by a teacher is an anathema. Fortunately, when we redirect our attention and energies toward teaching for inquiry, teachers benefit from a wealth of information about requisite knowledge. In what follows, I identify three categories of teacher knowledge which will contribute to teaching for inquiry: pedagogy to teach for inquiry, science content knowledge to teach for inquiry, and pedagogical content knowledge to teach for inquiry.

Knowledge of Pedagogy to Teach for Inquiry

Although specifically describing effective teaching practices when working in diverse classrooms, the standards Dalton (1998) offered within *Pedagogy Matters* has utility here. Indeed as has been the case over the years, publications from the Center for Research on Education, Diversity and Excellence (CREDE) have value beyond classrooms that are very heterogeneous in terms of race, ethnicity and language. Especially in regards to teacher knowledge, they offer five standards that supply inspiration, encouragement, and guidance (see Table 4).

From sociocultural theory the joint productive activity standard adds substance to an otherwise bland notion of group work. First, the activity upon which groups are working is to result in a tangible product: a document, a Web page, a plan of action, and so forth. More than just answering questions within cooperative groups, a material object is constructed. Second, the collaborations are not only among the students. The teacher also participates in the projects. Having the pedagogical skills to plan lessons where students create work products even as the teacher coparticipates is an important piece of teacher knowledge.

The language and literacy development standard reinforces the interplay between words and concepts within science learning. Knowledge required of teachers for this standard includes the appropriate use and timing of reading and writing tasks within the context of science teaching (e.g., Hand, Wallace, & Yang, 2004; Holliday, Yore, & Alvermann, 1994). Equally important is teacher knowledge about language development in the context of science learning including teaching techniques (Echevarria, Vogt, & Short, 2000), assessment (Kopriva & Sexton, 1999), and issues such as classroom environment (Lee & Luykx, 2005). This collection of literacy and language teacher knowledge can shed light upon how to think about teaching for inquiry.

The remaining three standards offered by Dalton are better known within the teaching profession. For those who wish to uncover more details about teacher knowledge for these standards, the following resources are recommended. For Standards III consider the book *Classroom Diversity* (McIntyre, Rosebery, & González, 2001); for Standard IV examine the science chapters within *How Students Learn* (Donovan & Bransford, 2005); for Standard V a good starting point is a CREDE research report that details the Instructional Conversations framework (Tharp & Gallimore, 1991). These materials provide deeper descriptions of the teacher knowledge as well as illustrating this knowledge being put into action in a wide variety of situations and grade levels, all of which readily connect to teaching for inquiry.

Science Content Knowledge to Teach for Inquiry

The previous section might lead a reader to believe that general pedagogical knowledge is all that is required—but this is not the case. Not only

Table 4. Standards for Effective Teaching Practice From the Center for Research on Education, Diversity, and Excellence (Dalton, 1998)

Standard I. Joint Productive Activity
Facilitate learning through joint activity among teacher and students.

Standard II. Developing Language and Literacy Across the Curriculum
Develop competence in the language and literacy across the curriculum.

Standard III. Connecting School to Students' Lives
Connect teaching and curriculum with students' home and community.

Standard IV. Teaching Complex Thinking
Challenge students toward cognitive complexity.

Standard V. Teaching Through Instructional Conversations
Engage students through dialogue.

---

is content knowledge important for science teaching to be effective, a very particular type of content knowledge must be acquired by science teachers. The science content learned by teachers at the college level during their teacher preparation program, and perhaps deepened during in-service coursework, is important and yet not sufficient. More than knowing fundamental and contemporary science content, teachers also should know about the historical development of scientific ideas. This knowledge is valuable as part of a teacher's instructional narrative, as shown by Mark Olson in his chapter, "A Framework Examining Professional Knowledge for Teaching Science via inquiry," but also has power because these notions often parallel the scientific misconceptions held by students.

Gunstone and White (2000) asserted that understanding the implications of students' "alternative conceptions is vital to discovering principles and methods for improving the quality of learning" within science (p. 303). Toward that end, teachers should be aware of a frequently updated compilation of alternative science conceptions by Reinders Duit titled "Students' and Teachers' Conceptions and Science Education" (accessible at http://www.ipn.uni-kiel.de/aktuell/stcse/). The form of teacher knowledge, the combination of science concepts and the typical misconceptions people hold about these scientific ideas, is very important in order to teach for inquiry. Awareness of potential misconceptions better prepares a teacher to steer students toward scientifically accepted alternatives, a process which can be readily accomplished as students are developing their inquiry skill-set.

Pedagogical Content Knowledge to Teach for Inquiry

Grossman, Schoenfeld, and Lee (2005) examined questions about teacher subject matter knowledge using pedagogical content knowledge to guide their efforts. This category of teacher knowledge describes the specialized teaching practices particular to the subject matter of science. In brief, teachers need to know how to assist students with negotiating meaning from their experiences as the class participates in the essential features of inquiry. Teachers' knowledge of science, combined with their pedagogical talents, becomes activated while supporting students who are doing inquiry. As a result, teachers promote students' "border crossing" (Giroux, 1992) between their previous ways of knowing at the specific cultural norms and practices of science.

Metz (2004) examined the role of uncertainty and how elementary school students navigate around uncertainty as they participated in scientific inquiry. The role of argumentation within the context of science classroom discourse (Jiménez-Aleixandre, Rodríguez, & Duschl, 2000) and the establishment classroom norms of argumentation (Driver, Newton, & Osborne, 2000) represent another realm of teacher professional knowledge. In total, teacher professional knowledge encompasses the spectrum described by the five essential features of inquiry, strategies for supporting students within these endeavors, variously called "nature of science" or "habits of mind." This is clearly a tall order but provides greater clarity than the pedagogy of students doing hands-on while teachers are strictly hands-off. The implication is that to accomplish this will require the combined efforts of science teachers and educational researchers.

Teaching For Inquiry and Developing the Skill-Set

Readers of this chapter are invited to join with others who resist a monolithic notion of classroom inquiry. Songer, Lee, and McDonald (2003) documented successful student learning in classrooms even though classroom instruction was not using open inquiry. Their position reveals that the idealized view of open inquiry—students conducting self-guided investigations with the teacher serving as an unobtrusive facilitator – is not only difficult to implement but may not represent an appropriate technique in all school settings. Songer et al. turned away from open inquiry in favor of strategies and practices which had a demonstrable benefit for students' learning of science. What this means for teacher knowledge is that inquiry should not be seen as either full and open versus more structured and hence less than true, but rather a range of possibilities that are responsive to a given situation. Therefore, teaching for inquiry represents an emphasis upon the five essential features of inquiry (NRC, 2000), which equates with the student inquiry skill-set.

It seems quite likely that we will need to attend to the development of teacher knowledge about inquiry in ways described by Fenstermacher (1994), wherein the generation of such knowledge must acknowledge the wisdom emerging from the actions of practitioners. The "knower" (i.e., the teacher of science) and the "known" (i.e., that which is required to support the development of students' inquiry skill-set) cannot be separated one from the other. Formal and practical knowledge cannot be differentiated into the realms and responsibilities of the researcher and the teacher respectively. Accordingly, there can be coordination between the two realms of knowing such that cognitive science and common sense are not held in opposition but are necessary components of the process and product of teacher knowledge about inquiry.

At the beginning of this chapter, the Tolstoy quote illustrated the difficulty involved with assigning essential meaning to an object. In *War and Peace*, he speculated about how different people might ascribe a purpose for the existence of bees: a child might claim bees have the purpose of stinging, a poet the purpose of drinking the perfume of blossoms, a beekeeper sees utility in bees as honey makers, an apiculturist would claim that bees gather pollen to sustain the queen, and the botanist would note that bees have the purpose of pollinating flowers. So who is right? Which perspective is correct? What does it mean to be a bee? Tolstoy claimed that we cannot know the answer and that the processes and purposes suggested by any of these people is insufficient. Such might be the view about inquiry: what is it *really*? The intent of the current chapter was to propose how to reorient ourselves to this question.

For the past 50 years in science education inquiry has been promoted as a worthy pursuit. On the one hand, open inquiry is touted as the path that will lead science teachers and their students out of the oppressive environment of stale textbooks (a 1960s effort) or as an antidote to standardized testing (a twenty-first century claim). Given how little progress has been made by promoting inquiry as pedagogy, I have proposed that inquiry should be reconceptualized as a student skill-set. In doing so, a semantic shift is advocated with inquiry becoming something we teach *for* rather than *by*—with the goal of students' science learning instead of an instructional model.

It has been suggested that within elementary classrooms, the science concepts can be regarded as nouns and the science process skills as the verbs (Settlage & Southerland, 2007). As has been alluded to in this chapter, this notion may be an oversimplification. After all, nouns, verbs, and modifiers sprinkled together could create a sentence; creating a narrative requires that the writer attend to a broader purpose or meaning. The requisite teacher knowledge is more than a combination of content and process. Furthermore, we have to discard the myth of open inquiry as the ultimate step reached by moving progressively upwards from confirmatory to structured to guided inquiry (Bell, Smetana, & Binns, 2005). By redirecting our attention to the essential features of inquiry (NRC, 2000) and embrace those as a student skill-set, the knowledge required of teachers becomes much more tangible, although not necessarily easier to achieve. With emphasis placed upon students doing inquiry, and by association, teachers teaching for inquiry, the professional knowledge of teachers can be situated within content knowledge and pedagogical content knowledge. Removed from the imprudent promoting of open inquiry, dynamic and substantive forms of teacher knowledge can be applied to advance students' science learning.

REQUISITE TEACHER KNOWLEDGE ABOUT INQUIRY: RESOURCES FOR THINKING ABOUT TEACHING FOR INQUIRY

John Settlage and Margaret Blanchard

In this section, we examine the knowledge teachers require in order to be effective when implementing inquiry within science classrooms. Although presented with the same classroom setting, the three vignette characters brought with them varied understandings and beliefs about inquiry. The intern represented a view grounded in the framework proposed by the National Research Council (NRC) (2000). Although the implementation of her ambitions fell short, we would applaud those who follow her lead in making the effort to use inquiry as a guiding principle of science instruction.

For his part, the mentor also could be regarded as a supporter of inquiry. Perhaps because of his years of service, he was more attentive than the intern to accountability issues impinging upon science teaching. However, the mentor relied upon a misguided definition of inquiry. His comments revealed that he believed inquiry teaching to be synonymous with student-centered investigations, a view we can trace to the post-Sputnik science education reform agenda and whose epistemological roots are much deeper (Rudolph, 2005). Unfortunately the mentor's knowledge of inquiry proves limiting since modes of inquiry other than open inquiry are considered less desirable.

Finally, the supervisor also might claim to support inquiry, but his definition represents yet another common interpretation. From his comments within the vignette we can surmise that he equates inquiry as paralleling the manner in which professional scientists go about their work. This scientific perspective pays scant attention to the cognitive differences between adults who have lived through a myriad of events in order to become scientists and the wide array of children who typically populate a science classroom. Perhaps the supervisor's referent for inquiry is based upon his experiences as a practicing scientist and/or through various portrayals about the ways in which scientific work progresses. In any case, his definition lacks a sufficient understanding about the difficulties of using an expert-novice framework as a means for describing how science ought to be taught at the precollege level.

Among these three characters with their three positions, the differences may be contrary but not necessarily contentious. Each holds a position emerging from their backgrounds, aspirations and responsibilities. Instead of trying to determine which individual is right, we will three different perspectives to interpret the circumstances. Along the way, we examine the implications each interpretative stance holds for teacher professional knowledge. In the conclusion, we review these efforts in order to draw some greater meaning.

THE WISDOM OF PRACTICE

Rather than situate practice and theory as adversaries, we follow the suggestion by Labaree (2003), who allows the perspectives of teachers and researchers to represent contrasting yet worthy perspectives about education. The benefits of wisdom derived from being a practitioner enhances our appreciation of the knowledge required by teaching for inquiry. But limiting our discussion to the practitioner's perspective ignores the contribution of theory in understanding inquiry in the classroom. On the other hand, theory that is never subjected to the bright lights of real classrooms and actual students is not sufficient.

In his chapter, "Teacher Knowledge About Inquiry: Incorporating Conceptual Change Theory," Meadows takes a very practical orientation to the challenges of inquiry. With the vignette as his starting point, Meadows illustrates how the competing forces depicted also permeated his year as a high school science teacher. His ambitions as a teacher were in seeming opposition to the desires of the students. The attempts to engage students in genuine science via open inquiry ran counter to the science learning standards that have become the trademark of contemporary education. When in the role of a university professor, Dr. Meadows was free to sort through conference papers and research articles with the luxury of time to mull over issues. In the role of "Mr. Meadows," the science teacher, the duration of each cycle of input and response was accelerated a thousandfold. The challenges were real and not mere ideas, taking the form of human beings who occupied his physical space by the dozens in 50-minute increments throughout the workday. Practicalities trumped deliberation, as the need to respond to problems in very short order became a necessity.

Dr. Meadows understood inquiry teaching to be a technique advocated for the doing of science while conceptual change was a theory about student learning. Rather than select between the two, he combined these by mapping the essential features of inquiry (NRC, 2000) onto conceptual change theory in a manner that is pedagogically sound. What emerged is an instructional approach that blends the demands to which teachers are subjected with the expertise of a university professor. The knowledge required of teachers involved a fusion of teaching techniques (e.g., orchestrating discussions, sequencing lessons, motivating adolescents) with research-based information (i.e., attending to misconceptions, recognizing gender differences, communicating high expectations). Without apology, Meadows made the limited time he had in the classroom as powerful as it could be for him and his students.

The Value of Theory

For all of the heat that inquiry has generated within science education for the past half-century, it is difficult to identify much in the way of theoretical light that has accompanied it (cf. Lee, Buxton, Lewis, & LeRoy, 2006). While teaching for inquiry might elicit images of its use in classrooms (e.g., students working with equipment, ideas being collaboratively discussed, etc.) we have lacked a theoretical framework about inquiry to assist researchers with making sense of what transpires in context. Some efforts have been made to explore links between teaching for inquiry and powerful explanatory frameworks such as conceptual change theory (e.g., Keys & Bryan, 2001), but each attempt only underscores inquiry's limitations as a dependable theory of teaching or learning. Mark Olson's chapter, "A Framework for Examining Professional Knowledge for Teaching Science via Inquiry," is an attempt to fill this void as he offers a framework to describe teacher knowledge and teaching for inquiry

Building upon ideas first articulated by Jerome Bruner and later expanded to science teacher knowledge by Fenstermacher (1994), Olson identifies two contrasting modes of knowledge. The narrative mode is represented in the "tales of science" told as instances of a particular phenomenon. The paradigmatic mode relies upon conceptual models or overarching categories as ways to connect processes and relationships, particularly those that are not directly observable. Olson contends that neither form of teacher knowledge is superior to the other. In fact, Olson calls for coordinating the paradigmatic with the narrative modes of knowing. He extends previous research he has conducted to consider the implications for building a knowledge base, replete with narrative and paradigmatic modes of knowing, for guiding and informing the support of teacher knowledge about inquiry. By combining "tales of science" with conceptual models, Olson shows how to enlarge teachers' views of inquiry even as he advocates for a fresh consideration of the requisite components of teacher professional knowledge.

A Shift in Focus

While Meadows discussed the pedagogical knowledge a teacher needs to effectively enact inquiry for student learning, and Olson describes aspects of the content knowledge a teacher may need, in the third chapter within Section V, "Moving Past a Belief in Inquiry as a Pedagogy: Implications For Teacher Knowledge," Settlage considers knowledge with a very different proposition, namely that inquiry be removed from the realm of pedagogy. He argues that treating inquiry as an approach to instruction has contributed very little to advances in the quality of science education. Drawing upon the NRC (2000) framework for inquiry, he advocates for an inquiry skill-set as a goal for science learners thereby avoiding the problems of creating a hierarchy (e.g., with open inquiry seen as somehow superior to guided) of inquiry teaching. By focusing on students' learning of the inquiry skill-set instead of seemingly endless considerations of the role of the teacher, we could focus on student actions as a litmus test for the effectiveness of inquiry.

Such an argument shifts the focus of the vignette from whether the lesson was too structured to how well students' proficiency with the inquiry skill-set was accomplished. However, what remains undefined in Settlage's contribution are specifics about the teacher knowledge required to teach inquiry as a skill-set. While discussions of a tangible "skill set" may be particularly helpful for teachers who are incorporating inquiry for the first time or who are constrained by such realities as time constraints, Settlage's argument creates an entirely new set of considerations that must be mapped, explored, and understood, perhaps side-stepping the alleged lack of progress inquiry-based teaching has made on science education.

TEACHERS' GOALS, VALUES, AND BELIEFS

> It is common to talk about barriers or obstacles that must be overcome for teachers to acquire an inquiry approach to teaching ... but much of the difficulty is internal to the teacher, including beliefs and values related to students, teaching, and the purposes of education. Teachers considering new approaches to education face many dilemmas, many of which have origins in their beliefs and values. (Anderson, 2002, p. 7)

While illuminating some aspects of teacher professional knowledge, the contributions in this section does not included teacher goals, values and beliefs. Keys and Bryan (2001) explain that research with science teachers who are implementing inquiry in the classroom is important because "such studies will reflect what may be realistically accomplished on a large scale" (p. 642). Indeed, teachers are the main agents of reform in the classroom and it is through teachers that classroom change ultimately occurs. Taking affective issues into account becomes appropriate within a discussion of requisite teacher knowledge.

Consider two goals prevalent at the secondary level: that teaching science requires "covering the material" and teaching science is efficiently preparing students for standardized tests. These beliefs are often promoted by the culture of the school. Teachers who highly value content coverage and efficiency in their teaching may find these goals to conflict with teaching in inquiry-based ways. Although inquiry-based teaching addresses content, inquiry's process-orientated approach often requires more time than traditional content delivery through lecture or cookbook laboratory activities. Kegan and Lahey (2001) discuss the notion of "competing commitments" as a useful framework when applied to an educational setting. Teachers may actually value both content coverage and science process skills, yet due to limited resources (frequently time) teachers must choose one over the other. As expressed within the *National Science Education Standards,* inquiry can coexist with traditional teaching methods. To pit content and process against each other is a false instructional dichotomy. For inquiry to become a part of a teacher's repertoire it needs to be selected at least some of the time by a teacher over possibly more efficient lecture methods.

One's general orientation to teaching is an important factor that can support or impede the use of inquiry-based teaching. These orientations emerge from teachers' beliefs about teaching and the meaning of learning. Teachers who use a traditional approach likely value an authoritarian model of teaching. Underlying this model is the belief that they, as the teacher, are the source of knowledge in the classroom. Blanchard (2006) studied ten secondary science teachers who participated in a 6-week research experience that modeled inquiry. When they returned to their classrooms, the teachers who operated primarily in authoritarian ways struggled to release control to the class, which in turn inhibited students' efforts to generate questions and their designs of investigations. In contrast, teachers who operated in more student-centered ways supported students' independence and were able to enact the lessons in ways that more were suggestive of inquiry-based teaching. Teachers whose methods were more oriented toward independence were a better "fit" with inquiry-based methods.

CONTEXTUAL AND CULTURAL ISSUES

Many teachers who encounter inquiry-based teaching do so via professional development experiences. In most cases, the training occurs in a classroom after school or during the summer, perhaps in a university setting. Then, teachers are expected to apply the knowledge acquired in one setting and transfer it to a new context. The differences in contexts include organizing students, managing schedules, monitoring supplies—along with the new purpose of teaching students instead of a focus upon the teacher's own learning. According to Osborne (1998), by changing the context in which we acquire knowledge, we change the knowledge itself. After teachers learn "how to do inquiry" in a professional development setting, they face demands not present in the original learning situation. These contextual differences are often more formidable than many expect and developing confidence with using the inquiry-based approaches requires additional patience and extra time. In addition the students may be encountering inquiry for the first time in these teachers' classrooms which makes the implementation all the more difficult.

Another adjustment many science teachers face is the cultural shift from an emphasis upon science to a focus upon instruction. Many science teachers emerge from undergraduate science degrees, and as such are immersed in the culture of science (Carlone, 2004; Eisenhart & Finkel, 1998). On one hand, this can be useful in that some of these teachers have had experience in research. Alternately, many see science and its teaching as a privileged way of knowing which can reinforce traditional instruction due to its putative rigor and claims to objectivity. We invite the reader to consider that the ascendancy of science to an exalted position as one that creates harmful isolation—of that field from others and from the ability for non-scientists to feel competent with thinking scientifically. We perceive that relying upon a cultural focus of science has underappreciated potential. When science is recognized as one of many alternative ways of knowing, and that this worldview does not rank higher than other cultural ways of knowing, it provides a unique entry point for a wider variety of science learners (Lee, 2003).

Glen Aikenhead (1996, 2000) has written extensively and published widely regarding science as a culture and has extended this work to an examination of the implications for making science more accessible to students with non-Western cultural backgrounds (Aikenhead & Jegede, 1999). Invoking the image of border crossing, Aikenhead represents science as a subset within Western culture, indicating that there are particular cultural norms that are at variance with other perspectives (e.g., First Nations people of Canada). Learning science, according to Aikenhead, becomes a process of being enculturated into the society of subculture represented by science (i.e., tools and objects, ways and norms, traditions and knowledge). Instead of discarding one's cultural heritage in order to apprehend scientific ways of knowing, the student could learn science so it becomes collateral knowledge to the forms of knowing fostered outside of school. Teachers may open themselves to change by realizing that their scientific way of knowing and presenting facts is but one way to come to know, just as is inquiry-based instruction and incorporating other knowledge students bring to science classrooms.

Finally, we wish to discuss a useful tool for understanding all of the changes involved in employing inquiry in one's teaching: reflection (Dewey, 1938/1997; Schön, 1987). There are many ways to reflect. One is to simply think back to what happened and consider ways in which the lesson could have been better. A more powerful way to deploy reflection is by systematically looking through evidence, such as classroom videotape data. For instance, one could look for who was generating questions, the teacher or the students, whether the teacher was simply answering questions or if the students began to ask one another questions rather than the teacher. Luft (2001) has made extensive use of reflection with both preservice and practicing teachers, documenting its use as an indispensable tool for teacher change, particularly with regard to employing inquiry in the classroom. Applied systematically, reflection is a powerful way to assist teachers to incorporate inquiry into their practices.

The preceding sections describe ways in which we can infuse aspects of inquiry into science classrooms. Yet, given the obstacles, what are the prospects for inquiry taking hold in American science classrooms? We would like to consider inquiry-based reform at the level of broader institutional reform. Tyack and Cuban (1995) identified four categories of educational reform that allow new ideas to move from novelties to become embedded in institutions. These categories are structural add-ons, noncontroversial initiatives, promoted by influential constituencies, and those that are legally mandated and monitored. Building upon Tyack and Cuban, in order for inquiry to become generally accepted practice, then it needs to fulfill at least one of these categories.

After sifting through their criteria, we reject inquiry as something likely to be structurally added on to current schools, and inquiry as non-contro-versial. Most teachers have experienced the juxtaposed values of college preparatory approaches to instruction and the intense focus on funda-mentals imposed on high-need populations (Haberman, 1991, 2000). We also doubt that adopting legislation is a useful or realistic goal. Instead, we turn our hope for institutional reform by suggesting a movement to create an unambiguous definition for inquiry. Promoted by the powerful constituency of scientists, science educators, and professionals who drafted the *National Science Education Standards*, we could finally work to achieve this overriding goal by clarifying the goal (Anderson, 2002). This could assist teachers in having a shared vision and purpose, while still allowing for appropriate contextual adjustments by teachers and students in different schools, districts, and states.

NEXT STEPS TO CONSIDER

A sure way to cause a gathering of science educators to avert their gaze is to request clear evidence that inquiry is an effective approach for educating science learners. Metz (2004) comes down quite hard on this fact claiming: "The research literature indicates that these claims about the benefits of inquiry-framed instruction may be more the rhetoric of desired outcomes than research-based findings" (p. 220). As others will certainly agree, considerable research remains to be conducted. With the expectation that others may be casting about for projects, we would recommend a focus upon requisite teacher knowledge to support teach-ing for inquiry.

Hashweh (1996) identified two typologies of teacher thinking. For those teachers he describes as knowledge and learning empiricists, rein-forcing students' understandings is the proper approach for developing students' understandings of the scientific method. In contrast, knowledge and learning constructivists embrace students' prior knowledge and employ a diversity of instructional approaches in an effort to engender conceptual understandings. It seems that research about approaches that account for the teachers' level of development, yet seeks to support them in moving away from empiricist views and toward constructivist mindsets, would benefit our understandings about teacher development. Certainly, focusing on this transition zone, and how to best encourage teachers in their development would go a long way toward overcoming preservice teachers' folk theories of inquiry that Windschitl (2004) has so capably described.

Finally, we see these efforts as an opportunity to contribute to the professionalization of teaching. Characteristics of professions include not only a recognizable collection of specialized practices and a community which self-monitors the quality of its members but also "a body of theory or special knowledge with its own principles of growth and reorganization" (Gardner & Shulman, 2005, p. 14). Moving toward consensus about teaching for inquiry is a crucial step and we nominate the NRC's five essential features of inquiry as describing an appropriate skill-set to be treated as a range of legitimate actions along the continua rather than the persistence of an idealized notion of true inquiry.

NOTES

1. Pulse glass image from Science Kit online catalog: http://www.sciencekit.com/category.asp_Q_c_E_439406

2. I would like to acknowledge with admiration the work of Eleanor Duckworth who compellingly argues for an expansion of the goals of inquiry to include affective outcomes as well as purely cognitive. Due to space limitations, I do not take up this set of worthwhile outcomes here, but to suggest that Duckworth might agree that it is in the exploration of a conceptualization of experience (the coordination of paradigmatic and narrative accounts) that contributes to the excitement of learning science.

REFERENCES

Aikenhead, G. S. (1996). Science education: Border crossing into the subculture of science. *Studies in Science Education, 27*, 1-52.

Aikenhead, G. S. (2000) Renegotiating the culture of science. In R. Millar, J. Leach, & J. Osborne (Eds.), *Improving science education: The contribution of research* (pp. 245-264). Buckingham, England: Open University Press.

Aikenhead, G. S., & Jegede, O. J. (1999). Cross-cultural science education: A cognitive explanation of a cultural phenomenon. *Journal of Research in Science Teaching, 36*, 269-287.

Anderson, R. D. (2002). Reforming science teaching: What research says about inquiry. *Journal of Science Teacher Education, 13*, 1-12.

Anderson, C., Mohan, L., & Sharma, A. (2005, August). *Developing a learning progression for carbon cycling in environmental systems.* Paper presented at the Pathways to Scientific Teaching of Ecology Education, Montreal, Canada.

American Association for the Advancement of Science. (1993). *Project 2061: Benchmarks for science literacy.* Retrieved May 12, 2005, from http://www.project2061.org/publications/bsl/online/bolintro.htm

American Association for the Advancement of Science. (2001) *Project 2061: Atlas of science literacy.* Washington, DC: Author.

Bell, R. L., Smetana, L., & Binns, I. (2005). Simplifying inquiry instruction: Assessing the inquiry level of classroom activities. *The Science Teacher, 75*(2), 30-33.

Blanchard, M. R. (2006). *Assimilation or transformation? An analysis of change in ten secondary science teachers following an inquiry-based research experience for teachers.* Unpublished doctoral dissertation, Florida State University, Tallahassee, FL.

Bransford, J. D., Brown, & Cocking, R. D. (Eds.). (1999). *How people learn: Brain, mind, experience, & school.* Washington, DC: National Academies Press.

Bransford, J. D., & Donovan, M. S. (2005). Scientific inquiry and how people learn. In M. S. Donovan & J. D. Bransford (Eds.). *How students learn: History, mathematics, and science in the classroom* (pp. 397-419). Washington, DC: National Academies Press.

Bruner, J. (1985). Narrative and paradigmatic modes of thought. In E. Eisner (Ed.), *Learning and teaching: The ways of knowing* (pp. 97-115). Chicago: National Society for the Study of Education.

Bruner, J. S. (1986). *Actual minds, possible worlds.* Cambridge, MA: Harvard University Press.

Bruner, J. S. (1996). *The culture of education.* Cambridge, MA.: Harvard University Press.

Bybee, R. (2002). *Learning science and the science of learning.* Arlington, VA: National Science Teachers Association Press.

Bybee, R. W. (1997). *Achieving scientific literacy: From purposes to practices.* Portsmouth, NH: Heinemann.

Carlone, H. B. (2004). The cultural production of science in reform-based physics: girls' access, participation, and resistance. *Journal of Research in Science Teaching, 41*, 392-414.

Chiappetta, E. L., & Koballa, T. R. (2006). *Science instruction in the middle and secondary schools: Developing fundamental knowledge and skills for teaching* (6th ed.). Upper Saddle River, NJ: Pearson.

Dalton, S. (1998). *Pedagogy matters: Standards for effective teaching practice.* Washington, DC and Santa Cruz, CA: Center for Research on Education, Diversity & Excellence.

Dewey, J. (1997). *Experience and education.* New York: Simon & Schuster. (Original work published 1938)

Driver, R., Asoko, H., Leach, J., Mortimer, E., & Scott, P. (1994). Constructing scientific knowledge in the classroom. *Educational Researcher, 23*, 5-12.

Driver, R., Newton, P., & Osborne, J. (2000). Establishing the norms of scientific argumentation in classrooms. *Science Education, 84*, 287-312.

Driver, R., Squires, A., Rushworth, P., & Wood-Robinson, V. (1994). *Making sense of secondary science: Research into children's ideas.* New York: Routledge.

Donovan, M. S., & Bransford, J. D. (2005). *How students learn: History, mathematics, and science in the classroom.* Washington, DC: National Academies Press.Duschl,

R. A. (1990). *Restructuring science education: The importance of theories and their development*. New York: Teachers College Press.

Egan, K. (1988). *Teaching as story telling*. London: Routledge.

Egan, K. (1997). *The educated mind: How cognitive tools shape our understanding*. New York: Teachers College Press.

Echevarria, J., Vogt, M., & Short, D. J. (2000). *Making content comprehensible for English language learners*. Boston: Allyn & Bacon.

Eisenhart, M. & Finkel, E. (1998). *Women's science: Learning and succeeding from the margins*. Chicago: University of Chicago Press.

Etheredge, S., & Rudnitsky, A. (2003). *Introducing students to scientific inquiry: How do we know what we know*. Boston: Allyn & Bacon.

Fenstermacher, G. D. (1994). The knower and the known: The nature of knowledge in research on teaching. *Review of Research in Education, 20*, 3-56.

Furtak, E. M. (2006). The problem with answers: An exploration of guided scientific inquiry teaching. *Science Education, 90*, 453-467.

Gardner, H., & Shulman, L. S. (2005). The professions in America today: Crucial but fragile. *Daedalus, 134*(3), 13-18.

Gess-Newsome, J., & Lederman, N. G. (Eds.). (1999). *Examining pedagogical content knowledge*. Dordecht, the Netherlands: Kluwer.

Giroux, H. A. (1992). *Border crossings: Cultural works and the politics of education*. New York: Routledge.

Gould, S. J. (1983). *Hen's teeth and horse's toes: Further reflections in natural history*. New York: W. W. Norton.

Grossman, P., Schoenfeld, A., & Lee, C. (2005). Teaching subject matter. In L. Darling-Hammond & J. Bransford (Eds.), *Preparing teachers for a changing world: What teachers should learn and be able to do* (pp. 201-231). San Francisco: Jossey-Bass.

Gunstone, R., & White, R. (2000). Goals, methods and achievements of research in science education. In R. Millar, J. Leach, & J. Osborne, (Eds.), *Improving science education: The contribution of research* (pp. 293-307). Buckingham, England: Open University Press.

Haberman, M. (1991). The pedagogy of poverty versus good teaching. *Phi Delta Kappan, 73*, 290-294.

Haberman, M. (2000). Urban schools: Day camps or custodial centers? *Phi Delta Kappan, 82*, 203-208.

Hand, B., Wallace, C., & Yang, E.-M. (2004). Using a science writing heuristic to enhance learning outcomes from laboratory activities in seventh-grade science: Quantitative and qualitative aspects. *International Journal of Science Education, 26*(2), 131–149.

Harvard-Smithsonian Center for Astrophysics. (Producer). (1997). *Minds of our own*. Retrieved May 12, 2005, from http://learner.org

Hashweh, M. Z. (1996). Effects of science teachers' epistemological beliefs in teaching. *Journal of Research in Science Teaching, 33*, 47-63.

Holliday, W. G., Yore, L. D., & Alvermann, D. E. (1994). The reading–science learning–writing connection: Breakthroughs, barriers, and promises. *Journal of Research in Science Teaching, 31*(9), 877–893.

Jiménez-Aleixadre, M. P., Rodríguez, A. B., & Duschl, R. A. (2000). "Doing the lesson" or "doing science": Argument in high school genetics. *Science Education, 84*, 757-792.

Kegan, R., & Lahey, L. L. (2001). The real reason people won't change. *Harvard Business Review, 79*, 84-93.

Keys, C. W., & Bryan, L. A. (2001). Co-constructing inquiry-based science with teachers: Essential research for lasting reform. *Journal of Research in Science Teaching, 38*, 631-645.

Koch, J. (2004). *Science stories: Science methods for elementary and middle school teachers*. Boston: Houghton Mifflin.

Kopriva, R., & Sexton, U. M. (1999). *Guide to scoring LEP student responses to openended science items*. Washington, DC: Council of Chief State School Officers.

Krajcik, J. S., Czerniak, C. M., & Berger, C. F. (2003). *Teaching science in elementary and middle school classrooms: A project-based approach*. Boston: McGraw-Hill.

Labaree, D. F. (2003). The peculiar problems of preparing educational researchers. *Educational Researcher, 32*(4), 13-22.

Laburú, C. E., & Niaz, M. (2002). A Lakatosian framework to analyze situations of cognitive conflict and controversy in students' understanding of heat energy and temperature. *Journal of Science Education and Technology, 11*, 211-219.

Layman, J. W., Ochoa, G., & Heikkinen, H. (1996). *Inquiry and learning: Realizing science standards in the classroom*. New York: Henry Holt.

Lederman, N. G., Lederman, J. S., & Bell, R. L. (2004). *Constructing science in elementary classrooms*. Boston: Allyn & Bacon.

Lee, O. (2003). Diverse students in science education: A research agenda. *Teachers College Record, 105*, 465-489.

Lee, O., Buxton, C., Lewis, S., & LeRoy, K. (2006). Science inquiry and student diversity: Enhanced abilities and continuing difficulties after an instructional intervention. *Journal of Research in Science Teaching, 43*, 607-636.

Lee, O., & Luykx, A. (2005). Dilemmas in scaling up innovations in science instruction with nonmainstream elementary students. *American Educational Research Journal, 42*, 411-438.

Lee, O., & Luykx, A. (2005). *Science education and student diversity: Synthesis and research agenda*. New York: Cambridge University Press.

Lubben, F., Netshisaulu, T., & Campbell, B. (1999). Students' use of cultural metaphors and their scientific understandings related to heating. *Science Education, 83*, 761-774.

Luft, J. A. (2001). Changing inquiry practices and beliefs: the impact of an inquiry-based professional development program on beginning teachers and experienced secondary science teachers. *International Journal of Science Education, 23*, 517-534.

Martin, D. J. (2003). *Elementary science methods: A constructivist approach*. Belmont, CA: Wadsworth.

McDiarmid, G. W., Ball, D. L., & Anderson, C. W. (1989). Why staying on chapter ahead doesn't really work: Subject-specific pedagogy. In M. C. Reynolds (Ed.), *Knowledge base for the beginning teacher* (pp. 193-205). New York: Pergamon.

McEwan, H. (1995). Narrative understanding in the study of teaching. In H. McEwan & K. Egan (Eds.), *Narrative in teaching, learning, and research* (pp. 166- 183). New York: Teachers College Press.Metz, K. E. (2004). Children's understanding of scientific inquiry: Their conceptualization of uncertainty in investigations. *Cognition and Instruction, 22,* 219-290.

McIntyre, E., Rosebery, A., & González, N. (2001). *Classroom diversity: Connecting curriculum to students' lives.* Portsmouth, NH: Heinemann.

Meadows, L. (in press). Change in secondary science settings: A voice from the field. In J. Gess-Newsome (Ed.), *Reforming secondary science instruction: NSF Foundations Series.* Washington, DC: National Science Foundation.

Metz, K. E. (2004). Children's understanding of scientific inquiry: Their conceptualization of uncertainty in investigations of their own design. *Cognition and Instruction, 22,* 219–290.

National Research Council. (2000). *Inquiry and the National Science Education Standards.* Washington, DC: National Academy Press.

National Research Council. (1996). *National Science Education Standards.* Washington, DC: National Academy Press.

Oblinger, D., & Oblinger, J. L. (2005). *Educating the net generation* [Electronic version]. Boulder, CO: EDUCAUSE.

Olson, M. (2005). *Interns' narrative and paradigmatic ways of knowing science.* Unpublished Dissertation, Michigan State University, East Lansing, MI.

Osborne, M. D. (1998). Teacher as knower and learner: Reflections on situated knowledge in science teaching. *Journal of Research in Science Teaching, 35,* 427-439.

Roehrig, G. H. (2004). Constraints experienced by beginning secondary science teachers in implementing scientific inquiry lessons. *International Journal of Science Education, 26,* 3-24.

Rudolph, J. L. (2005). Epistemology for the masses: The origins of "the scientific method" in American schools. *History of Education Quarterly, 45,* 341–76.

Rutherford, J., & Ahlgren, A. (1990). *Science for all Americans* [Electronic version]. New York: Oxford University Press.

Schwab, J. J. (1960). Inquiry, the science teacher, and the educator. *The School Review, 68*(2), 176-195.

Schön, D. (1987). *Educating the reflective practitioner.* San Francisco: Jossey-Bass.

Settlage, J., & Southerland, S. (2007). *Teaching science to every child: Using culture as the starting point.* New York: Routledge.

Shulman, L. S., & Tamir, P. (1973). Research on teaching in the natural sciences. In R. M. W. Travers (Ed.) *Handbook of Research on Teaching* (pp. 1098-1148). Chicago: Rand McNally.

Songer, N. G., Lee, H. S., & McDonald, S. (2003). Research towards an expanded understanding of inquiry science beyond one idealized standard. *Science Education, 87,* 490-516.

Southerland, S. A., Kittleson, J., & Settlage, J. (2005). Individual sense making and group meaning making in an urban third grade classroom: Red fog, cold cans, and seeping vapor. *Journal of Research in Science Teaching, 42,* 1032-1061.

Suping, S. M. (2003). *Conceptual change among students in science.* Retrieved May 12, 2005 from http://www.ericdigests.org

Tharp, R. G., & Gallimore, R. (1991). *The instructional conversation: Teaching and learning in social activity.* Washington, DC: Office of English Language Acquisition, Language Enhancement, and Academic Achievement for Limited English Proficient Students (OELA). Retrieved July 20, 2007, from http://www.ncela.gwu.edu/pubs/ncrcdsll/rr2.htm

Tolstoy, L. N. (1898). *War and peace.* New York: Thomas Y. Crowell.

Tyack, D., & Cuban, L (1995). *Tinkering toward utopia: A century of public school reform.* Cambridge, MA: Harvard University Press.

Watson, J. D. (1968). *The double helix: A personal account of the discovery of the structure of DNA.* New York: Atheneum.

Wilson, S. M., Floden, R., & Ferrini-Mundy, J. (2001). *Teacher preparation research: Current knowledge, gaps, and recommendations.* Seattle, WA: Center for the Study of Teaching and Policy, University of Washington.

Windschitl, M. (2004). Folk theories of "inquiry:" how preservice teachers reproduce the discourse and practices of an atheoretical scientific method. *Journal of Research in Science Teaching, 41,* 481-512.

Wiser, M., & Amin, T. (2001). "Is heat hot?" inducing conceptual change by integrating everyday and scientific perspectives on thermal phenomena. *Learning and Instruction, 11,* 331-355.

Windschitl, M. (2004). Folk theories of inquiry: How preservice teachers reproduce the discourse and practices of an atheoretical scientific method. *Journal of Research in Science Teaching, 41,* 481–512.

SECTION VI

STUDENT-SCIENTISTS PARTNERSHIPS: EXPLORING ONE EXAMPLE OF INQUIRY IN THE CLASSROOM

David M. Moss, Catherine Koehler, and Barrett N. Rock

EDITORS' NOTE

Describing Section VI's Use of
Inquiry in the Classroom

Throughout this volume, each section has illuminated just how complex classroom inquiries are and the equally complicated interaction of factors that influence the optimal nature of inquiry to be enacted. Perhaps because of these complexities many teachers rely on a relatively common approach to classroom inquiries—Student-Scientists Partnerships (SSPs). Much lauded due to their seeming convergence of teaching students "science" as students generate useful data to propel that very science, SSPs seem a natural answer to the call for inquiry in the classroom. However, as this section will suggest, this convergence is not without conceptual costs. Indeed, this discussion harkens back to the discussion Chinn and Malhotra's (2002) work described in the introduction. The detailed protocols required for students to generate useful scientific data may serve to make the data appropriate for an authentic scientific task, but a task authentic to the scientists who design the investigation. In contrast, the students may be participating in a simple task, one authentic only to the scientists that require the data. Thus, one of the dimensions of our inquiry definition to attend to in this section resides in authenticity—remembering that the same task may be authentic or simple to different partners in SSPs.

Inquiry in the Classroom: Realities and Opportunities, pp. 233–265
Copyright © 2008 by Information Age Publishing

233

As for the other points on the description of inquiry, the goals of inquiry suggested in the discussion of SSPs lie primarily in **learning to inquire**, as the authors suggest that by participating in scientific processes of data collection, students may learn to conduct their own inquiries. This primary goal is followed by **learning about inquiry,** as the authors describe that analysis of these procedures may allow students to develop understandings of how science proceeds. The final goal, **constructing scientific knowledge**, is mentioned but only briefly, almost as if discussions pertinent to science education in the "age of accountability" cannot afford to exclude such a goal. However it is clear that inquiry to better construct content knowledge is at best a distant concern as one discusses SSPs, at least in their current configurations.

In the SSP exemplar that is the heart of this section, GLOBE, students are collecting data to help their scientist partners pursue an answer to a scientific question. Because similar groups of students all over the world may also be collecting data for this question, standardized data collection protocols must be used. Thus, in our jargon of enactment, students are provided the question and the means of answering the question, making SSP's a Level 1/guided inquiry.

VIGNETTE

Central High School (CHS) is located in a large suburban town in New England. CHS is the only public high school in the town of approximately 55,000 people, and it suffers from overcrowded classrooms due to years of limited school budgets.

Ms. Horn is an experienced secondary science teacher with certifications in both general science and earth science. This is her seventh year of teaching, and she initially accepted the position in this school primarily because of their modified block schedule and the flexibility she believed that it offered. The block schedule is arranged so that every class meets on Mondays and Fridays, and the classes are the traditional 50 minutes in length. During the rest of the week the periods are 90 minutes long, however she meets with each class only 2 of the 3 days during the extended midweek periods. The district science curriculum places a heavy emphasis on covering a significant number of content topics, yet she has also found that CHS professes a philosophy which promotes inquiry skills as well. Although the school district advocates an inquiry-oriented learning model, she has come to see this as an "on paper" emphasis, as inquiry is not something she has seen in her school. From the day she arrived, the emphasis has been on content acquisition. This is driven by demands from the administration as CHS to overcome the mediocre scores that the 10th-grade classes have traditionally achieved on the statewide performance tests.

*Currently, she teaches five classes of 10th-grade integrated science, known sim-
ply as Year II in the science department. The curriculum for this integrated science
class is designed to address three general areas: Physical science (usually taught
September through mid-December), earth/space science (usually taught January
through March) and life sciences (usually taught April through June). In addition,
Ms. Horn teaches two sections of college prep and three of "general studies."
Absenteeism is not uncommon among her lower achieving general students, and
quite a few qualify for individual education plans. Although she has nearly 30 students in each of her general studies classes, she strives to maintain consistency
between her pedagogical approach in class and her epistemological underpinnings
guided by a constructivist perspective.*

*Over the course of the year Ms. Horn used mostly "canned" (verification) labo-
ratory activities designed to directly teach science standards approved by the district
science curriculum committee, but she is committed to provide her students with an
exciting, real science experience in the waning weeks of the school year. Ms. Horn
had spent 3 days of her winter break attending a workshop designed prepare her to
facilitate The GLOBE (Global Learning and Observations to Benefit the Environment) program, which is a worldwide, hands on, school-based science education
program. GLOBE brings students and their teachers together in partnership with
scientists, where scientifically valid measurements are collected, reported via the
Internet, and shared among the entire network of classrooms involved in this program. Ms. Horn was trained in data collection protocols along with other aspects
of the program during her professional development workshop and the time had
finally arrived for her to introduce this project to her classes.*

*The weather had turned agreeable in early May, and Ms. Horn was taking her
first class out during a morning block period to begin to survey the school yard for
a data collection site. Although she had identified a likely study plot based on the
protocols she learned at the workshop, she wanted to create a sense of ownership for
these students, hoping that ownership would translate into fewer management and
behavioral issues later. With clipboards and tape measures in hand, her first period
general studies class tromped out the double doors behind the gym and headed for
the strip of trees on the far side of the athletic field. Gathering the students around
in a semi-circle, she sensed a level of engagement which was atypical for this class,
and asked her students, "So, what do you see?" After a long pause, a male student
responded rather flatly, "trees." Gesturing with her hands in a rolling motion to
indicate she wanted a more detailed response, she replied with a barrage of questions, "Ok, what else? What kind of trees? Tall or short? Anything other than
trees?" Her students swiveled their heads around in silence. "We talked about this
in class all last week … remember?" she added. "The trees don't have leaves," a
student noted. "But they will," another replied. "Yes, yes!" Ms. Horn offered to
encourage this her students' tentative engagement. "Take 10 minutes, and write
down everything you see in the space provided on the cover page of your packet on
the clipboard—go!" And with that, the students broke from their formation and*

begin jotting things down as they meandered through this area of the schoolyard which had been previously the sole domain of students engaged in behavior best left unseen by the school officials.

Although the very start of the program was perhaps a bit rocky, Ms. Horn found that packets with explicit directions and places to record data, along with the strict deadlines she set, was very helpful to keep the project moving forward over the next several weeks. Weather permitting, students spent their 2 block days outside engaged in data collection protocols, and their Mondays and Fridays transcribing, organizing, and analyzing their data. Time was tight right from the beginning of this project. Once students had mapped the borders of what may eventually become a long-term study site, assuming Ms. Horn stays at the school and keeps up with the project, they began to collect land cover and atmospheric data such as tree height, canopy closure and ground cover, and temperature. Midway through the project, Ms. Horn began to feel she was making some strides toward bringing scientific inquiry into her teaching.

Several weeks into the project, two students from this same first period class approached their teacher with a puzzled look on their faces. "Our tree shrunk," they stated with a tone indicating they did not quite know what to make of this apparently remarkable finding. "Really," Ms. Horn offered as an open-ended reply. "See," one student countered as she held up her clipboard with a measurement which simply stated 44 feet, as if that had settled the matter. "The tree is 44 feet?" the teacher questioned. "It is now," the second student quickly replied, "but it was 50 feet last Tuesday." Ms. Horn slowly looked back and forth between the faces of the students to see if they were testing her patience, but made the split second decision that they were generally at an impasse. "Ok" she said in a newly invigorated voice, "Can both measurements be accurate? Could we have made an error here? How should we handle this conflicting data?" After a beat or two, the first student conceded that during the second measurement it was harder to precisely see the top of the tree now that the leaves had fully come out. "And" the teacher responded in that familiar tone which indicated she wanted that student to finish her thought. "And ... I suppose that is why the measurement is off." "The tree didn't shrink," the second student added in a confident tone. Ms. Horn nodded with a smile, in part because she recognized that her students realized that this tree didn't shrink, but most of her pleasure was because they were able to explain a plausible possible source of error in their data. "I suppose we could measure it again and see what happens," one student remarked to the other as they were turning away, "And average the two," the second replied. Before she could follow-up with a question about whether that might be an appropriate strategy they were a few paces away, and besides, during this conversation she noted a group of students well outside the study area and mentally was preparing to give them a holler and see what they were up to.

The balance of the data collection periods went relatively smoothly for Ms. Horn and her classes. Behavioral issues were kept to a minimum, along with absenteeism, and you could readily tell her students really looked forward to getting outside.

She wished they had brought this same enthusiasm to her class all year, and toyed with the notion of beginning next year with this project, but conceded that given the push for test preparation, it would be hard for her to get permission until after the statewide exam was given in April.

Other than another case of "the great shrinking tree" and data that suggested that there were a few days in which the ambient air temperature approached the boiling point of water, she was pleased with the seemingly extensive amount of accurate data collected from this year. When the dataset was finally posted on the Internet to the GLOBE site a few days before the end of school, she made an explicit point of telling her students that they had contributed to an actual scientific study, and they could now think of themselves as scientists. Unfortunately, she knew this would be the last science class many of these students would ever have given that only 2 years of high school science was required for graduation. Even if they believed they had made a scientific contribution it would likely be there last.

She wished she had more time. More time to compile their data and look for patterns. More time to look at datasets from other schools around the world. More time to encourage her students to actually think and act like scientists. After all, "Isn't that what inquiry science is all about?" she often asked herself. She felt this partnership between students and scientists held largely untapped potential. If her students could spend months and not weeks on this project by eliminating the mandated rote memorization of science facts for the statewide test, as she confided to a sympathetic colleague regarding this project, she could "Do it right." Although she was pleased that she went the extra mile to afford her students what she hoped was a memorable experience to finish up the year, she still had a nagging sense that she could had done things differently to ensure they really learned "the spirit scientific inquiry."

The principal aim of *National Science Education Standards* (National Research Council [NRC], 1996) and *Project 2061: Science for all Americans* before it (American Association for the Advancement of Science [AAAS], 1990) is the recommendation that individuals develop an understanding of the very essence science itself as a key precursor for attaining a scientifically literate worldview. This outcome serves as the rallying call for the present day science education reform movement, and for years has been widely advocated by scholars in this field (Rutherford & Ahlgren, 1990). Scientific literacy customarily refers to making the most of science understandings throughout the course of one's life through informed decision-making underpinned by an appreciation for the complex relationships between the institution of science and society at large. Although numerous research studies have concluded that purposeful instruction about the nature, or essence, of science should become an explicit, enduring component of science education (Lederman, Abd-El-Khalick, Bell, & Schwartz, 2002; MacDonald, 1996; Moss, Abrams, & Robb, 2001), how that approach is best accomplished is still very much open to investigation and discussion.

In this section we present one, somewhat common example of the way in which inquiry is "brought off" in schools, Student-Scientists Partnerships (SSPs). SSPs are often thought of as a way to bring authentic science, and sometimes scientists, into the schools (Moss, 2003). In the typical SSP scientists work in a variety of ways with students on a "real world" science project. Scientists become involved in SSPs because it allows them to engage K-12 students to help them collect needed data and many scientists have a desire to help excite students to learn about science through participation in their research. Many teachers welcome SSPs because they allow their students to have a window into authentic science, support is often available via the partnerships, and there is a prestige to working with scientists. SSPs are fairly common and can be a win-win situation in the right set of conditions. One of the goals of this section is to explore those necessary conditions, as well as the challenges and difficulties associated with SSPs.

The three authors of this section of the book come to this project with diverse, yet related, backgrounds with SSPs, science and science education. They have all taught science classes at the university level and have each engaged in scientific research resulting in publications in scientific journals. Dr. Barrett Rock, professor of natural resources, has dedicated his career to science and education, and has remained active in outreach efforts that have enabled him to work closely with students and schools for decades. Catherine Koehler began her career as a researcher in the health professions, and then became a licensed science teacher, and most recently has shifted her emphasis to the preparation of secondary school science teachers. Finally, Dr. David Moss has blended his work in environmental science and science education throughout his career. As a science teacher educator and environmental advocate he has worked with students and professional educators at all levels throughout his career.

In this section, three different perspectives will be offered about SSPs will be offered. The first essay discusses the goals of SSPs, the next essay explores the benefits of SSPs from a scientist's point of view. The final essay examines at the potential of SSPs through the rewriting and extension of the vignette. The section summary explores the conditions necessary for SSPs to be a sound pedagogical choice.

INQUIRY AND STUDENT-SCIENTIST PARTNERSHIPS

David M. Moss

Student-Scientists Partnerships (SSPs) are designed to involve students in authentic science activities in cooperation with scientists themselves

(Moss, 2003). Across the nation, there are numerous extracurricular SSPs, such as Forest Watch (Rock & Lauten, 1996) and The GLOBE program (Tinker, 1997). In these programs, students partner with scientists and collect actual data which is used to investigate environmental issues. In this configuration of a student scientist partnership, classes form a network of data collection sites, often share their local results, and essentially work toward contributing data to ongoing scientific research programs. For example, students might make measurements of the number of different plant species present in a field near their school. Given enough schools collecting and reporting such data, scientists could generate a very detailed map which might be too time intensive to otherwise produce. One substantial criticism of such a model is that students often are relegated to serve in a role which is analogous to technician (Moss, Abrams, & Robb-Kull, 1998). That is, students primarily serve as data collectors for scientists, and may not necessarily experience a full range of inquiry thinking which underpins the nature of science. One must also question the value of the knowledge gained from such work in relation to the established school curriculum. It is easy to imagine work which might benefit *either* detailed learning objectives or scientists specific data needs, but finding engaging pedagogically sound activities which meets the aims of both partners is often elusive. In an article which synthesizes the literature related to apprenticeship experiences in science education, Barab and Hay (2001) concluded, "SSPs are practical but much of the richness is lost when students participate in simplified science" (p. 76). In their exploration of a summer camp in which middle school students engaged in authentic research while apprenticing with scientists, they concluded that the greatest potential for learning occurs when students are closely mentored and learn to inquire within the context of a professional community. Although such intensive programs make a valuable contribution, if such one-on-one mentoring is required to make SSPs work, there is little hope such an idea can go a long way in meeting our aim of K1-12 systemic reform and science for all.

Another effective program which partners students with scientists in a different manner than the large scale data driven SSP or intensive apprenticeship model is The JASON Project (Moss, 2003). In this model of a SSP, students are not necessarily engaged in collecting data for scientists as their primary mission, but are invited to participate in and observe a broad range of activities in which the scientists themselves are engaged. The interdisciplinary JASON curriculum is much less focused on real science data collection activities, and combines science with mathematics and other disciplines so that students may see connections across content areas. Regardless of the model of SSP, whether they are international programs or one of the countless numbers of local initiatives bringing together schools and scientists, a common aim is to offer students a window into the realm of real science.

Ideally, SSPs would not merely afford students a passive role as simple data collectors, but would involve them deeply and deliberately in inquiry activities, such as formulating and refining questions for study, promoting a depth and breadth of thinking and doing. Hopefully this more "authentic" involvement in the creation of scientific knowledge would result in a perspective on the nature of science necessary for scientific literacy. There is presently no research to conclusively offer insight into which model of an SSP may be the most effective at meeting these aims.

SCIENCE AND PUBLIC PERCEPTIONS

As suggested by the discussions of Chinn and Malhotra (2002), very real tensions exist between science and school science when considering on one hand how actual science is conducted, funded, and reported as compared with so-called inquiry science curriculum in schools. When one considers the expert-novice gap between practicing scientists and high school aged students with regard to their experiences and motives, the issues appear even more complex. The institutions of schooling and science each have their own aims and roles to play in society, and yet it still seems as if there may be some form of a partnership which may serve both. A principal aim for this section is to explore such a possibility.

The common perception of science, both in the general public and in K-12 education, makes essentially three major assumptions:

- Science is based on a series of discipline-based facts, that if learned and committed to memory, makes a person a scientist;
- Since science is assumed to be based on a large set of known facts, each question asked about science must have a correct answer and that all one needs to do is look in the back of a book or conduct an experiment to find that correct answer;
- Conducting authentic scientific investigations are only seen as feasible once one has become a scientist and has been fully trained in a specific discipline. Only then can you *do* science.

This last perception gives rise to the notion that science is only accessible to scientists. This view also implies that students are not capable of doing real science and that they cannot be involved in authentic scientific investigations. I do not believe that any of the above perceptions are accurate, as I have been actively involved in engaging K-12 students in the process of learning science by doing actual science.

The reality of science is very different from these popular perceptions. I argue (supported in part by American Association for the Advancement of Science [AAAS] (1989) "scientific habits of mind"), science is a state of mind, one way of looking at the world that is driven by a curiosity of the patterns and change seen in the natural world along with a yearning to question and explore. In a sense, a scientist may be thought of as a detective, asking questions and looking for clues and using a set of standard methods and tools to investigate important phenomena and solve problems. At its core, science is really the ultimate inquiry-based learning activity, one in which questions are posed and refined, methods are designed to push our thinking toward a potential explanation, and then results are evaluated to determine if the educated guess or prediction offers a reasonable conclusion based on the evidence gathered. Thus, the one common thread in all of science is not learning facts, but rather learning how to ask the right question and gather evidence to evaluate potential answers. Throughout the process, knowledge is certainly identified, but is often modified or replaced as our understandings and measurement tools improve over time. Most importantly, K-12 students can become active participants in the process of doing authentic science. When students pose their own scientific questions, they are engaged in the principal activity of how we operationally define inquiry.

Since scientific studies often address very complex issues (climate change, air quality and water quality, and their impacts on living things, etc.), communicating scientific findings to the general public is especially difficult since the public often seeks and demands one-dimensional answers to these complex problems. Since scientists spend much of their time speaking with other scientists in their own field of research, "science-speak" is often characterized by its own language and culture. It has been said that asking a scientist to speak plain English is like asking a cat to bark. Scientists find it difficult to convey their culture, language, and thought into everyday language. This leads to the idea that science is only for the smart geeks, the elite few, those that know the jargon. Although this is a challenge often faced by teachers in the classroom, by carefully crafting a student-scientist-partnership program which takes this into account, this challenge can be readily overcome. Considering the implications for the pressing need of an engaged scientifically literate citizenry in this information age, we must make it a priority to make science accessible to all children regardless of whether they are from a so-called general studies or college track program.

If a scientific way of thinking is the common thread sustaining all science disciplines, I should address the embodiment of this line of thinking as it manifests itself in school curriculum. Although there is no one magical set of procedures that yield scientific findings, it may be beneficial to portray this nonlinear, complex way of looking at the world in a format which is accessible to the novice learner. Thus, the notion of the scientific method is common in schooling. I acknowledge right up front that there exists no single method for conducting science, and yet at the same time, from a pedagogical standpoint I have seen firsthand the value of a straightforward organizational schema which can make the nature of science explicit to those beyond the scientific community (Koehler & Moss, 2006). For example, we often articulate that the need for standardized research methods comes from the need to be certain that the measurement of the same variable in different organisms or under different conditions is always made in the same way. Thus, standardizing a method of measurement assures other scientists that different results are due to differences in the organisms or conditions, and not due to different ways of making the measurement. Assuring that measurements are always made in the same way often involves following a common outline and method, commonly referred to as a protocol. Within the context of a SSP, a standardized measurement protocol is helpful to assure that the data collected by students is both reliable and accurate.

In research that has focused on improving our understanding of how poor air quality affects the health of trees, some questions that Barry Rock, a coauthor of this section, has asked include, "What factors affect the growth rate and health of a tree?" "How does one specific type of air pollution, such as ground-level ozone (often referred to as smog), affect tree growth rates and health?" "Do all trees growing under the same smog conditions grow at the same rate?" "Are some tree species more suscepti- ble than others to smog damage?" Do different tree species grow at differ- ent rates?" "Are younger trees more susceptible to smog than older trees of the same species?" "How does acid rain or smog reduce the growth rate in trees?" In order to try to answer these complex questions, one can begin to see the need to have a standard way of measuring tree growth, and specific protocols and tools must be employed.

To follow this line of thinking, a standard way of measuring tree growth is to determine its diameter at a specific height above the ground—the diameter at breast height or DBH. The diameter of a tree is determined by measuring the circumference and dividing by Pi (3.14). Since both cir- cumference and diameter vary (becomes smaller) as the distance above the ground increases, there is a standard breast height (3.5 ft or 1.35 m above the ground) used by scientists around the world. By making this simple measurement annually, usually best done in the fall or early winter, for the same tree, you can determine how much the tree has grown. Dr. Rock and others have begun to answer some of the above questions by making the same DBH measurements on young trees and older trees, on pine versus maple, trees of the same species watered with controlled amounts of acid rain vs. those watered with neutral pH water, and so forth. Involving students in collecting such data will afford them an opportunity to experience science from the perspective of a scientist while opening their eyes to timely scientific questions.

One of the most significant questions in science today is, "Will increasing levels of carbon dioxide in the atmosphere, caused by emissions from burning fossil fuels, result in an increase in the growth rate of trees?" The answer will provide important input to global climate models used to project future climate conditions in 50 or 100 years. We need to know how much carbon dioxide is being removed from the atmosphere and converted into wood by terrestrial forest and marine ecosystems. Simple annual DBH measurements by schools across New England or throughout the United States, combined with maps of the amount and kind (young/old, pine/maple, healthy/damaged, etc.) of forest covering the land surface for a given area, would be invaluable data for climate modelers attempting to understand how climate is likely to change over time due to rising carbon dioxide levels now and in the future. Using the standard DBH protocol to make these measurements will insure that the data produced is accurate enough to be used in climate modeling efforts.

In the following essays of this section, we will discuss the The GLOBE Program; through the lens of a practicing scientist, through the viewpoint of a participating teacher, and an overview that offers recommendations for an "ideal" SSP model.

THE SCIENCE OF A STUDENT-SCIENTIST PARTNERSHIP

Barrett N. Rock

As was noted in the previous essay in this section, one of the criticisms of programs such as GLOBE is that because students are following preset protocols, they are only involved in a limited assortment of the activities underpinning the scientific enterprise—by and large the process skills involved in science, and little of its conceptual underpinnings. Perhaps most importantly, students are not encouraged, or even given an opportunity, to ask their own questions, which I, and a host of others argue, is at the very core of inquiry science (cf. National Research Council [NRC] (1996, 2000). However, I do not see the initial reliance on preset protocols (as allowed through SSPs such as GLOBE) to be as limiting as others might argue, As will be addressed in the conclusion of this section, it is my argument that when we introduce students to the protocols and equipment provided in programs such as GLOBE, these students may be in a far better position to raise their own scientific questions.

As I briefly describe the science underpinning the protocols described in the initial vignette, keep in mind the following question:

Are students learning the nature of science by being actively engaged in the selected GLOBE activities?

The measurements and the protocols the students in the vignette were using to make their land cover measurements include:

1. Laying out a 30m X 30m pixel-sized study plot;
2. Identifying the dominant species (trees, grasses, ground cover, etc.);
3. Determining tree height;
4. Determining tree DBH (Diameter at Breast Height);
5. Canopy closure and ground cover;
6. The use of Landsat satellite data to map local land cover types;
7. Maximum, minimum, and mid-day temperatures;
8. Precipitation; and
9. Cloud cover.

Establishing a pixel-sized study plot is the very first activity required in establishing a long-term database. The students are asked to follow a GLOBE Protocol to layout a 30m x 30m square study plot in a forested site adjacent to their school. The purpose of this exercise is to expose the students to the use of compass and tape measure to duplicate on the ground a 30m pixel from a satellite image of the area surrounding the school. A pixel is the smallest unit of data within a digital image. In laying out the pixel, students see the diversity within a forested setting, often with dense understory vegetation, topographic variability, and several tree types—not to mention poison ivy. Because of this experience, the next time the students see the pixels in a satellite scene they will be better able to understand what such a pixel actually looks like on the ground. If several pixels are investigated by different student teams, they will quickly understand why there is no one correct answer to the question of what's in a typical forested pixel. The answer depends on the age of the trees, the kinds of trees, and a host of other variables. This notion of there is no single correct answer to many scientific questions is an essential element of the nature of science (Moss, Abrams, & Robb, 2001). The GLOBE activities can provide the needed activities to build this important aspects of the nature of science.

Identifying the dominant species is typically the second protocol employed. Once the pixel-sized study plot has been laid out, the students then go about identifying the dominant tree species within the pixel. Students are introduced to the use of a dichotomous key to determine the species of trees (in the northeast United States where Central High School (CHS) is located they are typically white pine, red oak, sugar maple, etc.) and determining how many of each species is present. The level of identification is defined by the overall goal of the study. If the goal is to determine the cause of the color differences in two or more image pixels in a satellite image, then knowing the relative amounts of broadleaf versus coniferous trees within a pixel is adequate. If the goal is to locate a specific type of tree (i.e., locating white pines for study as bioindicator of low level atmospheric pollutants), then identification to the species level is required. Again, a key point in a broader understanding of the scientific enterprise is provided for in this activity: Scientists pose questions to guide their work.

The students are next introduced to the use of a clinometer to determine tree height. While this method of measuring the height of a tree is widely used in the forestry profession, it is prone to many sources of error and is only good for an approximation. As seen in the vignette at the opening of this section, trees may appear to shrink due to the error introduced by the student. Such notions as data reliability and validity are key elements of real world science and readily come up in the use of such a measurement instrument.

As described earlier, diameter at breast height (DBH) is a standard measure of tree size. Making annual measurements at the same time of year allows students to track the growth rate of individual trees or groups of trees over time. Student DBH measurements can be one of the most valuable contributions to a scientific database, and as such be a great value to researchers involved in the measuring of carbon sequestration capacity of various types of forests (broadleaf forests vs. conifer forests, young forests vs. older forests, etc.). Student data, such as DBH, can make a significant contribution to ongoing carbon modeling efforts for researchers around the world. Revisiting an earlier question from this section, we are left wondering if making such measurements are also valuable to the teacher and student from an educational standpoint? Phrased another way, even though making such measurements may make significant contributions to science, do they make significant contributions to the education of children? The answer is determined by the goals the teacher has and how he/she embeds this activity into his/her lesson plan.

Just as DBH measurements are potentially valuable data for carbon-sequestration studies, canopy closure data and tree type data are useful and valuable for satellite monitoring studies. Four types of data combined (DBH, tree height, canopy closure, and tree type) can be used to produce biomass data for large areas of the planet. Such biomass data do not exist for much of the United States, and an even lesser extent for the rest of the world, student contributions of such data will provide an extraordinary opportunity in terms of generating maps for much of the Earth's land surface.

Canopy closure is measured using a very simple tool called a tubular densiometer. It can be made from an item as affordable and available as a toilet paper tube to which a set of cross hairs of string or thread is attached at one end and a weight such as a washer on a string to the other. Even for schools with strained supply budgets, like CHS at the beginning of this section, can manage to get these into the hands of their students.

In the GLOBE program, K-12 students have the opportunity to use satellite image processing software, titled MultiSpec, which is made available as freeware by National Aeronautics and Space Administration (NASA). Satellite data of areas around their school are also made available free of charge. Since the Landsat satellite system has been in orbit continuously since July, 1972, an extensive archive of available data is available for the past 35 years. This means that multidate Landsat satellite images of a given school can be examined for the purpose of documenting change over time for the given area. Several GLOBE schools have produced such change over time data for city and town councils, regional planning boards, etc. Involving students in such community issues and concerns is yet another way of engaging them in addressing the larger issue of the nexus of science and society.

Meteorological data are also routinely collected utilizing GLOBE protocols. For example, students in Ms. Horn's class at CHS collected daily temperature measurements. While potentially tedious, such measurements provide students with insights into another important aspect of science—the value of a long-term database. Scientists themselves would acknowledge that doing real science is not characterized by endless excitement and frequent eureka moments. While collecting daily temperature measurements may be monotonous and seem to lack educational value, especially if they are taken every day of the school year, assigning different student teams to record these data each week may be a useful strategy in the classroom to share the responsibility. What has been stated about the collection of daily temperature measurements can also be said for the GLOBE precipitation data. Although making the measurements may be repetitive, the GLOBE rain gauge was selected because it allows for accurate measurements. Since the GLOBE weather stations are often co-located with the adjacent forest pixel-sized study sites, having access to local, and highly accurate, rainfall data allows students to compare amount of rainfall for a given spring with incremental increases in DBH measurements over the same time period. Interestingly, in an analysis of student versus professional temperature and precipitation data (Rock & Lawless, 1997), the student data were shown to be more accurate than the professional data. Such findings bolster the case for involving students in authentic scientific work, at least in terms of their ability to make real contributions to the broader project of science.

Finally, evaluating local cloud cover using the GLOBE visual method is a wonderful tool for making students aware of ever changing cloud cover conditions and identifying cloud types. By characterizing cloud type and amount, and comparing the data with rainfall and temperature records, students begin to see the interrelationships which exist between temperature, precipitation, and cloud cover as well as the interrelationships which exist between the major earth systems, including the atmosphere, the hydrosphere, the biosphere. This idea of the interconnectedness among the earth's systems is an essential element of literacy in science (NRC, 1996).

While using the GLOBE protocols discussed in this section may seem like it severely limits the students' ability to "do it their own way," in fact it may be an excellent means to prepare students to generate appropriate scientific questions. Once the students learn the protocols, they should be encouraged and supported in the pursuit of their own questions. This is a critical point to note, that is, once that students acquire some basic habits of mind and skills which are consistent with scientific reasoning and thinking, they may be able to better pursue questions in science and engage more fully in the ways of thinking which are characteristic of practicing scientists. Science education research is desperately needed to explore this supposition.

A second key point to make is that the *science* is important. We see throughout this section that at first blush making daily temperature measurements may not seem to meet any educational aim, but when we consider such measurements as a developing a long term database to monitor and understand the unifying concept of change (AAAS, 1989), we begin to see how closely following protocols can lead to meaningful learning in science.

Reflecting on the question of whether students can potentially learn the nature of science via this student scientist partnership model reminds us that SSPs are not standalone entities. They must be purposefully facilitated by real teachers and scientists, and a balance must be achieved between the science and educational aims if we are to portray this as a true partnership. It is a partnership that can be a "win-win" for science and education alike.

REAL SCIENCE IN REAL SCHOOLS?

Catherine Koehler

Within this section, I will explicitly revisit the vignette presented at the beginning of this section and address several organizational and management challenges of actually teaching science through a student scientist partnership (SSP) program. Given the reality that students are not scientists, I will explore a classroom teacher's perspective on how to approach a SSP program, motivate students to engage in protocols designed to ensure the collection of real data and weigh the very real pros and cons represented by such partnerships.

From somewhere deep down, Ms. Horn had to remind herself that she once learned about inquiry instruction and how it helped students to acquire a genuine understanding of science. She had first been introduced to this notion of inquiry in her preservice program nearly a decade ago, but she had seen very little evidence over the years that inquiry science had found its way into everyday science classrooms. Her teacher education program had introduced her to such reform minded documents as Science for All Americans: Project 2061 (American Association for the Advancement of Science [AAAS], 1989) and the National Science Education Standards (National Research Council [NRC], 1996), each promoted inquiry in science. At the very start of her teaching career she envisioned these works guiding her daily practice, but soon came to realize there were more local and pressing issues which served to dictate her lesson planning and instruction. Preparing her students for mandated state-wide testing at her grade level was the principal factor which drove what she did in class each and every day for much of the school year.

Just a few months back she was on the college campus where she pursued her teaching degree, and met with her old science education professor. She reminisced about her time on campus, and over a cup of coffee enjoyed their brief conversation about science education reform. Her professor reminded her of the works of Joseph Schwab (1962) and how his enquiry philosophy articulated nearly a half century ago still held relevance today. Following her campus visit she pulled out this old book, and noted the following passage highlighted from the text, "enquiry as a mode of investigation ... proceeds through uncertainty and failure, and eventuates in knowledge which is contingent, dubitable, and hard to come by" (p. 5). After thumbing through her notes from this class she reaffirmed her approach to the teaching and learning of science from a constructivist perspective, and right there and then is when she went on-line and signed up for the GLOBE workshop. She was committed to ending this school year on an instructional high note. The program description on-line immediately convinced her that if her students participated in this program, they would have an opportunity to explore state-of-the-art content and perhaps experience the very nature of science itself. She was concerned that her underperforming students would be a little perplexed and overwhelmed when they were initially presented with a real science problem, such as global change, but after looking more deeply into GLOBE, she became reassured by the detailed protocols which carefully steered this project. She knew all too well that her students had been drilled in the scientific method in science classes in recent years, and would be very unnerved to find that there is no linear, unwavering pathway for uncovering a single, correct answer to questions in science. On the other hand, she hoped they would be excited to learn how various scientists approach their discipline in so many different ways. She was also a little concerned that the frustration and confusion her students would experience while collecting data at their study plot might lead to behavioral problems which would serve to undermine the experience. This, however, was a challenge she was willing to take on given her renewed commitment to portraying science as a dynamic, human endeavor.

Prior to attending the GLOBE workshop, she found buried deep in her methods class notes the idea of inquiry which was taught by her professor as a means to incorporate science content, process, and reasoning with the explicit aim of providing relevance and motivation for students to learn the nature of science. She was reminded that inquiry as a teaching and learning strategy can be utilized in any science discipline and that ideally it should be grounded firmly throughout the curriculum. Her professor noted it was not something to come and go on a whim. She recalled that her professor told her that having students develop their own researchable questions was at the heart of student-centered inquiry. She considered using this instructional approach for GLOBE as this program certainly offers authentic science themes which might serve to foster an inquiry approach. She figured what better way to initiate a discussion about the very nature of science than to do it in with support from real scientists while working toward contributing data to timely scientific problems. The very essence of science, in Ms. Horn's mind, could never be learned through the rote memorization of facts and vocabulary words. It was most effectively learned through developing questions, generated by both the students and the teacher, and refining and revisiting those questions in small group discussions and through whole classroom discourse. To rush through lessons in order to merely cover sections in the text was not a strategy which benefited anyone, and she began to realize that it was, in fact, borderline educational malpractice to do so.

She laughed to herself as she considered an inquiry approach to science education when she thought about what many of her colleagues and her department chair at Central High School (CHS) might say. The omnipresent "teach to the test" mantra stood in stark contrast with an inquiry approach, and certainly created significant tensions regarding her beliefs about best practices in science education. But, following the GLOBE workshop another very real tension was slowly forming in her mind as well. This time, the tension between following strict protocols and the very student centered notion of inquiry she had revisited from her preservice days those many years ago was beginning to loom large. Closely following protocols certainly seemed to offer a clear organization to this kind of project which was appealing to her as a teacher planning to implement it for the first time. Those management issues, especially with certain classes are very real, and not easily dismissed. On the other hand, with time available for such a project at a premium, how much time should be spent training students to follow directions versus letting them pursue their own questions and interests?

For this year at least, attending the GLOBE professional workshop helped her resolve some of these issues. For the brief few days of the workshop, the constant pressure to cover adequate content for the state wide testing, along with administering practice tests with her students seemed to fade away. These practice tests were a conglomeration of released test questions from previous state exams along other multiple choice questions created by the faculty at CHS, and in her mind represented a real low point for the year. Essentially the entire month prior to the exam was taken up with practice testing. The professional development opportunity instilled in Ms. Horn a renewed vigor for science and learning. She had heard other science teachers in the state rave about the GLOBE program and was glad she was finally getting the opportunity to participate.

At the outset of the workshop, her facilitators noted that GLOBE provided the students with the opportunity to learn science by:

- *Taking scientifically valid measurements in the fields of atmosphere, hydrology, soils, and land cover/phenology;*
- *Reporting their data through the Internet;*
- *Publishing their research projects based on GLOBE data and protocols;*
- *Creating maps and graphs on the free interactive Web site to analyze data sets;*
- *Collaborating with scientists and other GLOBE students around the world.*

Since in the final months of the year she was in the life science portion of the curriculum, it was only natural that she chose the land cover-biology portion of the program to focus on initially. However, since she would be talking her class outside for the very first time, she could not pass up select atmosphere/climate protocols either. This combination of topics might also reinforce the earth science content the students' learned during the winter, which she felt was an added bonus. Although she might be embarrassed to admit it to anyone, she mentally toyed with the idea of only taking her more advanced classes outside, however her strong sense of equity prevailed, and she quickly decided to involve all of her students. Her decision to follow the protocols, as opposed to going with the inquiry model she learned back in college was in part based on her perceived need to carefully manage the time for her general science classes. Although she believed that all students can potentially learn what science is all about by collecting and analyzing real data, she knew she had to carefully plan her daily lessons to proactively manage any potential behavioral issues—especially those issues which would take her students off task. From a science standpoint, she also became convinced during the workshop that protocols would be necessary to ensure a high enough quality dataset so that students could submit their findings online. She thought this element of the program would motivate students in all of her classes.

Once students were actually outside and making measurements, she found that each protocol gave a concise and helpful description of the specific parameters that were to be investigated in that topic. Thus, she continued to give each group a copy of these protocols, which were firmly affixed to their clipboards each day, as a means to keep them on track. Again, considering the logistics of the project, she made a decision to divide her class into research groups with four or five students per group. Initially, it would be their task to divide the work evenly among members of the group, but she was ready to step in at any moment to scaffold the group process as necessary. She felt strongly that in a project such as this, it was essential for each group to take responsibility for their own work. Her experience as a teacher told her that this sudden change in classroom norms was likely to met with some frustration, but she was pleased that the block schedule afforded each class 2 solid field days per week, and that they could develop some momentum toward taking on these new responsibilities. However, it was her first Friday back inside after 2 days out collecting data which presented her with her first real challenge.

Ms. Horn had booked the computer lab at CHS all day so that each of her classes would have the opportunity to immediately begin to enter data and, time permitting, begin to look for any emerging quality control issues or patterns. She was a little dismayed by the students' reactions to this first class back inside, as her students were quite vocal about their confusion regarding the purpose of all this data. The reality that her college prep students as well as those in general studies seemed united in their resistance and confusion told her she had not done an adequate job of setting this project up the previous week. "What are we supposed to do?" was the question that echoed throughout the computer lab in every class. Although no students came right out and accused her of anything, each time they asked that question she also heard a hint of the accusation "Why are you doing this to us?"

All that following weekend she wondered how to remedy things on Monday. She had responded on Friday by essentially retelling the students what she had shared with them the week before. She again tried to convince them that participating in the GLOBE project was an exciting and unique opportunity—at least at CHS. She reminded them they were doing real science, contributing to real data to real problems, and members of a global network of schools. But this argument apparently did not resonate like she had hoped—either time that she made her case. She anticipated they might be a bit confused, but she certainly did not expect such an uproar. Sadly, she felt this was strong evidence that her students had been trained to be passive receivers of information. They understood the rules of that game: Listen quietly, take notes, give back the same information in the same form when prompted to do so. She did not want to give them answers, in fact there was no way for her to do so even if she wanted to, and she was committed to seeing this project through. She was frustrated. She realized she needed to change the rules.

After spending much of her Sunday planning for the following day, she hoped her more structured timetable would afford her students the opportunity to see more quickly the benefits of participating in such a project. Although she did not originally plan on in-class presentations of data, she told her classes on Monday that they had 3 weeks to collect and analyze data, and on that third Friday each group would be responsible for sharing with class their dataset and tentative findings. Real panic set in. "What, only six days outside to collect data and present it to the class?" her students responded, "Yes," she remarked, "we all have deadlines to in life—show me what you are made of." She threw down the gauntlet, and hoped they would rise to the challenge.

Although she knew her students were just happy they could go outside, and perhaps more than a few students did not care why, just that they were free from the confines of the building, this timetable and assignment provided a level of challenge these students rarely experienced in their day to day high school lives. Ms. Horn was serious about this project, and it showed. Her support along the way came in many forms. She must have said a thousand times that it was very, very important to write down everything on the forms they carried on their clipboards, as they would need this detailed information for their oral reports. At the beginning of the second week, she provided each class with a detailed rubric of how the presentations were to be evaluated. Criteria included presentations skills as well as details on how much and in what form data should be presented. It mentioned the need to discuss outliers as well as any general conclusions they might be able to make about the makeup of the study plot. Finally, she noted they must list any questions they have about their data to receive full credit.

*Her strategy worked. With few exceptions, the groups made reasonable presentations, especially given the compressed nature of the assignment. Most importantly, many of the questions regarding the reason for doing this project seemed to fade away. Unfortunately, she felt the abatement of frustration was perhaps more to do with the fact that her students were busy, and less about them coming to an understanding regarding the importance of scientific reasoning. For the balance of the project, students' certainly appeared to be on task "doing" science by collecting data, but she had a nagging sense that what they were really doing was following "cookbook" data collection strategies not too dissimilar from virtually every lab for the entire year. Did she teach them that there was no single way to conduct science? Were students actually engaged in doing real science? Was this **inquiry**?*

MAKING A STUDENT-SCIENTIST PARTNERSHIPS WORK

David M. Moss

As we conclude this section and examine the notion of inquiry within the context of student scientist partnerships, it would be prudent to place this discussion within a larger context of educational discourse. When considering a framework to initiate this discussion I wanted to underscore the tensions that have emerged throughout this section, and yet avoid the false dichotomy of right versus wrong that is so prevalent in education today. Issues of educational reform are complex, and the role of inquiry in science classrooms and the nature of partnerships between schools and scientists are no exception.

I begin my discussion by revisiting the seminal work of John Dewey (1938) which was published in the first half of the twentieth century. In *Experience and Education*, Dewey offers a straightforward framework that is best summarized by the frequently cited passage from this text, "The belief that all genuine education comes about through experience does not mean that all experiences are genuinely or equally educative" (p. 25). Dewey describes that in worst case scenarios certain experiences may be mis-educative and ultimately may serve to limit a student's power of judgment or impetus to learn. In contrast, *educative experiences* are those which serve both the here and now in terms of interest and motivation, and set in motion a desire to learn and engage across many facets of life well beyond formal schooling. High quality educative experiences are consistent with promoting the participatory ideals of democracy. Quite sadly and perhaps most common are experiences that are noneducative. Although these may not immediately work against a long term passion for learning and willingness to engage in communal discourse, the accumulation of such dreary experiences will surely result in such a disconnect.

Making use of these criteria, it is essential I acknowledge right up front that I see no indication of a mis-educative enterprise in anything that we have outlined in this section. Unfortunately, convincing evidence for educative work may also be sparse. As we look back to the opening vignette, although there is a hint of promising work to be done by Ms. Horn and her classes, the project as depicted appears noneducative at best. I do not mean to imply that students were standing idly by and learning nothing as they engaged in data collection protocols, but when we consider the potential enduring lessons to learned by participating in such a project, it becomes hard to argue that students have undergone an experience that fundamentally shaped how they view science and society, and their role and responsibility in such a relationship.

If you question if I am setting the bar too high in terms of student involvement in a project such as this, I would respond by noting several key points to keep in mind. First, as noted in the opening vignette in this section, it is quite likely this is the very last science course many of these students will ever take. The obvious question then follows is if they do not learn about the nature of science in public schooling, what opportunities will be available for them to acquire an informed scientifically perspective they deserve and does not a robust democracy requires of all of its citizens to be informed? My second point centers around the notion of resources. Taken broadly, Student Scientist Partnerships (SSPs) take such things such as the time and money required by teachers to attend professional development workshops, not to mention the years of behind the scenes preparation to even facilitate such opportunities from the perspective of the provider. In the case of the GLOBE program, this represents millions, perhaps tens of millions, of dollars and countless hours of work by educators, scientists, technicians, and programmers. Then, of course, there is the time it takes for teachers to plan to implement such a curriculum. This work, more often than not, comes at the expense of teachers' personal time and usually requires an out of pocket expenditures for supplies. An investment of such resources surely deserves significant results.

Finally, and perhaps not readily apparent, is the normative decisions to be made when considering such partnerships. Although virtually every educational decision requires a value judgment, most go unnoticed. In the opening vignette, Ms. Horn struggled against a culture of test preparation which was prevalent at Central High School (CHS). Her decision to "afford her students what she hoped was a memorable experience to finish up the year" was not merely a decision between a boring and exciting curriculum for her students, it was a much more profound choice. Her motivation was not about generating excitement, it was fostering an experience which gave her students a firsthand look at the "spirit of scientific inquiry." As such, the stakes were very high, and the bar for ensuring worthwhile outcomes should be as well.

As it stands now, when we consider the entire academic year in which our vignette was situated, we see an all too familiar series of events unfold. The primary objective of the 10th grade science curriculum is to prepare students to perform well on a statewide science exam. The reality is that these students have likely been in this test preparation mode for most of their middle school years and were most certainly being taught under this model the previous year. Sadly, this exemplifies a "coverage of content" mentality. Only after an extensive landscape of content is traversed, as dictated by released test items and the like, are teachers encouraged to even consider breaking from this mandated undertaking. As noted, with essentially a full month set aside for actual practice testing and the exam, this leaves precious little time for work on projects such as GLOBE.

Continuing to follow our vignette from this section, after an adequate volume of content has been taught, although perhaps not learned, students are then trained in the protocols. Earlier in this section, Dr. Barry Rock emphasized the importance of introducing students to the use of protocols and standardized equipment to ensure a precise and reliable dataset. As such, these tools provide the opportunity for allowing the scientific community to access these datasets which might simply be unavailable otherwise. Additionally, we noted that rather than limiting student inquiry, these important tools are perhaps essential precursor for facilitating an inquiry oriented experience ultimately characterized by student driven questions.

This sequence of *content—protocols—inquiry* lies at the very heart of our most significant source of tension to arise out of this work. That is, this linear progression seems a very long road to travel to finally be able facilitate inquiry opportunities for our students. Moving beyond a false dichotomy of right versus wrong, we see the issues of how much content and when, the educational value of scientific protocols, and the background knowledge and experiences students need to engage in meaningful inquiry as intertwined and multifaceted, and still quite open to exploration from the science education community.

On one side we defer to our scientists who authored an essay in this section and clearly see the critical need for the use of scientific protocols from a quality assurance and science perspective. Although there is no single path to be followed that yields scientific findings, protocols offer an established set of guidelines which have been proven to ensure reliable and accurate data. Protocols can be an important catalyst to ultimately help students to pursue their own questions. Since students have much less training than scientists, protocols make sense from a practical standpoint--if the goal of such a partnership is to collect useful scientific data. Those of us closely involved in GLOBE_experiences have come to believe that the more students know how to do in terms of scientific methodology the greater their ability to generate and pursue their own questions. Certainly, it is an interesting line of thinking for further research.

As previously noted, we do not wish to minimize the importance of content as a key element of education in science. We must be cautious however not to make the coverage of content our only aim. In recent work which addressed the challenges of developing curriculum supported by a numerous content aims, Moss, Osborn, and Kaufman (2003), caution science teachers not to solely let subject matter drive our curriculum or it "may overwhelm the curriculum, creating a territory of content so vast that the learner has no time to learn the skills needed to navigate the territory, much less to explore the landscape itself" (p. 4).

Many reform documents note that inquiry as a teaching strategy is perhaps the most effective way to promote learning in science, but also reserve a prominent place for what turns out to be an extensive amount of topics to be learned (American Association for the Advancement of Science [AAAS], 1989; National Research Council [NRC], 1996). At the end of the day, relegating inquiry to the waning weeks of a given school year, or worse, to the final science course a student will ever take, seems irresponsible and shortsighted given our ultimate goals is to help our students to be scientifically literate citizens.

Although recognizing and encouraging a much needed research base for understanding the role student scientist partnerships play in science education, we feel it prudent to move toward a series of recommendations which may help to dissolve some of the tension seen between the aims of science and those of science education. Although it may be unfair to portray these constructs as polar opposites, certainly we have seen that what might be essential for science, such as strict protocols, may or may not be necessary for education. In all fairness, the opposite may be said of student driven questions, as actively researching scientists participating in partnerships with schools bring their own established research for investigation and are not looking to students to set their agenda.

When I consider the GLOBE program as a model for student scientist partnerships, perhaps one of the more significant outcomes is the global reach and interconnectedness of program. Since scientists are working toward documenting and characterizing global change, it seems quite appropriate that this SSP connects classrooms via world wide network of actively participating schools. Developmentally, Sobel (1996) argues students in high school are ready to tackle such global issues. He cautions against placing the burden of large scale serious environmental issues on younger students, but in high school addressing such issues may offer much needed motivation for the adolescent learner. In effect, a SSP may offer motivation for students in terms of contributing to a global project, and yet may fall short from a relevancy standpoint if students are merely working toward providing data for questions and issues which have been provided for them. In contrast, an inquiry model may offer a high level of relevancy for students in that they can essentially pursue questions derived from their own interests (as suggested in this volume in the section on student diversity), but merely presenting student data to their classmates certainly lacks the motivational kick of contributing to an authentic and actively investigated issue in science. So why not do both?

Before outlining several fundamental elements of what we consider to be an ideal student scientist partnership, I wanted to briefly speak to one other key aspect of why in our vignette Ms. Horn, and perhaps countless other dedicated teachers like her, often implement programs with only minimal deviation from their design. In a recent case study which examined the JASON project model of a student scientist partnership from the perspective of describing changes in student conceptions of the nature of science, the findings indicated that the teachers implemented the activities, and only those unembellished activities, that were experienced firsthand in the professional development workshop designed to introduce the program (Moss et al., 2003). This report concludes,

All SSPs need to recognize that curriculum initiatives and professional development should exist as reciprocal elements along a single continuum. We cannot expect teachers alone to bear the responsibility of science education reform. As much effort should be placed in fostering professional development opportunities which are designed to complement these curricular products as in the energy placed in their development, so that teachers can make informed instructional decisions consistent with a broad vision for science education reform. (p. 28)

The implication here is that programs that are essentially extracurricular in nature often have explicit aims of impacting science education from a reform-minded perspective. Yet, the materials and associated professional development opportunities often place this burden of reform squarely on the shoulders of teachers. This is especially problematic given the teacher proof design these curriculum materials often present, and the mixed messages that are a result. That is, the materials are designed in such a way as to stand alone, and yet at the same time there is an implicit expectation that teachers should go beyond what is covered in a workshop and, in fact, in the very materials themselves.

It is simply not adequate to suggest to teachers to utilize the GLOBE program as a catalyst for students to pursue their own questions and ultimately experience a greater range and depth of scientific thinking. That aim should be central to the program and meticulously scaffolded. Professional development workshops typically emphasize content (and in the case of GLOBE, protocols as well) and assume teachers will be able to take back to their classroom and be able to plan for and implement experiences well beyond the scope of the workshop. I do not mean to suggest that teachers do not have the capability to adapt curriculum or understand the larger implications of their work. However, given the time constraints in classroom teaching, it is unrealistic, and perhaps unfair, to assume that teachers have the adequate time and resources to go beyond the materials as presented to them. We should not assume the curricular sum of a program will add up to a greater reform-minded whole, unless the necessary professional development offers explicit opportunities for teachers to consider the complex and long-term learning considerations to achieve that aim.

AN IDEAL STUDENT-SCIENTIST PARTNERSHIP

Let us consider the notion of an ideal student scientist partnership. First, I must place this notion of an ideal in a specific context. Given the reform-minded thread of this section, we can easily assume that our SSP is, in fact, designed to serve the current reform agenda by fostering student understandings of the nature of science so that students may begin to move toward a scientifically literate perspective. Although noted earlier in this section that making informed decisions is at the heart of literacy in science, I further clarify this notion by noting that a scientifically literate person is one who that makes those decisions in both civic and personal contexts (Moss, Settlage, & Koehler, in press). As such, one must develop a fairly clear understanding of the nexus between science and society, and perhaps most importantly, explore one's own epistemology underpinning of science as a way of knowing. This point of view immediately demands that this ideal SSP must be able to be fully integrated within a science curriculum.

Student scientist partnership programs are typically run as extended in class field trips, with varying degrees of preparation, depth of experience, and follow-up or closure. Such detached experiences are certainly nice enhancements to the core curriculum, but they are not essential to fostering core ideas such as scientific literacy. The reality that they are by design self contained and thus, extracurricular, lies at the crux of my line of reasoning. If we once again consider the vignette from this section, Ms. Horn spent the bulk of the academic year following a prescribed curriculum with the singular aim of preparing her students to perform well on a single, standardized test. Even if certain elements of the test might be consistent with the outcomes for science education as previously stated, I view this path to be shortsighted, especially given the untapped promise of a project such as GLOBE. The next research step might be to pilot the feasibility of making student scientist partnerships elements of the core curriculum. A careful research design to support such a move would yield evidence which would enable us to determine the effectiveness of not merely adding more on to an established curriculum, but actually replacing aspects of what we already do. For many districts this would be a bold move, and the key question of feasibility and effectiveness would center around the impact of such a move on testing initiatives. Although I am often tempted to jump on the test bashing "bandwagon" to critique those institutions that develop and support such testing, I am resigned that in this age of narrowly defined accountability any reform proposals must work with and not against the tests themselves to gain an initial foothold.

So, what might a fully integrated student scientist partnership program look like? First, I recommend not merely setting aside a few weeks sometime during the school year, but carefully considering one's curricular aims along with the notion of what a partnership means. Realistically, given that school teaching is the primary responsibility of teachers, while practicing scientists are charged with conducting research, we are not implying a full-time commitment to each other is necessary. Instead, a committed reciprocal arrangement should be the norm. That is, this partnership should not merely be mutually beneficial in certain respects, but should serve to fundamentally impact the quality of both education and science.

In the case of Ms. Horn and her class, this would require seeing how the aims of the GLOBE program overlap with what she is required to already teach. The SSP program then replaces certain elements of her integrated science curriculum on an ongoing basis throughout the year. Making the case that a program such as this could indeed serve as an alternate model for teaching the established curriculum is no easy charge, and the responsibility should not fall solely on the teacher. Although most SSP programs cross reference their materials to state or national standards in hopes that their programs can be justified as being timely and relevant, this simply does not go far enough. Although this referencing could be done ahead of time to initiate a discussion, time during professional development workshops should be set aside for the very purpose of helping teachers understanding how the aims of the program meet their local curricular needs. The implications here are that program facilitators are not merely well versed in the project activities, but hold expertise in curriculum theory and design. From the perspective of the school, ideally teachers do not attend such workshops alone but a team of teachers, or better yet teachers and administrators are required to attend this aspect of the workshop. Attendance by such a team of professional educators would go a long way to ensuring that such a program would, in fact, be substantially integrated into the school.

Once back at the school, it would be essential for teachers to be committed to providing an inviting context for students in which they would be interested in generating their own questions for study. For example, we could begin with that same plot of trees behind CHS that served as the study plot for Ms. Horn's classes, but instead of jumping immediately into canned protocols after the initial field visit as was done in the earlier vignette, students would have the opportunity to consider questions about the very things they noted on their clipboards when the completed their preliminary survey. Our experiences have shown many students are interested in questions pertaining to the amount and type of trash at a site, looking for evidence of various kinds of wildlife as well as numerous other topics of immediate tangible interest. Inquiry is only a tool to promote learning and is most successful when the questions underpinning them are relevant and interesting to the student and provide adequate focus for designing and conducting investigations. Student choice of topic helps yield engagement, relevancy, and motivation, especially in the initial stages of an inquiry experience. Ultimately, this introductory series of lessons in which students propose and refine questions and pursue simple investigations will show them the very real need for standardized measurements. As such, it will serve as catalyst for moving into activities which are more traditionally supported by GLOBE.

At this point in the program, access to scientists becomes essential for an effective partnership. We specifically do not describe this access as on-demand communication, because it may not be feasible to match a relatively small number of scientists with each and every classroom from around the world. Of course, in regional or local programs this personal, sustained dialogue would be preferred. The nature of the communication is what is most important. At this early stage of our proposed program we are primarily looking for additional scaffolding by scientists with regard to the generation and refinement of questions. We want to know what interests scientists from a research point of view. We would like to see made explicit the nonlinear path traveled from the early stages of an idea to a full blown investigation. An online research BLOG written by a scientist would perhaps meet our needs. Preferably such entries would capture the authentic thinking of a diverse group of scientists exploring a wide range of topics.

Once students see the questions scientists themselves have posed and why, they can select one they wish to contribute to in terms of collecting data. The various protocols discussed in an earlier section now come directly into play. This element of the SSP proceeds as it is currently designed to do, however there is potentially an underlying difference in terms of motivation and relevance in that students have made an informed choice regarding the topic. Although at this stage the differences may seem subtle, as they engage with protocols they now do so as part of a continuum of increasingly challenging experiences in which they encounter a more authentic sense of what scientists actually do. This stands in contrast with the current model where students are in essence serving as mere technicians on a project (Moss, Abrams, & Robb-Kull, 1998), following a conceptual and procedural blueprint which has been provided for them. Although there is clear justification for establishing strict protocols from a quality assurance standpoint, having those serve as the principal connection between science and students cheats them out of the opportunity to think scientifically or even consider what that means.

Before I discuss the final changes I propose to the current configuration SSPs, I wanted to address this notion of thinking through a science lens, as it lies at the very heart of our notion of an ideal student scientist partnership and is the primary justification for recasting the model toward an inquiry stance. When we consider the earlier descriptions in this section, we can see that a deep level of thinking underpins the scientific endeavor—and our argument demands that we foster this level of thinking and not simply highlight it in a prepackaged and polished from.

To accomplish this, students must engage in scientific reasoning, which we believe can most readily be promoted through inquiry. For example, the notions of inductive and deductive reasoning provide an excellent starting point to explore the nature of science (Okasha, 2002). Here students will learn that even with a preponderance of evidence there can be quite a bit of uncertainty, or at least numerous unanswered questions, in explanations regarding natural phenomena. To support challenging thinking such as this in science, recent research has pointed to an explicit/reflective approach as showing promise. We see clear implications for the role for inquiry, specifically the development, refinement, and pursuit of questions as a central element for programs designed to bring students and scientists together.

I'm suggesting that "it's all about the questions"—and inquiry is all about the questioning. We must go to great lengths to encourage students to first have the opportunity to pursue questions of interest to them. Next, they must come to understanding how scientists themselves develop researchable questions. Following, there is a clear role for protocols to scaffold students in their thinking so they develop the tools necessary to pursue questions even further. After students participate in protocol driven data collection activities which contribute to ongoing research programs, they then should ideally go back and pursue new or variations on questions consistent with the aim of the program. This critical final step affords students the opportunity to consider questions and questioning across multiple contexts which represent a balance between their own interests and the opportunity to contribute to actual ongoing scientific work. To carry our example even further in the case of GLOBE, after students might have engaged in an investigation about what wildlife may be present at their plot, and then worked toward collecting biometric measurements about the site to be included in the international database, they could pose a question about what wildlife might be present at varying times of years. Perhaps they might wish to develop the first biomass maps of their area. This could take other groups toward such related topics as forest succession in which they can build upon their experiences in generating questions and collecting data to complete a meaningful science investigation. An inquiry approach, underpinned by questions and questioning, to SSPs may yield the greatest potential to teach students the essence of real science in understanding the real world.

Conclusion: Partnerships and Possibilities

As I conclude this section, I wanted to reiterate several key points which we as authors found to be authentic sources of tension as we developed the ideas for this section. First and foremost is the role technical protocols play in a science curriculum. For the first time in this section we now refer to them as technical, and not scientific protocols, because of their procedural nature. Certainly there were questions and interesting investigations which went into the development of these, but that process remains largely invisible to the student as they are typically presented as all too familiar cookbook-like directions to follow. When this occurs, we obfuscate the nature of science which may best serve our aims of fostering literacy in this domain. Since we largely defined literacy in science as making informed decisions, when we portray science as a series of steps to complete, even if those steps are underpinned by an authentic context, it does not serve our needs to effectively educate our students for lifelong engagement in scientific issues. If students have experienced science as merely a series of procedures, what hope can we hold for them to feel empowered to critically question science and its role in society. Although we acknowledged science is often characterized by few periods of startling discovery, and to portray it as any different would be disingenuous, portraying science as a "connect the dots" enterprise is just as misleading.

I have made recommendations to shift the nature of the student scientist partnership programs toward one characterized by questions and questioning. This essentially makes operational our notion of inquiry. In doing so we have not fully resolved the many tensions which exist, and perhaps have created others as you consider our discussion of inquiry and SSPs, but we argue our position represents a doable set of recommendations which help make explicit the nature of science. There is a clear distinction between engaging in activities that are scientific in nature and actually doing science. Student scientist partnerships must be true to all participants, students and scientists alike, and thus afford students the opportunity to scientifically question while at the same time add value to the work of scientists. Our "ideal" SSP aims to accomplish just that.

Another significant source of tension centers around the very role SSPs play in an educational era defined by a very narrow notion of accountability. The question of whether there is a role for such programs altogether is fundamentally important. To simply reject standardized testing is not a productive line of discourse, and any curricular reform initiatives must address this issue. However, I cannot resist the notion of suggesting a fundamental change, but not to tests directly, to standards. Imagine the implications of a national standard in science education which stated something to the effect of:

> Working in partnership with scientists, student will develop and refine questions, design and pursue scientific investigations, and report findings to the

scientific community with the aim of contributing both data and findings to an authentic research program. Such partnerships should be designed to promote lifelong engagement in issues underpinned by science.

There is much work to be done with regard to the reform of science education. In this section we offer a discussion of the potential of bringing together schools and scientists with the explicit aim of fostering a sense of the nature of science for students. If the recommendations for implementing a more inquiry-inclined SSP were in place, perhaps the opening vignette might have included the following description instead of what was seen:

> With clipboards and tape measures in hand, her first period general studies class tromped out the double doors behind the gym and headed for the strip of trees on the far side of the athletic field. Gathering the students around in a semi-circle, she sensed a level of engagement which was atypical for this class, and asked her students, "So, what seems interesting to you out here?" She reminded her students that science is all about inquiring by pursuing questions, ideally questions which are both personally interesting and important to society. She notes there are no guarantees in uncovering answers, but eventually you will learn precise protocols for collecting and analyzing data, and will have the tools to follow those questions to wherever they take you. She states that not all class members will follow the same path, but everyone will develop an insider's perspective on what scientists do, how they think and solve problems, and learn this very special way of looking at the world so that they will be empowered to participate in decisions about pressing issues facing our society.

Such a description reads quite a bit different from the one presented earlier—that difference could mean everything with regard to ensuring our present day students are prepared to contend with the many ethical, environmental, and technological challenges which await them as citizens of the twenty-first century.

REFERENCES

American Association for the Advancement of Science. (1989). *Project 2061: Science for all Americans.* New York: Oxford Press.

American Association for the Advancement of Science. (1990). *Science for all Americans: Project 2061.* New York: Oxford University Press.

Barab, S. A., & Hay, K. E. (2001). Doing science at the elbow of experts: Issues related to the science apprenticeship camp. *Journal of Research in Science Teaching, 38*(1), 70-102.

Chinn, C., & Malhotra, B. (2002). Epistemologically authentic inquiry in schools: A theoretical framework for evaluating inquiry tasks. *Science Education, 86,* 175–218.

Dewey, J. (1938). *Experience & education.* New York: Collier Books.

Koehler, C., & Moss, D. M. (2006, April). *Can You "Force Feed" NOS enlightenment? Two experienced teachers' pedagogical journeys teaching the nature of science.* Paper presented at the annual meeting of the National Association for Research in science Teaching, San Francisco.

Lederman, N. G., Abd-El-Khalick, F., Bell, R. L., & Schwartz, R. S. (2002). Views of nature of science questionnaire: Toward valid and meaningful assessment of learners conceptions of nature of science. *Journal of Research in Science Teaching, 39*(6), 497-521.

MacDonald, D. (1996). Making both the nature of science and science subject matter explicit intents in science teaching. *Journal of Science Teacher Education,* 7(3), 183-196.

Moss, D. M., Abrams, E. D., & Robb-Kull, J. (1998). Can we be scientists too? Secondary students' perceptions of scientific research from a project-based classroom. *Journal of Science Education and Technology,* 7(2), 149-161.

Moss, D. M. (2003). Exploring the JASON project: A window on science. *Journal of Science Education and Technology, 12*(1), 21-30.

Moss, D. M. Abrams, E. D., & Robb, J. (2001). Describing student conceptions of the nature of science over an entire school year. *International Journal of Science Education, 23*(8), 771-790.

Moss, D. M., Osborn, T. A., & Kaufman D. K. (2003). Going beyond the boundaries. In D. K. Kaufman, D. M. Moss, & T. A. Osborn (Eds.), *Beyond the boundaries: A transdisciplinary approach to learning and teaching* (pp. 1-11). Westport, CT: Praeger.

Moss, D. M., Settlage, J., & Koehler, C. (in press). Beyond trivial science: Assessing understandings of the nature of science. In D. M. Moss, T., A. Osborn, D. K. Kaufman (Eds.), *Interdisciplinary education in an age of assessment.* Mahwah, NJ: Erlbaum.

National Research Council. (1996). *National science education standards.* Washington, DC: National Academies Press.

National Research Council. (2000). *Inquiry and the National Science Education Standards.* Washington, DC: National Academy Press.

Okasha, S. (2002). *Philosophy of science: A very short introduction.* Oxford, England: Oxford University Press.

Rock, B. N., & Lauten, G. (1996). K-12th grade students as active contributors to research investigation. *Journal of Science Education & Technology,* 5(4), 255-255.

Rock, B. N., & Lawless, J. G. (1997). The GLOBE program: A source of datasets for use in global change studies. *IGBP Global Change Newsletter, 29,* 15-17.

Rutherford, F. J., & Ahlgren A. (1990). *Science for all Americans.* New York: Oxford University Press.

Schwab, J. J. (1962). The teaching of science as enquiry. In J. J. Schwab & P. F. Brandwein (Eds.), *The teaching of science* (pp. 1-103). Cambridge, MA: Harvard University Press.

Sobel, D. (1996). *Beyond ecophobia: Reclaiming the heart in nature education.* Great Barrington, MA: The Orion Society.

Tinker, R. F. (1997). Student scientist partnerships: Shrewd maneuvers. *Journal of Science Education and Technology, 6*(2), 111-117.

INDEX

Printed in the United States
136559LV00004B/6/A

9 781593 118358